Nursing Fathers

American Colonists' Conception of English Protestant Kingship, 1688-1776

Benjamin Lewis Price

LEXINGTON BOOKS
Lanham • Boulder • New York • Oxford

LEXINGTON BOOKS

Published in the United States of America
by Lexington Books
4720 Boston Way, Lanham, Maryland 20706

12 Hid's Copse Road
Cumnor Hill, Oxford OX2 9JJ, England

British Library Cataloguing in Publication Information Available

Library of Congress Cataloging-in-Publication Data
Price, Benjamin Lewis, 1951-
    Nursing fathers : American colonists' conception of English
  Protestant kingship, 1688-1776 / Benjamin Lewis Price
        p. cm.
    Includes bibliographical references (p.) and index.
    ISBN 0-7391-0051-3
    1. United States—Politics and government—To 1775. 2. Political
  culture—United States—History—18th century. 3. Colonists—United
  States—Attitudes—History—18th century. 4. Monarchy—Great
  Britain—Public opinion—History—18th century. 5. Public opinion—
  United States—History—18th century. 6. United States—Relations—
  Great Britain. 7. Great Britain—Relations—United States.
  I. Title.
  E195.P93   1999
  973.2—dc21   98-53034
                                                          CIP
Printed in the United States of America

Contents

Acknowledgments

I would like to thank Professor Robert Becker of Louisiana State University for his assistance and encouragement during the creation of this work, and Professor Victor Stater of Louisiana State University for his help with the English material, especially in the first chapter. Gregory Hospodor's assistance was also invaluable. Numerous useful insights grew out our discussions and arguments on this subject, and on themes that related to both this work, and his own dissertation research on the Southern mind and the Mexican War. I would also like to thank Dean Karl Roider of Louisiana State University for his careful editing and advice, and Ann Lang of Louisiana Public Broadcasting for her help in the last minute editing and preparation of this manuscript.

Abbreviations

The following abbreviations are used in the notes:

Cal. St. P.   *Calendar of State Papers, Colonial Series, America and the West Indies, 1661-1668, Preserved in Her Majesty's Public Record Office*

C.R.N.C.   *The Colonial Records of North Carolina*

D.H.N.Y.   *Documentary History of the State of New York*

N.J.C.D.   *Documents Relating to the Colonial History of the State of New Jersey*

N.Y.C.D   *Documents Relative to the Colonial History of the State of New York; Procured in Holland, England and France*

N.Y.H.S.C.   *Collections of the New York Historical Society*

Introduction

New York, July 15. On Wednesday last the Congress's Declaration of Independence of the United States was read at the head of each Brigade of the Continental Army posted in or near this city, and everywhere received with the utmost demonstration of joy. The same evening the equestrian statue of George III erected in the year 1770, was thrown from its pedestal and broken to pieces; and we hear the lead wherewith this monument was made is to be run into bullets. — *Pennsylvania Gazette*, July 17, 1776.

In July of 1776 a group of angry New Yorkers dragged the equestrian statue of George III from its pedestal and dismembered the gilt lead likeness of the King. According to the newspaper reports of the event, the lead from the statue was "run into bullets" to be used to defend the colony from British troops.[1] Scholars and others who are interested in the American Revolution are familiar with this event, but rarely do they pause to question why that statue was erected in the first place. George III didn't build it to commemorate himself. It was the product of an outpouring of gratitude, loyalty and affection that New Yorkers felt for their king, who, in their view, had taken an active role in bringing about the repeal of the Stamp Act in 1766, and in so doing, defending the liberty of his American subjects. Colonists had not always viewed their king as a tyrant and oppressor. Americans did not always characterize their king, even George III, as a "Royal Brute." In fact, the notion that Hanovarian English kings were, and had always been, tyrants, came to Americans as late as 1776. This was one of the truly revolutionary concepts that grew out of the Revolution.

Historians understand the American Revolution to be both a defining event of colonial history and the seminal moment in the history of the United States. As a result they often tend to view colonial political culture through the narrow telescope of hindsight. Historians often place local colonial political crises and the arguments that surrounded them into a Revolutionary context, even though the actors in those distant political dramas were certainly unaware that American colonists would take up arms against their mother country to gain their independence at some future date. Often, to view the Englishmen who lived in the colonies before the American Revolution as proto-Patriots leads one to forget that most of the residents of English North America *were* Englishmen, who thought and behaved much the same as their cousins did an ocean away.

Eighteenth-century colonists themselves viewed another revolution, that of 1688, as the seminal constitutional event in their own history, and particularly in the history of their relationship with England. In their interpretation of the Glorious Revolution, colonists claimed that they had allied with William of Orange to bring down a tyrant and to restore the ancient constitution both to their motherland and to their own colonies. The ideology and constitutional thought of the Glorious Revolution, as transmitted across the Atlantic during the spring of 1689, provided colonists with beliefs about kingship, religion and government that had a lasting effect on colonial political thought. Colonists agreed with the majority of the English people that Prince William of Orange had invaded England in order to defend their liberty, property, and Protestant faith against the tyranny of the Catholic James II. Once on the throne, William III and the rulers who followed him were viewed by colonists as protectors of the rights that they had secured by means of the Glorious Revolution.

William and his successors were also conceived of as protectors of English Protestantism. Although previous rulers of England claimed the title "Defender of the Faith," the church that they defended was the Church of England. From the reign of Queen Elizabeth, English monarchs had often defended Anglican orthodoxy against the proliferation of Calvinist thought and other schismatic Protestant creeds which they viewed as a threat to the religious and political consensus in England, and ultimately to their own authority. William and his Hanoverian successors exhibited greater tolerance toward dissenting Protestant sects and were concomitantly portrayed by their supporters as bulwarks against the threat of Roman Catholicism. This view of the ruler as a model Protestant Prince who was the defender and protector of Englishmen of all Protestant religious persuasions made it possible for dissenters, both in England and in the colonies, to accept their nominally Anglican rulers as godly defenders of their liberty of conscience. Henceforth, Quakers, New England Puritans, Dutch Reformed Calvinists of New York, Presbyterians, Baptists, and members of other Protestant denominations could, with clear consciences, join with the Anglicans in praying for and praising their king. At the same time, they could stand firm and united with their ruler as allies against the threat of Romanism.

Colonists' understanding of government was also affected by the political philosophy that grew out of the Glorious Revolution, and by the Whig political culture and discourse that followed the Revolution and continued to develop during the Hanoverian Era. They accepted the Whig premise that the first goal of government was the protection of the liberty and property of the subject from encroachment by any one element of the nation—be it king, peers, or the mob—and from foreign invaders. The post-Revolutionary interpretation of the English constitution cast off earlier notions of absolute kingship and divine right, replacing the former with the doctrine of the king in Parliament, and the latter with the idea that English rulers, though guided by God's providence, nevertheless ruled by the consent of their subjects. Additionally, post-Revolutionary political thinkers claimed that the king's first goal, in harmony with the duty of the peoples' representative assembly, was the preservation of the liberties and property of his subjects. Colonists chose to believe that if the king ruled England through Parliament, then he must rule his colonies through their own representative bodies.

Colonists' acceptance of the political premises of the Glorious Revolution had several effects on colonial political thought, and on the constitutional relationship between the people of each colony and royal government. First, Americans' notion of the "king in assembly" brought the royal colonies into a more intimate relationship with the king than had heretofore been the case. Secondly, it made the position of the colonial governor precarious because, although he was the titular representative or agent of the Crown in the colony, he was not the king, but a servant, and while the king could do no wrong, the governor certainly could. A succession of colonial assemblies would claim that they represented the king's and the people's interests (which were one and the same) against greedy, corrupt royal governors, often even when the governors were attempting to carry out instructions that they had received directly from their royal master. Finally, colonial politicians embraced the ideas and mastered the language of Whig political discourse and its ideological conventions of Court and Country, the first dedicated to stable secure government, and the second employed in opposition to ministerial authority.[2] In their local struggles with the representatives of the Crown, colonists practiced both Court and Country arguments and applied them skillfully at home and in their dealings with the government in London.

As the Whigs gained ascendency during the reigns of the first two Hanoverian kings and came to view their party as the nation's only security against Jacobite plots and foreign invasion, their ideology changed from libertarian to authoritarian. They achieved political stability by becoming more authoritarian and conservative. They avoided the libertarian radicalism of Locke and other political theorists of the English Civil War and the Glorious Revolution with their troublesome theories of social compact, popular sovereignty and the right of revolution. Instead, these institutional Whigs embraced the security of the Crown with its comforts of power, office and patronage, and enthusiastically assimilated from the Tories the maxim of government that political power should follow property. To a great extent under the Hanovers, establishment, or Court Whigs achieved a synthesis between the Tory commitment to property, prerogative authority and order, and the basic Whig premise that a mixed and balanced representative government best served to secure the peoples' liberties. This synthesis was, at least in part, made manifest as Court Whigs gradually reduced the franchise in England and increased the severity of laws that protected the property of freeholders. Interpreting John Locke to their own ends, Court Whigs argued that once the people had delegated their powers to the government, they were obliged to obey the unchallengeable authority of Parliament.

Without serious political opposition from any other English political movement, Whigs lost their cohesion and broke into factional groups based on both genuine political differences and competition for power and places in government. The earliest opposition to both William and to George I was couched in Tory terms. Post-Revolution Tories came to accept William's right to rule, but had considerably more difficulty accepting the Whig notion that the sanction for the powers of the Crown rested with the people. Fearing the threat of anarchy more than absolutism, they still supported the doctrines of divine right, non-resistance and passive obedience so long as the ruler was Anglican.[3] Tories were "High Churchmen" who feared dissenters of all kinds, viewing them as anti-monarchical and a threat to the established order of church and state. They opposed any attempts by Whigs to promote tolerance of dissenting Protestant groups in the realm, or to reform the Church of England so that dissenters might be able to attend Anglican worship and thus meet the requirements of the various tests and oaths that were conditions for government service. Although Tories initially had the support of many English voters, especially the rural freeholders, their association with Jacobitism and with the "High Church" civil disturbances of the first years of George I's reign damaged their credibility. The Whigs grew to dominate both the government and the political discourse under the Hanovers. Tory opposition, successfully equated by the Whigs with Jacobitism and Catholicism, virtually disappeared.

During the 1720s a primarily Whig opposition to the government replaced the Tories. This "loyal opposition" accepted the basic assumptions of the Whig constitution, supporting the king, the balanced constitution, and the protection of property as the first order of government. It also stood with the Court against Jacobitism and Catholicism. Since the language of Tory opposition had become tainted and was thus no longer an acceptable mode of criticism, Whig factions (and a few Tories), eager to acquire office from those Whigs who dominated the Court, employed Country political thought to criticize the government.

Country ideology contained components of several strains of English political thought. Its content was influenced by the country squires who as either Whig or Tory backbenchers in the Parliaments of William III and Anne had seen their independence threatened by Court politicians with their train of patronage and corruption. These Country gentlemen were also deeply troubled by a growing tendency to repose ever greater power within the executive. They were joined by the radical Whigs (also called Real Whigs or Commonwealthmen) who "developed a more positive ideology and offered a more coherent vision of the ideal society."[4] Libertarian visionaries, Radical Whigs offered a prescriptive analysis of current politics with a view toward restoring the "ancient constitution" to its pristine form: a mixed and balanced government with more clearly separated and independent branches. They alleged that corrupt courtiers and placemen had destroyed the separation between, and independence of, the three branches of the government, transforming the commonwealth into an oligarchy. They argued that the nation should not be guided by career politicians whose only ambition was to maintain their places and power, but by agrarian freeholders whose strict adherence to civic virtue made them ideal leaders for the nation.

Tories like Henry St. John, Viscount Bolingbroke comprised another element of the Country party opposition. In the late 1720s they emerged from the political wilderness, or in the Viscount's case the Stuart Pretender's retinue in France, to claim membership in the opposition. These ex-Tories claimed that they held principles virtually identical to those of the Radical Whigs, but that there was no longer any need for party distinctions in any case since "the proper and real distinction of the two parties expired" in the age that followed the Glorious Revolution.[5] By the

1720s many of the Country alliance joined with a growing Whig opposition whose chief goal was to attain power and places in the Court, and who found in Country criticism themes that evoked the Glorious Revolution and resonated among English freeholders.

In the summer of 1716, while George I was in Germany, Charles Townshend took advantage of the King's absence and a growing rift between the King and the Prince of Wales to form an opposition. He was soon joined by Lord Sunderland, Robert Walpole, and numerous other Whigs. Their "sole object was to embarrass their erstwhile colleagues" in the government.[6] They employed "obstructionist tactics" and appeals increasingly couched in terms of Country opposition, to win the support of independent Country members of Parliament.[7] They claimed to represent all honest Englishmen against the corrupt policies and practices of the ministry, and alleged that the overweening power of the Court threatened to bring down the balanced constitution. From the 1720s on, the Whig opposition promoted the reduction of the standing army, opposed new taxes, "and attacked placemen and pensioners with a vehemence that ill became men who had so recently quitted office, and whose sole desire was to force their way back into it."[8]

The transparently political use of Country opposition criticism of the government by Whig politicians whose only goal was to retake offices in government and the power and patronage that went with them, has led some historians to assume that the "country creed" amounted to little more than "camouflage for other interests."[9] Sir Lewis Namier, in response to the self-interest that he found inherent in the opposition's use of Country criticism, proposed that the "ideas and principles of eighteenth-century politicians were merely rationalizations of selfish ambition and base motives."[10] Namier and his followers dominated the scholarship of eighteenth-century English history from the 1920s until the 1960s. Under their influence, English historians adopted a cynical approach to the study of political ideology, claiming that political behavior could only be explained if the facade of political arguments and declared principles were stripped away to expose the baser self-interests that drove politicians to seek power.

At about the same time American Progressive historians such as Charles Beard, Carl Lotus Becker, Merrill Jensen and Philip Davidson argued that American Revolutionary rhetoric, and indeed all political rhetoric, represented an effort by a self-interested minority in the colonies to delude fellow colonists by manipulating public opinion in their favor. For Progressives, political rhetoric was composed substantially of demagoguery and rationalization.[11] Like Namier, they believed that interest provoked action and ideas were rarely prime motivators. Those Progressives who, like Charles Beard and Philip Davidson, studied ideas, argued that rhetoric was the tool employed skillfully by the colonial economic/political elite to mold and control the behavior of the largely disenfranchised poorer elements of society in order to garner their support for independence.[12] In the late 1960s and 1970s the Progressive interpretation gave way to Neo-Progressives, who took a more decidedly interest-based Marxian approach to historical interpretation, focusing on class conflict and the development of class consciousness in the colonies. Neo-Progressives, unlike either the Progressives or the Namierites, stressed the importance of approaching history from the bottom up in order to explain the "concerns of the common man and the inarticulate masses."[13] Neo-Progressives also largely discounted ideas as motivators of men or movements.

The patriotic euphoria of the late 1940s prompted a new conservative approach to American history. The "consensus historians" began to reassess the causes and results of the Revolutionary and Constitutional periods. Whereas Progressives had probably overstressed class differences during the period, the new nationalist historians largely ignored them. Historians like Robert Brown and Daniel Boorstin, argued that, in general, the defining factors of the period were social and economic homogeneity, and that free Americans had been united in their goals of achieving independence from Britain. Having succeeded, they established a nation in which they preserved the traditional rights of Englishmen.[14] Most consensus historians stressed that although Americans' intellectual, political and cultural roots were grounded in British traditions, there was a practicality about them, an aversion to ideology and an innovativeness spawned by exposure to the wilderness, that made Americans qualitatively different in these areas from their British cousins.

Interestingly, throughout the period of historiographical wrangling, the waters of intellectual history of the Revolutionary and Early Federal periods remained largely untroubled. The intellectual origins of Revolutionary thought and the development of a federal nation were placed generally within the framework of Enlightenment thought, and specifically at the feet of John Locke. Locke was viewed as a revolutionary thinker whose ideas on government had sprung up, virtually *ex nihilo,* to guide American Revolutionaries to their own independence. Here Whig historians found agreement with the Progressives who studied colonial thought. For both schools, American Revolutionary ideology, as it was embodied in the *Declaration of Independence* " was pure Locke. As Carl Becker put it, 'The lineage is direct, Jefferson copied Locke.' For the historian Merle Curti, the 'Great Mr. Locke' was 'America's philosopher.'"[15]

By the mid-1960s, however, this historiographical tradition was beginning to come under fire. First British, and somewhat later American, historians began to search for the origins of eighteenth-century political thought, and began to find them in the political ideology of the later English Commonwealthmen of the late seventeenth and early eighteenth centuries. The historians who most influenced this turn in intellectual history were Bernard Bailyn, Caroline Robbins and J.G.A. Pocock. After studying Revolutionary pamphlets and documents, Bailyn asserted that the ideas which supported opposition to Britain predated the Enlightenment, and had been in America since the 1730s, and at least in part since the turn of the eighteenth century. In *The Ideological Origins of the American Revolution*, Bailyn, following Caroline Robbins' lead, traced the origins of American revolutionary thought to the Country opposition of the early Hanover governments, and from thence to the rhetoric of opposition to the Stuarts in the 1640s and 1680s, and finally back via the Renaissance republicanism of Machiavelli to classical republican thought. Revolutionary propaganda emphasized corruption as a historical process and civic virtue as a limited prophylactic against political corruption, and pitted the virtuous nature of agrarian republicanism against the corrupting influence of mercantile urban interests and government ministers and jobbers. For Bailyn, the American Revolution was an English Revolution fought in America by Whigs against a corrupt Tory government. This conclusion was a difficult pill for both the right and the left. Consensus historians were critical of Bailyn because his study made an "American Exceptionalist" view of the Revolution untenable; in fact, for Bailyn, the American revolutionaries were more English than their British contemporaries. Since Englishmen of the late eighteenth century had sacrificed their republican concerns for domestic and European security and international mercantile dominance, Bailyn argued, the Americans could claim to be the true heirs to the traditions of the English Commonwealth and the "Ancient Constitution." Other historians (especially Joyce Appleby) were perturbed, not so much that Bailyn focused on English political thought in order to find the origins of the Revolution, but that he focused on the conservative, even reactionary, country opposition rather than on the liberal tradition of Locke and the Enlightenment. Historians on the left viewed the "republican thesis" as another attempt by the right to extol American homogeneity and to avoid focusing on social and economic diversity and class divisions.[16] It may be added as a criticism of Bailyn that he was very selective in time and content in his choice of historical sources from which he framed his argument. Whereas Caroline Robbins traced a reasonably continuous line of English commonwealth thought and thinkers from Milton to Thomas Paine, Bailyn provided little evidence for a similar continuity in American colonial thought. Because few of the pamphlets that he used were written before the 1750s, and the few earlier works that he selected he often discussed without describing the context that inspired them, Bailyn gave the impression that Country ideology appeared rather suddenly in the American colonies just before the French and Indian War and was the only language that Americans who considered themselves Whigs employed in political discourse. It is one of the objects of this study to modify that conclusion.

To a great extent historians have divided into two camps. The first follows Namier, Marx and the Progressives, who argue generally that interest, in one form or another, is the primary determinant of action, and thus ideas should be largely discounted as significant agents of historical causation. The second group, generally labeled "Whig" historians and epitomized by Lord Macaulay, Bailyn and Robbins, largely discount interest, and stress the importance of ideas as the drivers of actions in history. Recently, several historians, in reaction to both Whig and Namierite interpretations of politics, have argued that ideas and interests exist side by side and interact, each often informing the other. H.T. Dickinson, Geoffrey Holmes, and John Brewer on the English side, and Gordon Wood and Joyce Appleby on the American, exemplify historians who study the interaction of interest and thought on the political stage.[17] These historians have taken a more holistic view of political culture, focusing on the development of political ideas and political behavior over time. Americans' political ideas were formed not only from their own special colonial circumstances, but also from ideas that made their way across the Atlantic from England. American colonists' understanding of their relationship with the British government and how they fit into the British constitution had an effect on their own domestic politics and the political culture peculiar to each of His Majesty's Colonies in North America.

Historians like Dickinson and Appleby note that members of society are motivated to some degree by self-interest and behave accordingly; but self-interested responses can take many forms, and thus, scholars need to study those specific responses that men take to specific stimuli. Do the actions that self-interested politicians take simply serve to further their own ends without regard to the social costs of their behavior, or do they make "principled" responses that serve the needs of the public as well as their own desires for power? Every society has its own set of cultural assumptions within which are included certain political ideals. These ideals motivate leaders to act in ways that the public will find acceptable, and even virtuous. Political principles differ from culture to culture, and may change over time in response to historical events and new intellectual contributions (which may include the propaganda engineered by leaders or parties in order to influence public opinion). Political behavior changes apace. Thus, for H.T. Dickinson:

> The historian . . . must recognize those actions which that society is prepared to regard as admirable or "principled" and those actions which it will condemn or deplore. If he does not understand the political values of a particular society, then he will not understand the political agents of that society. To understand the political values he must examine the political rhetoric, the arguments, prejudices and assumptions of the age.[18]

The specific language that political actors employ to achieve their goals provides evidence that the society in which they act embraces certain broad values and principles; otherwise, there would exist no basis for principled rhetoric. Politicians' actions are guided by intelligence and forethought; they use the themes that they think will work. They invoke the images and ideas that they hope will achieve the desired response from their listeners.[19]

What images and ideas, then, resonated in the British political world of the eighteenth century? The evidence indicates that the broad constitutional principles that Englishmen on both sides of the Atlantic confirmed and responded to positively after the Glorious Revolution were the concepts of mixed monarchical government, Protestant kingship, and the preservation of the people's liberties, property and Protestant religion. Time and again, English and colonial writers employed these themes in their editorials, sermons, pamphlets and speeches. If these ideas were not intimately tied to the fabric of English political culture, self-interested politicians and other political actors would not have employed them in their rhetoric. The ideas had power when invoked because they held meaning to those who received them. The study of these ideas provides historians with a means of comprehending the politics and the events of the age.

It is thus appropriate to inquire into American colonists' interpretation of the British constitution and their place in it. What had emerged by the reign of George II was an interpretation of the origin and nature of political society that was quite English in terms of its antecedents, and contained elements of both Court and Country political thought. When colonial thinkers inquired into the nature and origins of government, they appear to have been influenced by both Thomas Hobbes and John Locke. They agreed with Hobbes that men in a state of nature, or in a society unrestrained by some sovereign authority, would quickly slide into anarchy in which the stronger would inevitable prey upon the weak, and human institutions that required cooperation would dissolve into what eighteenth-century Englishmen called licentiousness—what John Phillip Reid called "the darker side of liberty."[20] Colonial thinkers were also influenced by John Locke and by the constitutional thought that grew out of the Glorious Revolution and the Whig ascendency of the early Hanover period. They understood that government should be divided and balanced so that the various elements and interests of society were equally represented and could exercise restraint upon each other. Simply put, their notions of the origins and constitution of civil government were little different from the English Whig ideas of the same period that informed them.

Like other Britons, American colonists perceived the British constitution to be the most well-balanced, fair and enduring system of law and government in the world. They agreed that government was created by men for the purpose of preserving their liberty against anarchy at one extreme, and despotism at the other, and that the British constitution, and the form of government that grew out of it, best fulfilled those goals. Colonists viewed their own provincial governments as models based on the English system. Each had a representative assembly, a council (which they equated with a House of Lords), and an executive. Colonists who lived in royal colonies viewed the king, and not the royal governor, as their executive. This placed royal governors in an ambiguous position in so far as their duties to their royal master was concerned. If they suggested legislation to the provincial assembly at the behest of the king, and the assembly construed it as a threat to the welfare of the people, then the governor, and not his master, was accused of a despotic exercise of authority. The colonial assembly claimed the high ground on the issue, at once asserting that they were the defenders of the people's liberty, and that their actions were taken out of loyalty to the king whose goal was identical to their own, namely to preserve and defend the liberties, rights and privileges of his subjects.

While colonial government institutions became increasingly independent and autonomous in the first half of the eighteenth century, under what is often referred to as British "salutory neglect," American colonists still felt a strong attachment to the mother country. They felt a special relationship, a strong bond, between themselves and their Hanoverian rulers. They viewed the king as the linchpin connecting their distant provinces with Britain. The king was also a substantive part of their own individual colonial constitutions. Even in the proprietary colonies, where the constitutional link between king and colony was less distinct, colonists evinced support, loyalty and affection for the monarch. Indeed, some in the proprietary colonies looked upon the Crown as an essential counterweight to the abuse of power by the proprietors or their agents in the colony. Colonists viewed the king as their protector whose first goal was to preserve and defend their English religion, liberties and property. Thus, colonists believed that the king's duty with respect to his subjects was in harmony with the professed aims of their own local popular political institutions.

American colonists gave evidence of their loyalty and devotion to the king and his family in many ways. They named counties, parishes, towns, colleges, taverns, inns, and ships after him and members of his family. They prayed for his continued health and prosperity. Colonial ministers of all denominations preached sermons explaining why the king should be loved, honored and obeyed. They extolled his virtues, calling him a providential ruler, a nursing father, the breath of his people's nostrils. They celebrated royal events, birthdays, weddings, births, accessions, and military victories, and mourned the passing of their king and members of the royal family. Ironically, although colonial political thinkers, like most of their English cousins, abhorred the notions of divine right and unlimited submission associated with Stuart monarchs, they often spoke of their rulers, especially George II, in terms that are, to modern readers, remarkably similar. Hanoverian kings were extolled as both chosen by the people, and anointed by God. Divine support was not given lightly, however; it was contingent upon the good behavior of the monarch. So long as rulers were considered good, exercising tolerance toward English Protestants, and jealously protecting the liberty and property of their subjects, they had the support of both the people and, according to two generations of American ministers, the Almighty. The good king's subjects were prepared to give freely and amply that loyalty that Stuart kings could only demand.

Hanoverian rulers were set in sharp contrast to Stuart monarchs, the former being the best of kings and the latter being the worst. This contrast became most stark on those occasions, like the Jacobite rebellions of 1715 and 1745 and the Atterbury Plot of 1722, when Whigs in England and America perceived themselves threatened by a possible Stuart restoration. American colonists made it clear in their newspapers, sermons and letters that they feared the Stuarts as much as their brethren in England did. And like English Whigs, Americans equated the Stuarts with Romanism and arbitrary government. Thus colonists claimed that a restored Stuart Pretender could only endanger the liberties, property and Protestant religion of his subjects, wherever they might reside. On the other hand, colonists viewed the Hanovers as the special friends of both orthodox Anglicans and English Dissenting Protestants. As the protectors of the Protestant religion, the Hanovers simultaneously became the protectors of English liberty. Protestantism and liberty went together in the minds of English political and religious thinkers on both sides of the Atlantic, in the same way that they linked Popery and slavery. Hanoverian rulers thus acquired a reputation as protectors and defenders of the civil liberties of their subjects. In fact, their reputation as rulers who were especially attentive to the liberty of their subjects was better in the colonies than it was in Britain, where, at least into the 1740s, a Jacobite minority and civil unrest threatened the Hanover Whig consensus. Colonial religious and political leaders characterized George II as an ideal English ruler—a benefactor to his subjects. If the Stuart Pretender was stereotyped as a model tyrant, Popish and arbitrary, then George II was most often characterized as the benevolent father of his country.

But what of the Country ideology in American colonial political thought before the reign of George III? It was frequently employed by one side or the other in local controversies, but very rarely in controversies with the government in London. The popular party in Massachusetts accused Royal Governor Jonathan Belcher of corruption and arbitrary rule when he stood against a paper money infusion in the colony in the late 1730s. And in that same colony, opponents of the new excise of 1754 copied the arguments against the taxes from Bolingbroke's *Craftsman* series of the 1730s to condemn the policy of the provincial assembly. In New York, the Presbyterian party leader, William Livingston, published *The Independent Reflector* to criticize the colonial government dominated by the Anglican party. He modeled his arguments after the English opposition *Independent Whig*, authored by John Trenchard and Thomas Gordon.[21] As often as not, however, until the 1760s, each side in colonial controversies mixed

Country and Court rhetoric, alleging in the press and in memorials to London that their opponents' behavior was an act of disloyalty to the king and to his subjects in the colony. Country opposition rhetoric was by no means the sole possession of the colonial assembly or the popular parties in the colonies. On more than one occasion royal governors borrowed from "True Whig" writers like Bolingbroke, Bishop Hoadly or Thomas Gordon when they responded to attacks from their provincial assembly. Governors employed Country opposition language to argue that annual salaries voted by the colonial assembly undermined the independence of the executive, unduly bound the office to the party that dominated the assembly, and thus unbalanced the colonial government. Peter Zenger attacked the popular majority in the New York Assembly, and was arrested for seditious libel for his troubles. He and his lawyer "turned for authority to Trenchard and Gordon's *Cato's Letters*" for grounds to defend the newspaperman against the charge.[22]

In fact, the colonial political ideology of the age of the Hanovers was not very different from that of England. Political discourse in the American provinces was couched in Court and Country Whig terms as it was in the mother country; however, the difference was that in the American colonies there was no Court *per se*, and so the roles, and thus the language of Court and Country opposition, were not bound permanently to any set of government institutions or factions within any colony. Individuals and factions chose the language that might be used most effectively against their opponents, and mixed their rhetoric to suit their needs, but all sides continuously and enthusiastically claimed loyalty to the king.

From the accession of William III until the sixth year of the reign of George III, American colonists viewed their kings as active participants in the great work of governance—as protectors of their lives, liberties, and property, and the preservers of their Protestant faith. Colonists characterized their rulers as "nursing fathers," benevolent and just, who employed their authority to protect and defend their subjects. This notion of English Protestant kingship was the wellspring of a powerful bond of allegiance between colonists and their kings that was not broken until the summer of 1776 when Americans perceived that King George III had forsaken them, had severed the connection between king and people, and had thus, in effect, separated the American colonies from the British Empire.

Notes

1. "New York," *Pennsylvania Gazette*, July 15, 1776.

2. For the genesis of Court and Country political arguments in the second decade of the eighteenth century, as a discourse between the "ins" who employed arguments in support of the Court, and the "outs" who employed Country arguments and policies to rally support from Tories and country backbenchers in order to attain political power, to become "ins," see H.T. Dickinson, *Liberty and Property: Political Ideology in the Eighteenth Century* (New York: Holmes and Meier Publishers, 1977), 121-122.

3. Dickinson, *Liberty and Property*, 45-46.

4. Dickinson, *Liberty and Property*, 103.

5. Bolingbroke, cited in Dickinson, *Liberty and Property*, 178.

6. John B. Owen, *The Eighteenth Century, 1714-1815* (New York: W.W. Norton & Co., 1974), 12.

7. Owen, *The Eighteenth Century*, 13.

8. Owen, *The Eighteenth Century*, 13.

9. John Brewer, *The Sinews of Power: War Money and the English State, 1688-1783* (Cambridge, Massachusetts: Harvard Press, 1990), 157.

10. Dickinson, *Liberty and Property*, 2. See also Gordon Wood, "Rhetoric and Reality and the American Revolution," in *In Search of Early America: The William and Mary Quarterly, 1943-1993* (Richmond, Virginia: William Byrd Press, 1993), 68; Lewis Namier, *England in the Age of the American Revolution*, 2nd ed. (London: Macmillan & Co., 1961), 131.

11. Wood, "Rhetoric and Reality," 59-60. A few influential Progressive works include Charles A. Beard, *An Economic Interpretation of the Constitution* (New York: Macmillan & Co., 1913); Carl Lotus Becker, *The Declaration of Independence: A Study in the History of Political Ideas* (New York: Alfred Knopf, 1922); Philip Grant Davidson, *Propaganda and the American Revolution, 1763-1783* (Chapel Hill: University of North Carolina Press, 1941); Arthur Schlesinger, *Prelude to Independence: The Newspaper War on Britain, 1764-1776* (New York: Knopf, 1958). For a study that takes a similar approach to ideology and the Glorious Revolution in Massachusetts, see Viola Florence Barnes, *The Dominion of New England: A Study in British Colonial Policy* (New Haven: Yale University Press, 1923).

12. Davidson, *Propaganda and the American Revolution*.

13. Gerald N. Grob and George Athan Billias, eds., *Interpretations of American History: Patterns and Perspectives*, 6th ed., 2 vols. (New York: The Free Press, Macmillan, Inc., 1992), 1:125. Grob and Billias provide a discussion of Neo-Progressives, 1:124-126.

14. See Robert Elton Brown, *Middle Class Democracy and the Revolution in Massachusetts, 1691-1780* (Ithaca, New York: Cornell University Press, 1955), and *Virginia, 1705-1786, Democracy or Aristocracy?* (East Lansing, Michigan:

Michigan State University Press, 1964); Daniel J. Boorstin, *The Americans: The Colonial Experience* (New York: Random House, 1958).

15. Gordon Wood, "Virtues and Interests," *The New Republic;* Feb.11, 1991, 32. Important works by Merle Curti include *The Growth of American Thought* (New York: Harper & Row, 1943), and *Human Nature in American Historical Thought* (Columbia, Missouri: University of Missouri Press, 1968).

16. See Caroline Robbins, *The Eighteenth-Century Commonwealthman: Studies in the Transmission, Development and Circumstance of English Liberal Thought from the Restoration of Charles II until the War with the Thirteen Colonies* (Cambridge, Massachusetts: Harvard University Press, 1959); Bernard Bailyn, *Ideological Origins of the American Revolution* (Cambridge, Massachusetts: The Belknap Press, 1967); J.G.A. Pocock, *The Machiavellian Moment: Florentine Political Thought and the Atlantic Republican Tradition* (Princeton, New Jersey: Princeton University Press, 1975); Joyce Appleby, *Economic Thought and Ideology in Seventeenth-Century England* (Princeton, New Jersey, 1978) and *Liberalism and Republicanism in the Historical Imagination* (Cambridge, Massachusetts: Harvard University Press, 1992). For a compilation of neo-Progressive scholars' critiques of the "neo-Whig" point of view, see Alfred F. Young, ed., *Beyond the American Revolution: Explorations in the History of American Radicalism* (DeKalb, Illinois: Northern Illinois University Press, 1993).

17. See, Dickinson, *Liberty and Property*; Geoffrey Holmes, *British Politics in the Age of Anne* (New York: St. Martin's Press, 1967); Brewer, *The Sinews of Power*, and *Party Ideology and Popular Politics at the Accession of George III* (Cambridge: Cambridge University Press, 1976); Gordon Wood, *The Radicalism of the American Revolution* (New York: Alfred A. Knopf, Inc., 1992); Joyce Appleby, *Economic Thought and Ideology*.

18. Dickinson, *Liberty and Property*, 5-6.

19. Dickinson, *Liberty and Property*, 6-7.

20. See John Phillip Reid, *The Concept of Liberty in the Age of the American Revolution* (Chicago: University of Chicago Press, 1988), 32-37.

21. Bailyn, *Ideological Origins*, 52-53.

22. Bailyn, *Ideological Origins*, 52-53.

1

Images of Authority

[We,] being deeply impressed with the Divine Goodness brightly displayed in the late Revolution, begun and carried on by King *William* of Glorious Memory, and in bringing in our only Lawful and Rightful Sovereign King GEORGE to the peaceable Possession of the Throne of his Royal Ancestors, not withstanding the many open and secret Practices that have been used of late Years to defeat the Succession, cannot sufficiently adore the kind Providence, which has so often and so seasonably interposed to save this Nation from Popery and Slavery. — "A Seasonable Admonition by the Provincial Synod of *Lothian* and *Tweeddale,* to the People in their Bounds, with Respect to the Present Rebellion," *The Flying-Post or the Post-Master,* London, November 1, 1715

Nor have the People *any Authority* against or over the Legislature; for while the *Constitution* is Preserved, the *original* Power of the People in their *collective* Body can't exert itself, or indeed have a *Being,* because it is *lost* and *swallowed up* intirely in their *Representatives.* — "Some Reflexions on the *Rights of Parliament* and People," *London Journal,* May 5, 1733

The Atlantic Ocean is the central geographical feature that affected Colonial Americans' relationship with their mother country. American historians describe it as both a road that connected the colonies to the homeland, and as a barrier whose dangerous shoals, deadly storms and broad expanses made travel and communication perilous. The Atlantic was also a road over which ideas were carried between the British Isles and the British colonies. Ideas were transmitted by newspapers, letters, and travelers arriving in American ports upon the ships that constantly sailed between the Old World and the New. The news and ideas that traveled across the Atlantic kept colonists in America socially and politically up to date with the mother country as it developed and changed from the end of the Stuart dynasty and the Glorious Revolution to the American Revolution. The ocean was also a barrier to the transmission of information, however, because the ideas, or at least the language that shaped those ideas, often arrived in the New World bereft of the contexts and political nuances that gave them meaning in the mother country. Inevitably, American colonists provided their own contexts when they assimilated new political ideas that arrived from so far away. Frequently they understood these new political ideas not as the products of the politics of the moment in London, but rather in the light of England's history and their own relations with the mother country. In the process, history as they understood it was palpably changed. And sometimes colonists reinterpreted their own history in light of these incompletely understood new ideas that had been generated under other circumstances in another land an ocean away.

Often images that arrived on American shores were tailored by politicians in England to mold public opinion and garner public support for themselves or their policies at home. So it was with the images of Prince William of Orange that Americans received in 1689, and when George, the Elector of Hanover, arrived in England to ascend to the throne. So it also was when Whigs dominated government in London after 1715, and began to employ an energetic Whig press to promote their policies. In each of these cases (especially the last), the issues and controversies that lay behind the rhetoric that Americans read in the news from England were downplayed. The underlying issues were, in fact, often unreported in the British press. Supporters of the Crown and government found it prudent to argue that their patrons were preserving the liberties, property and religion of Englishmen against social disorder and conspiracy at home and foreign powers abroad, and so to deflect criticism that they supported foreign invaders (William and George I), or promoted policies, such as the Septennial Act, the Riot Act, a large standing army, excise taxes, and other measures that might defy the traditional understandings of the constitution and English liberties. Opposition papers could criticize government, but were forced to do so circuitously, because their editors were constrained by the laws of seditious libel as they applied to the Crown, magistrates and Parliament.[1] After 1716, Whig accusations that Tories were traitors who plotted to restore a Catholic monarch and enslave the people were so successful that the Tory opposition press declined both from decreased popularity and from fear of prosecution or mob action. What few Tory papers continued to circulate, like Nathaniel Mist's publications, offered only lukewarm criticism of Whig politicians and the measures they promoted. Tory editors chose instead to criticize the corruption and immorality of their opponents and of the age in general, and to glorify Queen Anne's reign and her government against her detractors. Eventually Tory opposition was subsumed within that safer and more acceptable branch of English political thought that was associated with the English Country political thinkers. So, while both government and opposing presses energetically promoted their agendas in the English press, neither did so by debating the issues themselves in detail. They sought instead to mold popular opinion by criticizing the honesty and morality of their opponents (generally the only means of criticism available to Tories) and by arguing that it was they who were the true guardians of the constitution and the liberties, property and religion of the nation, while their opponents conspired to reduce the nation to misery and slavery.

Across the sea, colonists received English news from a number of sources. They corresponded with friends and relatives in England and conversed with newcomers, but the majority of their information came from the colonial press. Colonial editors garnered information from interviews with mariners and newly arrived immigrants, from correspondence with American travelers in England and Europe, from colonial agents residing in London, and from other colonial newspapers, but the vast majority of their information came directly from English newspapers.[2] Except during war, news from other colonies amounted to the announcement of ship arrivals or coverage of communications between colonial assemblies and governors. Colonial editors also garnered news stories from England from other colonial newspapers. The vast majority of news that colonial papers carried was about Europe and the British Isles. Historian Paul Langford notes that "in the typical weekly or semiweekly edition" of any colonial newspaper, "the heading 'London,' with its attendant columns and rows of articles, had a way of driving more local information either to an inferior position, or indeed off the page all together."[3]

By 1700 English newspapers were political organs as much as news vehicles. They were edited by partisans and sponsored by politicians. In 1694 the statute that the government had used to control political content in the press, the Licensing Act, was allowed to lapse. This gave publishers the opportunity to print a wider range of political news than had been previously possible. It also gave them an opportunity to publish political editorials that could be used to promote party interests and the careers of their politician sponsors. Partisan periodicals proliferated in the first half of the eighteenth century in spite of various attempts by the government to weed out those that were unfavorable to its measures. Often these attempts were only half-hearted, because by the 1720s Whig ministers and their supporters were well aware that the political future was always precarious, and the government men of today might well become the opposition of tomorrow. When Queen Anne's Tory government passed a stamp tax to raise the cost of publishing opposition journals, these same Tories had to pay the tax a few years later when they published opposition papers and tracts of their own against the Whig-dominated government of George I. A series of ministers under the Hanovers blasted the opposition press, only to find themselves patronizing opposition publishers of their own when the vagaries of political life cast them out of office. This sort of turnover took place so frequently that even the editors of partisan journals might cynically ask "is there a *Patriot* now of any Distinction or Eminence, who has not heretofore been a *Place-Man*? or any *Place-Man* of Note or Figure that has not been a *Patriot?*"[4] All in all, politics in the eighteenth century encouraged a vigorous press devoted to the editorial promotion of party men and party measures.

The great demand for political writers made it possible for the first time for editorialists and publicists to make a comfortable living from their pens. B.W. Hill comments that it "is not always realized by the modern readers of 'Augustan' literature, with its urbane social instruction and tolerant satire, how many of its writers served their apprenticeship in the fierce political infighting" of the early eighteenth century.[5] Literary figures such as Jonathan Swift, Daniel Defoe, Joseph Addison, and Richard Steele, as well as political hacks like John Trenchard and Thomas Gordon, and the lesser known machinators like Tom Brown, George Ridpath and Jean de Fonvive all made a good living practicing the art of the political squib.[6] By 1714 dozens of political serial publications proliferated in London alone. Some of them, like the *London Gazette* and the *Flying-Post*, were fairly long lived, while others died after a scant few issues. These papers thrived in the political atmosphere of the nation, where ready advertisers and political patrons supported them and growing numbers of literate and politically aware consumers bought them.[7] Newspaper circulation increased prodigiously during the middle of the eighteenth century. Coffee houses that carried a wide range of papers for their patrons to browse and discuss accounted for some of the increase in circulation. Most of the increase, however, must have been filled by subscribers who chose papers that best reflected their political persuasion, or through the sales by street hawkers who had become a ubiquitous feature of the street life of London and other English cities by mid-century.[8] By 1740, seventeen London papers filled the demands of their customers, printing one copy of a newspaper each week for every four inhabitants of Great Britain.[9]

Much of the content of early eighteenth-century newspapers was political, and it reached a wide reading public. It was not the Englishman's only source of political information and commentary, however; sermons, tracts and pamphlets, plays, songs, broadsides, pageantry, and even riots all served political purposes. Nevertheless, newspapers are among the most important to this study because of their portability. They were easily transported to the colonies where they were eagerly awaited, read and reprinted in colonial papers.

Because Americans received and were influenced by so many ideas about the English constitution, politics and kingship developed in the mother country, it is necessary to trace the development of these ideas at their source. While the press was employed with varying degrees of success by English monarchs from at least the reign of Elizabeth, and by politicians and Parliament from the 1620s, the public relations campaigns that had the most profound influence on Americans of the decades before the American Revolution were those sponsored by William of Orange in his bid for the English throne of 1688/9, and by the Whig supporters of the Hanover succession and dynasty who dominated government from 1714 through the eighteenth century.

For Englishmen everywhere, the Glorious Revolution was the event that defined eighteenth-century political culture and thought. In the political perceptions of English Whig thinkers this event marked a period of national unity when, according to the legend of William's invitation, arrival and accession, distinctions of politics and differences among English Protestants were put aside and an "entire concord among all intelligent Englishmen" was attained against the Catholic and tyrannical James II in favor of the Prince of Orange.[10] The Revolution was also viewed as the event that restored the English constitution to its ancient roots: government by consent, frequent Parliaments, and a balanced government that preserved the liberties and property of English subjects. At the same time William was seen as a defender of Protestantism and as the deliverer of England from the evils of Catholicism.[11]

William himself worked hard to help create these perceptions. He realized that he faced problems in making his case before the English people on the one hand, and the European states on the other, if he invaded England with a foreign army. If he entered England only as a champion of the Protestant cause, he must alienate his Catholic allies on the Continent. At the same time, if he did not make a strong enough case against James II, one that included and, in traditional English fashion, related James' political transgressions with his religious ones, William might well find himself treated as a foreign invader rather than as the nation's deliverer. To smooth the path, William and his closest Dutch and English advisors created a pamphlet to make their case against James and to clarify the Prince of Orange's intentions toward England. The *Declaration of His Highness William Henry, Prince of Orange, of the Reasons Inducing Him to Appear in Arms in the Kingdom of England for Preserving of the Protestant Religion and for Restoring the Lawes and Liberties of England, Scotland, and Ireland,* and its sequel, *The Second Declaration,* were devised to sway English public opinion toward the Prince while making a strong argument against James. William, avoiding any specific direct attack upon the King himself, declared that James had been led astray by Jesuits and wicked advisers to violate the fundamental laws of the kingdom, endangering the liberties and property of the people and subverting the constitution. The *Declaration* alleged that James had illegally favored Roman Catholics over his Protestant subjects, and had persecuted Protestants for their faith and for their love of liberty. William also cast aspersions on the origins and legitimacy of the infant Prince of Wales, declaring that "evil councillors" had published "that the Queen hath brought forth a son," that "not only we ourselves but all the good subjects of the Kingdom do vehemently suspect . . . was not bourne by the Queen."[12] William declared that it was his intention to bring these, the grievances of the people of England, before a freely chosen Parliament for investigation and settlement.

William claimed that he did not come as a foreign invader, but because of his own, and his wife's interest in the succession, the affection that English subjects had shown in the past to himself and to his family, and at the express invitation of a "great many Lords, both Spiritual and Temporal, and by many Gentlemen, and other Subjects of all Ranks."[13] He claimed that he was not actually invading England, but was accompanied by a small army (and, significantly, though he did not mention it, a printing press) in order to defend his person from James' wicked councillors.

From Torbay to London, William's press worked harder than his army did, printing two weekly papers and a vast array of pamphlets supporting the Prince, and attacking James. Many of these pamphlets were designed, not so much to castigate James, but to illuminate the character and appearance of the Prince of Orange. William, who was asthmatic, frail and weak, and whose appearance could only be described as homely out of a charitable act of kindness, was portrayed by his supporters as healthy, robust and handsome. Pamphlets and tracts published by William and his allies praised his morality and integrity, his justice and virtue, and paraded his Protestant piety at every opportunity. Though the Prince was irritable, distant, cold and aloof, William's allies depicted him in their myriad tracts on his character as amiable, sweetly tempered, and even charming. The Prince was declared valorous and brave on the battlefield, and unambitious, courteous, and unassuming in his dealings with others.[14] In short, the Orangist press endowed its patron with the traits of the ideal prince, comely in his physical, social and spiritual attributes, manly in battle, exemplary in his piety, and mild and solicitous toward his subjects. William's character, as painted in his propaganda, went a long way toward creating the mold for the model English Protestant king. At the same time, the characterization of James in William's *Declaration* and in the flood of pamphlets, tracts and cartoons produced by the Prince and his English and Dutch supporters employed traditional anti-Stuart motifs from the English Civil War, the Popish Plot and the Succession Crisis, to portray James as an evil Popish tyrant, duped by coreligionists and wicked power-hungry advisors.[15] This propaganda effort did much to consolidate an array of previous sketches of bad rulers into one ideal, and thus helped to create a stereotype of the evil English monarch.[16] At the same time William also set a precedent when he declared that he would rest his case and the case of England in the hands of a Parliament. In doing so he confirmed the nascent Whig assumption that Parliaments chose kings rather than vice versa, and that good English rulers were willing to subordinate their prerogatives to parliamentary constraint.

Once he arrived in London in late December 1688, the Prince called the Lords Temporal and Spiritual together and summoned the membership of Charles II's last Parliament (excluding members of James II's first and only Parliament as an illegal body). This assembly advised William to create a provisional government, and to call a convention in order to create a new government. The first task of this new Parliament was to bring some degree of legitimacy to the coup that had unseated the legitimate and constitutional hereditary monarch. The second was to replace James with a new ruler. Although William still maintained that he had no desire to rule, and that his only objective in invading England was to resolve the grievances of the English people, only the most naive observer could believe that William did not want the throne. In fact, he had already begun to exercise royal authority in both foreign and domestic affairs of state. He expelled the French ambassador in early January, a provocation that was in effect an act of war. He also had the Lord Chancellor (the notorious

Judge Jeffries) arrested and incarcerated in the Tower and dismissed all of James' high court judges, replacing them with others of his own choosing. As J.P. Kenyon notes, "He was not acting in James' behalf, and lawyers acknowledged that the King's legal authority had lapsed from the moment he left the country."[17] In short, William had already begun to exercise a *de facto* regal power, even before the Convention was seated.

The Convention Parliament met in late January of 1689. From the start it was plagued with constitutional complications. First, there were questions concerning William's place in things. Most members of the Convention agreed that James had forfeited his right to rule by his unconstitutional behavior while on the throne, if not by fleeing his kingdom. The Convention had no desire for his return. On the other hand, there was little constitutional precedent that might legitimate placing William on the throne apart from declaring him a conqueror, an act that was unacceptable to most members. To declare William of Orange a conqueror was to surrender the nation to a foreign power. This would hardly sit well with the English populace. Additionally, according to some prevailing political philosophers a foreign conqueror was by definition a despot. For Thomas Hobbes, for instance:

> Dominion acquired by Conquest, or Victory in war, is that which some Writers call Despoticall, . . . and this Dominion is then acquired to the Victor, when the Vanquished, to avoyd the present stroke of death, covenanteth either in express words, or by other sufficient signes . . . that so long as his life, and liberty of his body is allowed him, the Victor shall have the use thereof.[18]

In short, Hobbes continued, the vanquished are the slaves of the victor. It would not do to trade one sort of tyrant for another.

There was a minority within the Convention who called for an outright disposition in favor of William, that is, to simply declare the throne empty and install the Prince in it. There were similar, if not identical, precedents for such a disposition, one being the accession of Henry Tudor (Henry VII) in 1485. Henry had employed an army to supplement a tenuous claim to the throne based on family affinity. As the nephew and son-in-law of James II, William had, his supporters argued, as strong a claim as Henry in both particulars. The comparison was, however, strained by facts. There had been no Bosworth field; James still lived over the water; and the existence of a legitimate heir to the throne, the infant James, Prince of Wales, further strained the analogy.[19] Additionally, the prevailing Whig understanding of the first Tudor ruler made the idea unpalatable. Henry was popularly believed to have been a despotic and arbitrary ruler who raised extortionate and unconstitutional taxes, created the Court of Star Chamber to punish political enemies and enforce his tax schemes, and was allegedly manipulated by grasping and cruel councillors.[20] These were hardly the qualities that William's supporters wanted to attribute to the Prince by association.

The Orange Prince's constitutional status was not the only problem. The Convention's existence and purpose were also open to debate. It was not properly a Parliament, since it was not called by a reigning monarch. In fact it was called by an extra-constitutional body and created when the throne of England was vacant. The traditional paraphernalia required to call a Parliament were even absent because James, in a last act of political sabotage, had countermanded the writs to select a new Parliament and thrown the Great Seal into the Thames on his way out of the city. Not only might the constitutionality of the Convention be questioned, but also its purpose. At one extreme, some conservatives wanted to avoid acknowledging William as king at all, and establish a regency instead.[21] Other conservatives argued that the purpose of the Convention Parliament was to establish William on the throne as quickly as possible, to preserve the Anglican Church against both Roman Catholicism and English Dissenters, and to punish James' accomplices and supporters as quickly and decisively as possible. At the other extreme, a few supporters of the Revolution who were present at the Convention asserted that the nation had been thrown into a state of nature at James' abdication, and thus, the Convention represented a new constituent assembly with a mandate to alter the English constitution in any way that it saw fit. These members desired that England be transformed from a monarchy to a republic.[22] Some members proposed a regency. Others called for Mary, the daughter of James, to succeed her father rather than her husband.[23] A very small minority, primarily of Lords, argued that King James, while he lived, could not be deposed, and that the proceedings of the Convention amounted to "accumulative treason."[24]

When the Convention met on 22 January, 1689, it chose a speaker and promptly moved on to consider the state of the nation, and what might be done to solve the problems at hand. The result of their deliberations was the *Declaration of Rights*. The majority of those seated agreed with William's *Declaration of Reasons* when they opened debates with the premise that James had "endeavored to subvert the constitution of the Kingdom . . . by the advice of Jesuits and other wicked persons."[25] After much discussion over wording, members reached a consensus resolution stating that James had, on the advice of evil councillors, violated the fundamental laws of the land, and had deserted his kingdom, and hence was no longer king. After settling this question, the committee moved on to find a successor. The committee quickly eliminated the infant Prince of Wales from the succession by excluding any Catholic monarch from sitting henceforth on the throne of England. On 24 January, Commons passed a resolution that "it hath been found, by experience, to be inconsistent with the safety and welfare of this Protestant kingdom to be governed by a Popish Prince."[26] Thus, the Commons, by declaring the throne vacant and the immediate heir incapacitated by virtue of his religion, left the field open for William. A resolution to offer the throne to him had been proposed and seconded in Commons on 29 January, when Anthony Cary, Lord Falkland, a Tory lawyer, intervened. He questioned the wisdom of filling the throne without defining the powers of the executive. "It concerns us to take such care," he said, "that as the Prince of Orange has secured us from Popery, we may secure ourselves from Arbitrary Government." Falkland argued that before the throne should pass to any new monarch, the Convention should "consider what powers we ought to give to the Crown, to satisfy them that sent us hither."[27]

Falkland's recommendation found support from the vast majority of members. Whigs supported it as a means of explaining James' abdication in order to forestall public disorder and to punish their political enemies who had supported the Stuart monarch. They saw that both goals might best be reached if "the nation's grievances" were published in detail.[28] Tory members were just as eager as their Whig colleagues to resolve the matter. Discussion of the possibility of placing constraints on the king had been circulating among the Tory leadership since the previous October. They regarded this as a necessity both to preserve the Church and to prevent arbitrary rule and taxation without parliamentary oversight. William had also tacitly endorsed this when, in his *Declaration* and in other tracts published by his supporters, he advocated that a parliament be called to judge the nation's grievances, and restore the liberties and rights of the kingdom, and the "ancient constitution."[29] Some Tories, like their Whig colleagues, also wanted to see James' followers punished.

The result of Falkland's proposal was the *Declaration of Grievances*, which was renamed the *Declaration of Rights*. The *Declaration of Rights* presented a list of actions, attributed to James II, that came to define arbitrary rule. The document also confirmed the supremacy of Parliament. Its creators claimed that it represented no constitutional innovations; it merely reaffirmed the undisputable ancient rights of English subjects, and at the same time reiterated the ancient first principles of the constitution by giving Parliament pride of place in government.

The *Declaration* began with a list of allegations against James II. It claimed that the Stuart ruler, "by the Assistance of divers Evil Councillors, Judges, and Ministers, employed by him did endeavour to subvert and extirpate the Protestant Religion, and the Lawes and Liberties of this Kingdom."[30] He had pretended the right to dispense with laws, to set up unconstitutional courts, and to prosecute defendants in his own courts who, by right, should have been tried only by Parliament. James levied taxes without consent, and raised and maintained a standing army in time of peace without consulting Parliament. He allowed Catholics to go armed and disarmed Protestants. He inflicted cruel and unusual punishments, "all which were contrary to the known Lawes and Statutes and Freedome of this Realm."[31]

Having summed up James' perfidy, the document declared that William, "whom it hath pleased Almighty God to make the glorious Instrument of delivering this Kingdom from Popery and Arbitrary Power," had come by the invitation of Englishmen of all classes to resolve the nation's grievances.[32] In response to this call the Convention proposed thirteen items as the best means to resolve their grievances and "for the vindication and asserting of their [the people of England] antient rights and Liberties."[33] They declared it illegal for the Crown to dispense with or suspend laws, to raise money without the consent of Parliament, to create courts of special jurisdiction, or to raise or keep standing armies in times of peace without the consent of Parliament. They confirmed the right of Protestant subjects to keep arms "for their defence Suitable to their Condition and as allowed by Law," and the right of English subjects to petition the king.[34] It also called for frequent Parliaments, and declared that freedom of speech and debate within that body ought not to be hindered by the Crown or the courts. The document then declared William and Mary to be the co-rulers of the realm.

Like William's *Declaration of Reasons* before it, the *Declaration of Rights* clarified, indeed codified, the behavior of arbitrary rulers, and by contrast, good rulers as well. It redefined the relationship between king and people and also elevated William to defender and savior of English Protestantism and liberty. As is so often the case in English constitution making, the framers of the *Declaration of Rights* who were, at the time, most concerned with the specific problems at hand (reversing James' abuses, increasing parliamentary oversight over the executive and filling a vacant throne) created two political myths. The first was that the Convention had restored the ancient constitution, thus preserving the ancient rights and liberties and the "primitive Christianity" of the English people. The second was that the *Declaration* confirmed and sharpened the dichotomy between good and evil monarchs, as represented by James Stuart and William of Orange. The Convention also created a new political reality: that henceforth the behavior of the Crown was to be constrained by Parliament, and that the succession of English monarchs was not entirely hereditary, but might be changed by the people through their representative body.[35]

Although the Crown as redefined by the *Declaration of Rights* was subordinated to Parliament, it was still intended to be able to exercise the constitutional powers necessary in order to function as an institution of government. This was necessary because political thinkers understood that the English government was built on a republican model, in which the three branches (Crown, Lords and Commons) employed checks and balances to protect the people's liberties. The king still had the power of appointments—"of disposing of all Places of *Honour, Profit,* and *Trust*"—to positions of church and state, and the judiciary and the military.[36] He still had the power to create peers, and, so long as he did so frequently, to summon and dismiss Parliament. He still had a negative over Parliamentary statute, though he was forbidden from giving specific dispensations or from suspending laws once they were on the books. In short, William was not to be a titular head of state, but "a real, working, governing king."[37]

The myth-making continued in the coronation ceremony of 11 April, 1689. Instead of employing the Archbishop of Canterbury, William Sancroft, who did not support the new regime, William and his advisors gave the responsibility for arranging the ceremony to Henry Compton, Bishop of London. Compton, one of the signers of the Invitation and Mary's former tutor, had a reputation for militant anti-Catholicism and was respected among Dissenters and Whigs as well as Williamite Churchmen. The Anglican communion ceremony, absent from James' coronation, was reinstated, and its importance stressed by placing the coronation ceremony in the middle of the Eucharist. A large (quarto-sized) and richly adorned Protestant Bible was featured prominently among the regalia. It was presented to the royal couple during the ceremony at Westminister Hall that preceded the coronation, and was carried in the procession to the Abbey and shown from time to time to the spectators along the way.[38] The couple kissed the Bible after placing their hands upon it during the oath, copying the practice of witnesses when they took the oath in the law courts. They were then admonished by Compton to make the Bible "the rule of [their] whole life and Government."[39] The prominence of the Protestant Bible in the coronation ceremony confirmed the religious character of the Revolution, and reminded spectators that the new king was the rescuer and defender of English Protestantism. The text of the coronation sermon preached by Dr. Gilbert Burnet, an English refugee of conscience who had returned from Holland with William, was "The God of Israel spake to me, He that ruleth over men must be just, ruling in the fear of God."[40] This passage from the Book of Samuel was significant as it was God's exhortation to David after He had shown His favor by placing him on the throne of Israel in preference to the children and line of Saul, whom God had punished with death for their transgressions. Hence, to biblically conscious Englishmen, the sermon both admonished the new monarchs to rule in a godly fashion and equated William's coronation with the act of divine providence that had placed David on the throne of Israel.

The coronation oath was changed. It required the king not only to follow and uphold the laws and customs of the realm, as had traditionally been the case, but also to govern "according to the statutes in Parliament agreed on, and the laws and customs" of England, significantly placing parliamentary statute in the oath for the first time and giving it a place of precedence before the other elements of the Common Law.[41] The new oath clearly implied that monarchs were not above Parliament, and that statute took precedence over the traditions and customs of the nation.[42]

The symbolism that equated William with English Protestant kingship appeared in the memorabilia of the coronation as well as in the regalia. A medal struck for the occasion featured the two monarchs surrounded by a floral wreath of oranges and roses. A single crown was placed above their heads, and above the crown were the eye and sun rays that symbolized divine providence. Below the couple was an open book captioned "LEGES ANGLIAE," and resting upon the open book was a liberty cap. The new monarchs were thus portrayed as providential liberators of the English people, whose rule was the rule of law.

William's propaganda machine did not rest after the coronation. The king's supporters published articles, pamphlets, plays and songs during his reign that were intended to keep a proper understanding of the Revolution fresh in the minds of his subjects.[43] These works continued to stress anti-Stuart and anti-Catholic themes, and the idea that the nation had been unified under William. Over time the incidents and rumors of James' reign became stock props for the popular press, and crafty priests, Catholic worship, evil advisers, bed warming pans, French *agents provocateurs*, violent, half-witted and belligerent Irishmen, and royal cowardice became the potent symbols of tyrannical rule.[44] At the same time Williamite authors and poets praised their master in increasingly flowery terms. The themes of the model ruler and some of the props of the model tyrant are evidenced in this "clearly unperformable" stage instruction from the closing of the last scene from *The Abdicated Prince* of 1690:

> Enter *Prince Lysander*, attended with the Nobility and Gentry of *Hungary*, and Guards in a magnificent manner, with Drums beating, Trumpets sounding, Colours flying, the People shouting, and the Guns round the great Tower firing; at which the Skies clear up, the Sun shines, and all the enchanted Pagan Mosques, Priests, Jebusites, Crosses, Beads, Quo Warranto's, Dispensators, Ecclesiastic Commissioners, &c., vanish in a Moment.[45]

William was able to sustain a long argument about his place in history that eventually won out over any opposition views. In the process of creating his own persona he also succeeded in creating a general stereotype of the ideal monarch.

His successor was not so fortunate. Although Queen Anne's reign has undergone a degree of revision over the last two decades, the characterization that Whigs gave her after her reign (1702-1714) certainly had an enormous influence over Englishmen's understanding of the history of the eighteenth century.[46] She was remembered as a poor monarch who was manipulated by friends and advisors who would have had her resume arbitrary government to support their interests. Whigs argued that but for their vigilance, Anne's Tory favorites would have brought in the Pretender at her death. In most important particulars, Anne was not really very different from her predecessor. She, like William, was a military monarch who presided over a nation that was at war through most of her reign.[47] Like William, she viewed the English parties as a threat to the power of the Crown.[48] She was less fortunate than her predecessor in that the growth of religious dissent and political differences over both domestic and international issues "produced a strong polarization, pulling men into the Whig or the Tory camp."[49] Her reign saw fairly frequent party turnovers in both Parliament and in her cabinet. In fact, until the last six months of her reign Anne's ministry, like William's, was usually comprised of both Whigs and Tories "which could act in the interests of the nation rather than those of faction."[50] It is perhaps unfortunate for the Queen's reputation and our understanding of her reign that at her death on 1 August, 1714, a Tory majority existed in both houses of Parliament, and her cabinet was dominated by Robert Harley, and the Duke of Ormonde, both despised by the Whigs, and the arch-Tory Henry St. John, Viscount Bolingbroke.

Anne's successor, George, the Elector of Hanover, was received peacefully, if not particularly enthusiastically, when he arrived at Greenwich on 30 September, 1714. He was cheered by crowds on his arrival in London, but at least one historian has ascribed the cheering crowds to the "very impact of majesty, the awe which the mythology surrounding the sovereign imposed even in the age of the Early Enlightenment."[51] His arrival was greeted with enthusiasm by at least some of his new subjects. Dissenters welcomed the new monarch, whose reputation for religious toleration in his German state preceded him. They hoped that he would end the persecution that they had suffered during the last years of Anne's reign, and ignore enforcement of the Schism Act, passed by Bolingbroke in the Spring of 1714.[52] Whigs also had good reason to cheer George's arrival. Although he made it quite clear that he intended to rule rather than to defer his prerogatives to any party and declared that he intended to choose his government based on ability rather than affiliation, his behavior tended to belie his rhetoric. When he sent his list of regents for an interim government to rule until his arrival, fourteen of nineteen were Whigs.[53] While dissenters and Whigs viewed the new monarch's future, and their own, with great anticipation, most of the nation waited to see what the future would bring.

The Whigs' enthusiasm for the new king was well founded indeed. Elections for a new Parliament to meet in March returned a huge Whig majority. The new Whig government, emboldened by the results of the election, moved to lay articles of impeachment against Harley and Bolingbroke. Charges against the former were quietly dropped when he declared that he intended to move to the country and retire forever from politics. When Bolingbroke, fearing treason charges, escaped to France, he was attainted by Parliament. He became the Secretary of State to the Pretender at St. Germain. The King dismissed all but a very few Tories, most of them able, experienced and moderate statesmen, from the government, but promised that he would try to find places for them in minor positions at a later date. George was shocked when they angrily left government altogether.[54] The new Whig cabinet quickly set to work filling every patronage position from undersecretary to shire justice of the peace with their fellows. This purge, and the judicial revenge against the Tory leadership of the previous administration, contributed greatly to civil disturbances in England and to the Pretender's decision to challenge the Hanover succession.

From March of 1715, Scots and disaffected English conservatives of all stripes began to rally behind the Pretender as an alternative monarch. Many Scots felt that James was the legitimate ruler of Scotland, and longed for independence from England. Many Tories, even the most moderate, viewed the wholesale weeding out of their party from both national and local government and the prosecution of their leaders with anxiety, not only for the future of the nation, but for their own political and personal well-being as well. Religious conservatives, the high churchmen, feared that the growth of religious dissent and the support that Whigs gave to Dissenters would have dire effects on the Church of England. They did not so much gravitate toward the Pretender as retreat from the Elector. Political and religious anxiety and frustration led fairly quickly to anger and violence. On 23 April, the anniversary of Queen Anne's coronation and St. George's Day, crowds marched through the streets of London crying "God Bless the Queen," and "Save the High Church."[55] By 28 May, George's birthday, the popular movement had spread to all parts of the kingdom. Jacobite, or at least anti-Hanover, mobs cut church bell ropes to prevent them being rung in celebration of the monarch's birthday, scattered burning logs from celebratory bonfires (occasionally burning down houses in the process), and threw bricks through windows that George's supporters had illuminated for the occasion.[56] Rioting continued through the summer. The greatest part of the rioters' fury fell on the most visible evidence of Protestant Dissent as mobs all over England tore down or fired the meeting houses of Dissenters in much the same manner that their fathers had attacked buildings suspected of housing the Roman mass.[57]

In response to the disorder, Parliament passed the Riot Act, or, as one Tory wag christened it "the Bill of Riots."[58] The law stated that riotous assemblies of twelve or more people were guilty of a capital felony if they refused to disburse within an hour of being commanded by a magistrate, by proclamation, to do so in the king's name.[59] Public disorder increased, especially in London, where gangs of "Jacks" and "loyalists" engaged in gang fights and raided the coffee houses and taverns of their political adversaries, sometimes in groups as large as five hundred.[60] In the midst of popular turbulence in England, John, the Earl of Mar, raised the Stuart standard and summoned the clans in Scotland, and disaffected Highlanders began to rally behind it.

Thus, within a year, George, whose succession had been supported before the fact by a wide range of Englishmen, reigned over a deeply divided and unstable nation. His government set out to restore order from the turmoil that it had created, to rehabilitate the tarnished image of the king, and to define the place of the Whig party in history. Whig leaders created the tools necessary for the restoration of order in the summer and fall of 1715 when Parliament passed the Riot Act, and suspended the Habeas Corpus Act for six months. The Whigs also had an active press that was eager to place its services at the disposal of the new king and his party.

Shortly after Anne's death, and even before George's arrival, the Whig presses began to sing his praises in conscious imitation of the style and themes invoked by William and his public relations machine. Whig editors and publicists took every possible opportunity to link the two monarchs in the minds of their readers. "The illustrious GEORGE," one editor intoned, "cannot well be sounded by Britons without bringing to Remembrance the Great Name of WILLIAM."[61] This would certainly be the case if the press had anything to do with it. Whig papers stressed the unity of the nation that had extended an invitation to the Elector and the new ruler's interest in preserving the liberties, religion, and laws of England.[62] Just as William and his press had denounced James' evil councillors, the Whig press blasted Queen Anne's Tory administration. Apart from left-handed compliments to the late monarch based on her gender, Anne fared better from publicists' barbs than her father had, but her government and closest advisors and friends received no mercy, as evidenced by this piece published less than two weeks after her death:

Her Majesty certainly [was] one of the best of Women, the Ornament of her Sex, but it does not hence follow that she could not be grosly [sic] abus'd; the best and wisest Princes are sometimes forc'd to see and hear by the Eyes and Ears of their Ministers, and if they betray them by their ill Advice, . . . it in no way reflects on the Honour or Justice of the Prince . . . What Prince (tho' as wise as *Solomon*) could ever detect the Treason of a *Judas* Statesman, that plots and contrives his Ruin under the specious Pretence of Loyalty? And this, Alas! Was exactly the case of her Majesty with respect to that Jacobite Treason which has been so long hatching by her pretended Friends to bring in the Pretender, Popery and Slavery.[63]

National unity, a theme that William had used so successfully, ceased to resonate in the face of Whig supremacy in government, the Tory purge, and the popular disorder that followed it. Instead, Whig publicists stressed the disloyalty and treachery of their opponents, equating them with Jacobitism, Romanism and rebellion. At the same time they felt the need to justify the legitimacy of the Hanover claim to the throne. It is apparent that Whigs believed that some stronger and more traditional claim than a Parliamentary statute was necessary in order to forge a national consensus for Hanover rule. This need became more pressing as an increasing number of Englishmen called, often loudly and violently in the streets, for their king over the water, drank toasts to Queen Anne of glorious memory, and rang church bells in celebration of the Stuart claimant's birthday. Sometimes simple solutions are best when it comes to image making. From the Spring of 1715, publicists began to declare that George, the great grandson of James I, had an hereditary claim to the throne of England that was, by implication, at least as good as that of the Pretender—better, in fact, since the former was Protestant and the latter Catholic. Joseph Addison remarked that, although no one doubted George's bloodline, and therefore his right to occupy the throne:

> many believe that you [the Pretender] are not son to King *James* the Second. Besides all the World acknowledges he [George] is the nearest to our Crown of the Protestant Blood; of which you cannot have a Drop in your Veins, unless you derive it from such Parents as you don't care for owning.[64]

Thus armed, Whig publicists, following very much in the footsteps of William, asserted that George had both a hereditary and providential claim to the throne, and a mandate to defend the liberties and religion of the nation from disorder and treason at home and absolutist Catholic incursion from abroad. The following passage from an address to the ruler illustrates their arguments:

> [We] being deeply impressed with the Divine Goodness brightly displayed in the late Revolution, begun and carried out by King *William* of Glorious Memory, and in bringing in our only Lawful and Rightful Sovereign King GEORGE to the peaceable Possession of the Throne of his Royal Ancestors, notwithstanding the many open and secret Practices that have been used of *late* Years to defeat the Succession, cannot sufficiently adore the Providence which so often and so seasonably interposed to save this Nation from Popery and Slavery.[65]

The events of 1715 were concluded swiftly and efficiently. The Duke of Argyle suppressed the rebellion in Scotland and Parliament dispatched troops to guard those areas of England where potential support existed for the Scots rebels. Popular disorder in London ceased when five "Jacks" were hanged in July of 1716, for their riotous behavior.[66]

Although the rebellion and popular unrest never really threatened either the new dynasty or the Whig regime, they had a serious effect on the politics of the realm. From the 1680s to 1715 competition between Whigs and Tories for political supremacy, prestige, and places in government had defined the English political landscape. The events of 1715, however, cast a pall on the Tories, who were henceforth associated with hypocrisy, Jacobitism and treason. George I and his successor were convinced that Tories could never be trusted with political responsibility again, and so looked exclusively to Whigs to steer the course of the government. The Whigs, in their turn, set about to solidify their political victory. They consolidated their position in the country by purging virtually all of the remaining Tory magistrates and J.P.s, and removed the last Hanover Tory, Nottingham, from government.

In May of 1716 Whigs ensured their supremacy in government by passing the Septennial Act which extended the life of the existing Parliament by four years. To gratify Dissenters and reward them for their support, Whigs repealed the Occasional Conformity and Schism Acts in December of 1718. George's ministry was prepared to go even further to consolidate Whig primacy in government. Ministers recommended the creation of legislation to give control of Cambridge and Oxford universities to the government, to repeal the Septennial Act and thus prolong the current Parliament indefinitely, and to limit the prerogative of the Crown in the creation of new peers. The first two suggestions were never acted upon, and the last was defeated by a Commons that viewed the Peerage Bill as a stumbling block to the honors that they saw as their reward for government service. Robert Walpole, the rising star in the Whig constellation, helped to defeat the Bill when he argued that it would close "the avenue of honour and promotion to which all country gentlemen might aspire, if not for themselves, then for their children and their children's children."[67]

In the process of completing their domination of government, Whigs found themselves promoting measures that ran against the grain of the prevailing interpretation of the constitution as outlined in the *Declaration of Rights* of 1689. The Septennial Act clearly violated the doctrine of frequent Parliaments, and the Peerage Bill represented a rather severe restraint upon an executive branch already so beleaguered "since the *Habeas Corpus* Act, and the great and numerous *Limitations* of the *Successions Acts*," that some felt that the Crown would be hard pressed to provide a check against the growing power of the Commons.[68] Additionally, Parliament felt the need to maintain a large standing army in order to defend the new regime from domestic disturbances and foreign incursion in spite of the fact that the nation was at peace. A coalition of Whig opposition and country members forced the government to accept a cut in the size of the army in 1718, but the ministry continued to campaign for an enlargement of the armed forces.

Even though Whigs had been successful in their bid to purge the government of any Tories who might oppose them, their authoritarian measures angered the country gentlemen of the back benches and provided fodder for a new Whig opposition. The former were members of Parliament who were always distrustful of central government, and who treated their seats not as a means to their own aggrandizement, but as a trust from their constituents. They were characterized by the Court Whigs to possess a "restless aversion to all government . . . against which the best Minister is no more secure than the worst."[69] Although the country back benchers rarely comprised a formidable threat to the administration, by 1716 a Whig opposition composed of disappointed office seekers had begun to grow in the nurturing atmosphere of the "court" of the Prince of Wales. Their primary goal was simply to bring down the current government in order to raise themselves to power. As a matter of policy they courted Tories, country gentlemen, and anyone else who disapproved of current policy. In order to garner Tory support they denounced measures which they had previously supported in George's early reign, such as the repeal of the Occasional Conformity and Schism Acts. They attacked proposed tax increases, the expansion of the army, and other policies of the administration in order to gain the support of the country independents.[70] This "loyal" opposition that usually surrounded the current Prince of Wales became a feature of the politics of the first three Georges.

In the face of growing criticism from country writers and a nascent Whig opposition movement that gathered around the Prince of Wales, the Government depended upon their loyal presses, especially the *St. James Journal*, where the publicity campaign was ably led by Thomas Gordon and John Trenchard, to promote their policies and control the political fallout that so often ensued from them.[71] The Court Whig press promoted specific measures primarily by means of arguments based on practicality. It argued that the Septennial Act saved gentlemen from the prohibitive cost of standing for election every three years. Since elections were events that promoted factiousness, and thus occasional civil disorder, they argued that it was for the best if they were held less frequently. The press tried to calm the fears of those who worried that longer Parliaments might more easily be corrupted by reminding them that the king, ever mindful of his subjects' welfare, still had the power to dismiss a Parliament that threatened the liberties of the people. Administration publicists protested that the Peerage Bill was not meant to keep the present king from enlarging the House of Lords to promote his evil designs, because he was the best of princes, and had none; it was to forestall future monarchs, who might not be as benign as the present ruler, from doing as Queen Anne had done under the late Tory administration. A large standing army was necessary to promote peace at home and abroad. The representatives of the people, the House of Commons, raised and supported the army, not the Crown; therefore it would never be placed at the disposal of a tyrannical monarch.[72] The present armed forces were small and England's enemies great, and so a larger army was necessary to "support the Peace and Liberties" of Englishmen. Editors were quick to point out that the loudest critics of a bigger army were those "whose Master must be a Vagabond abroad 'til those forces are disbanded."[73]

The administration's supporters in the press argued that whatever Parliament did was, and could only be, for the good of its constituents: the freeholders of England.[74] "'Tis certain," wrote an editor of the *St. James Journal*, "that Parliaments are the constant Security of the Subjects' Rights and Liberties . . . they have never intirely [sic] forgot their Duty and Obligation to the People, their Electors."[75] The Parliament was, after all, chosen by the honest freeholders of England. It was dominated by Whigs, the party that had always promoted the people's liberty and exhibited "a Spirit of Opposition to all Exorbitant Power in any Part of the Constitution."[76]

The claim that the Whigs represented the interest of the county freeholders was itself novel. The Tories had traditionally held this place, while the Whigs had been understood to represent the towns and cities and the trading interests. When county voters returned a sizeable Tory majority in the election of 1710, as they had in the past, Jonathan Swift claimed that "the *Whigs* themselves have always confessed, that the bulk of the Landed Men in *England* was generally of *Tories*."[77] But in 1715 Whigs won more county seats than they ever had previously. This convinced Joseph Addison to name his series of tracts that promoted the Whigs and the Hanover king *The Freeholder*. He hoped to persuade readers that the Whigs represented country landowners as much as they did the other interests of the nation.[78] "A Free-holder in our Government," wrote Addison, was "of the Nature of a Citizen of *Rome* in that famous Commonwealth, who by the Election of a Tribune, had a kind of remote Voice in every Law that was enacted."[79]

Members of Parliament found that their constituents believed that if the Commons existed to serve the electorate, as was so frequently professed in the Whig press, then perhaps the voices of the freeholders should be less remote, and their representatives ought to be more eager to receive their instructions on the issues of the day.[80] Members quickly found the frequent instructions from their constituents to be inconvenient and somewhat alarming, as those instructions often ran counter to the measures that the Whig regime supported. The Septennial Act had freed members from actually feeling any real immediate pressure to gratify their constituents, but it was rather embarrassing to receive numerous and frequent instructions calling for the reduction of the army, more frequent Parliamentary elections, place bills, and other measures that ran counter to the administration's program.[81] Members and the government Whig press began to explain to constituents that representatives were not under any obligation to receive or follow the instructions of their constituents. As a *London Journal* editor put it, "to send threatning letters, and authoritative orders and commands, to those in whom we have lodg'd the supreme powers of legislation . . . is an unexampled piece of licentiousness, tending to the total dissolution of government."[82] Institutional Whigs created an analogy based on John Locke's premise that the people gave up their natural liberties to their rulers when they created civil government. The Court Whigs gave a new twist to Locke's premise, arguing that the people of the nation had, in time long past, tacitly consented to be governed by a commonwealth that consisted of King, Lords and Commons, and that compact could not be broken unless the government defaulted by abusing the trust of the people.[83] Constituents could petition any branch of the government for redress of grievances and instruct a candidate for the House of Commons, and, of course, they were always "at liberty, when the time is expired, to chuse others" to sit in Parliament, but that was the limit to which they should go.[84] As the *London Journal* editor noted, "that part of the power of legislation which belongs to the people is no longer in them collectively, but is devolv'd upon, and remains solely in their representatives."[85] Whigs claimed that sovereignty, though derived from the people in ancient times, was vested in the legislature, and not the people, and rested upon the laws of reason and divine will.[86] Once the People delegated "this Power . . ., into the Hands of Parliament, it becomes legally absolute, and the People are by their very Constitution oblig'd to a Passive Obedience."[87] Taking a cue from the Stuarts but applying it to the legislature instead of the king, Whigs claimed that political power "is from God, in opposition to Those who suppos'd it to be a Gift from the

People."[88] Simply put, by 1722 the Whigs who controlled both the Crown and Parliament employed very similar general arguments (passive obedience and divine right) to substantiate their sovereign and unchallengeable authority that the Stuart monarchs from James I had used to support absolute monarchy. They reasoned that these means were amply justified to defend the ends of maintaining the Hanovers on the throne, ensuring domestic order and British liberties, and not incidently securing their own predominance on the political stage.

After the Conspiracy of 1722 (the Atterbury Plot), the administration continued to follow in the footsteps of the Stuarts when it suspended the Habeas Corpus Act for a whole year instead of the traditional six months. This outraged country members and even some moderate Whigs. The government press went to work to put a good face on the unpopular measure, claiming that the state had an obligation to the people of the nation to preserve order and protect them from domestic conspiracy fomented by the enemies of their liberties—Tories, Jacobites, Catholics and Non-jurors. After all, one writer argued, the preservation of the people's safety was the first goal of government—*salus populi suprema lex esto*; "this is a Divine Law, by which all other, merely Human, Laws are to be controlled, qualified, or interpreted."[89] Whigs believed that the public welfare could best be secured through the preservation of public order, and thus, for them, the Roman maxim demanded that government restrain popular unruliness the better to insure the public welfare. To that end Parliament suspended the Habeas Corpus Act and passed a tax of five shillings upon every Catholic in Britain in order to pay the expenses incurred by the government in suppressing the conspiracy.[90] The *St. James Journal,* working tirelessly for the people's welfare and to promote the ministry, proposed that Parliament go further. Although the editor professed an aversion "against Persecution of all kinds," he recommended that the government place all Papists and Non-jurors into custody because they were all suspect and collectively represented a threat to the order of the nation. "The bare Suspicion of a Man's being concerned in any such pernicious Contrivances," the editor argued, " is sufficient to justify the securing of his Person, whether anything directly or positively can be proved or no." The editor stated that those guilty of conspiracy should be punished, and should be held until their guilt could be ascertained to prevent them from escaping. The innocent "will never have any Resentments rise in him," against the authorities, any more than a healthy person should be "displeased with a Physician, who, in a Time of Contagion, was appointed to inquire, whether he was [sick] or no, when the

Sick and Well mingled together, and every body was, by that means, in danger of receiving the Infection."[91] While this political quarantine was a road not taken, its recommendation is indicative of the extent to which some Whigs were prepared to go in order to preserve the people, the king, and their own place in the nation.

The Whigs gradually developed an historical interpretation of the constitution during their dominance over government under the first two Hanoverian rulers. Although it was rather short on philosophy and long on practicality, it contained a fundamental coherence at its root. Whigs preferred to look back no further than the Glorious Revolution for the basis of English government. The revolutionary settlement provided them with a firm foundation to support their assertion that Parliament had a limiting power over the prerogatives of the Crown, and, at the same time, defended them from any admission that sovereignty was derived (except in some dim past) from the people. Although Whigs asserted that their constitution was influenced by the Glorious Revolution, they also claimed that the settlement that resulted from the Revolution was not an innovation, but simply a return to its true and ancient constitutional principles.[92] Whigs believed that the constitution was fundamentally a mixed and balanced government that preserved the peace and protected the rights and property of the freeholders; that is, the landed and moneyed interests of the nation.[93]

Whigs held Aristotle's view on mixed government. They understood that the English Commonwealth was a republic or combination of the three pure forms of government—monarchy, aristocracy, and democracy—with each exerting a check on the interests of the other. Each branch possessed its own particular privileges, and each performed specific functions. The monarch was the fount of all honors and the source of justice. He retained prerogative powers meant to check the other branches, including a negative on legislation, the right to hear petitions from his subjects and redress their stated grievances, and the right to summon, prorogue and dissolve Parliament. The peerage, sitting in assembly, enjoyed the highest honors in the state: they could originate legislation, and constituted the highest court in the realm. The House of Commons represented the English polity, and was thus the proper place for the discussion and correction of any matters that aggrieved the people. It also held the purse-strings as supply bills had to be initiated there. No legislation could become law and no tax could be levied unless it met the approval of all three branches of government during the same session of Parliament. Thus, in theory, the English government was a mixed and balanced tripartite republic.

In practice, however, constitutional divisions were blurred by party government. By George II's accession, Court Whigs believed that the unification of the government obtained by having sitting members of Parliament in the ministry was beneficial and even necessary to the ends of government—that "harmonious relations between the executive and the legislature could be maintained only if there were close links between the two."[94]

Although country critics had cried foul at the employment of legislative members in judicial, military and ministry positions since the reign of Charles II, Court Whigs viewed the practice as a "form of constitutional lubricant," necessary for the promotion of legislation, and the survival of any particular ministry.[95] The government was never able to insure a majority for its policies, no matter how much "influence" it exerted on the legislature, however. Even when Walpole and Newcastle, both consummate manipulators of patronage, guided elections and found places in Parliament for their clients, the best they could do was create a small nucleus of supporters to advocate their policies. Historian John Owen estimates that office holders in the House of Commons before 1750 never amounted to much more than about one-quarter of the whole assembly, and even they could not always be depended upon to vote in support of the government.[96] Ministry Whigs primarily viewed "influence" as a vital link between the Crown and Commons, but they understood that the passage of their legislation depended on majorities that could not be obtained without a wide consensus of the members of the House of Commons. The government was thus dependent upon the representatives of the boroughs and rural freeholders for support of its policies.

Whigs believed that political power followed property. In this particular sense they differed little from Tories. Whigs, however, recognized that landed property was not the only measure of wealth in the nation, and claimed to speak for the merchants, manufacturers and financiers as well as the landholders. These new men were not expected to take as active a role in national politics as those whose wealth was built upon the firm foundation of landed property, but the Whigs recognized that the prosperity they provided contributed to the stability and wealth of the nation.[97] To protect the interests of the propertied classes, Whig governments created laws that made property more secure. Parliament increased the number of capital crimes for offenses that involved property. They passed the Black Act in 1723 against poaching, and other legislation to protect dogs, horses, fences, grain, cattle, and hedges.[98] In addition to the passage of legislation that protected property, Whigs lowered property taxes and made up the loss of revenues by introducing excise taxes on a wide range of domestically produced consumer goods. Taxes on such basic commodities as coal, soap, salt, candles, beer and cider shifted the burden of taxation from the landowners to the whole population, but the overall effect of the excise policy, as Nathaniel Mist asserted, was to "increase the Expense of the laboring and manufacturing People more, in proportion, than that of others in a higher Rank."[99] Through these means and others the Whig government leaders forged a steady political consensus that brought in majorities on their most important and least controversial measures.

That is not to say that Whigs ever enjoyed the support of all of the landholding country members. A group of "independent country gentlemen," one of three classes of men that Sir Lewis Namier called the "predestined Parliament men," held more or less permanent seats in the House of Commons. These country squires, elected to their seats from their home counties or respectable rural boroughs, had family influence and prestige that practically guaranteed them "the seats that were in that sense hereditary."[100] They comprised a more or less permanent standing opposition to the government throughout the eighteenth century.[101] Government Whigs categorized them as Tories, but Namier's characterization of them is more just. They were neither gifted with great political acumen, organization, or experience, but were of "an independent character and station in life," and indifferent to the temptations of office.[102] They believed that they had been elected to reflect the interests and sentiments of their constituents and behaved accordingly. They were nearly impossible to affiliate with any particular party, because these independent country squires lacked both the interest and the time to involve themselves in political matters in London when Parliament was not in session– "fox-hunting, gardening, planting, or indifference" occupied their time in the country "till the very day before the meeting of Parliament."[103] Though never much more than one-fifth of the total members, and never sufficiently disciplined to oppose the government alone, they were a significant force in English politics, and had a serious impact on the development of political thought throughout the century.

The British government was not, as French commentators like Voltaire, Montesquieu, and Lolme asserted, "a republic disguised as a monarchy," but neither was it the aristocratic despotism that country critics described.[104] What it had in fact become was an oligarchy dominated by various interrelated groups of people, all of whom held an adherence to a common ideology and all of whom were devoted to the preservation of domestic tranquility, national prosperity, and their own continuation in government. They had learned from bitter experience during George I's reign that an authoritative and unified government was required if their goals were to be promoted and sustained.

The first premise of Whig government—authority—was assured by the unification of all the branches of government under the influence of Crown and ministry. Whigs were able to monopolize government from the 1720s until at least 1754, primarily because they were able to convince the first two Hanover rulers that they were the only party that was trustworthy and completely loyal to the German House. Implacably anti-Tory, the first two Georges also accepted single party rule as their best security as well as the best means of promoting the interests of Great Britain and their own continental ambitions. So long as the kings accepted and identified with the Whig interests and were themselves essentially Court Whigs, "single-party government and the existence of 'a sense of common identity' were mutually reinforcing and dependent."[105] The theoretically separate interests of the three branches of government lost their distinction when the king, his ministry, and majorities in both Lords and Commons all shared the same ideology and, to a great extent, the same aims and goals. Historians have argued that the power of the Whig oligarchy rested upon the authority that the executive branch held over the legislature.[106] It is worth noting, however, that most of the politicians who rose to dominance in the age of Carteret, Walpole, Pelham and Pitt built the power base that sent them to Whitehall in the corridors and upon the benches of Westminister. The authority that they wielded was derived from their ability to play all of the branches of government, each with their separate and different strengths and weaknesses, in harmony. It might be more truthful to say that it was not so much the grip of the executive upon the legislature that drove the state as the directorial skills of the Whigs, who dominated the mix at any given time and kept the government in concert. Specific Whig ministries rose and fell, but since the king chose his new cabinet only from among the Whig factions, all of whom shared the same basic conceptions of government, the Whig tune continued.

Attempting to define the philosophical sources of Court Whig ideology can be frustrating. The premises of government by popular compact and the right of popular revolution were all admirable when a change of government was desired. John Locke's theories on the subject were taken down from the shelf, dusted off, and displayed on those occasions when he could safely be employed to reflect the government's zeal for liberty. The Whigs who governed the nation generally felt, however, that such notions were far too inflammatory to be allowed as the permanent basis for government. Only a small radical minority of Whigs accepted Locke's premise that an original contract was made by the express and explicit consent of the English people, or that such a contract constituted the foundation of the English government.[107] Court Whigs faced the uncomfortable prospect that post-revolutionary rulers often experience: what can be created by one revolution can be destroyed by another. Whigs felt that Lockean concepts like popular consent and the popular right to revolution were at odds with public order and with the effective, authoritative governance required to maintain it. Instead, they argued that once men had agreed to live together in civil society, they relinquished their sovereignty to their rulers, so that the power of government "should be absolute, and have the Sovereign Disposal of the Properties and Persons of all Individuals" who lived under it. But Whigs softened the threat of a government with so much power by arguing that its authority, though "as absolute as that of the grand Turk," could only be employed for the good of the nation because the governors themselves were constrained by the same laws as their subjects.[108]

In general, Whigs asserted that the first goal of government was the preservation of liberty. Ministry Whigs argued that the best means by which to promulgate that goal was through a strong government that could preserve domestic order and maintain a strong national defense. To achieve these ends the government promoted measures that inevitably brought an increased presence of national government into areas of the country that it had touched only lightly before. Excise men and other features of the complex excise apparatus appeared all over the nation, and people who had never previously paid taxes paid the excise on everyday products. After 1715 the army was more visible in rural areas and country towns. The Riot Act replaced local processes that had traditionally been employed by the shire and town elite to pacify popular disturbances. All of these innovations increased the visibility and authority of the national government in localities where previously it had only rarely been sensed.

Instead of employing any science of politics to support the policies of successive Whig ministries, their supporters in the press devoted themselves to making their political detractors as unpopular as possible, as well as bolstering the power and legitimacy of the ruling Whig oligarchy by portraying them as the defenders of the freeholders' liberty and property and the fittest representatives of the people of England. Whig ideology was dominated by party thinking. Court Whigs asserted that there had been, at least since the Reign of Charles II, two parties in England, Whigs and Tories. The Whig party was "well affected to the Memory of King

William," and "extremely zealous for his Majesty King George."[109] Whigs
labeled their critics Tories and equated them with Jacobitism. Government
Whigs sustained this characterization of opposition even after 1745, when
so few actual Jacobites remained in England as to make them irrelevant to
the politics of the nation. By characterizing their opposition in this manner,
Court Whigs intimated that all of their critics were devoted to the Stuart
Pretender and were thus a threat to the liberty, property and religion of the
English people. Court Whigs argued that they were the legitimate heirs to
the legacy of the Glorious Revolution, the preservers and defenders of the
constitution and the Hanoverian dynasty, and that the opponents of Whig
government were at least the unwitting dupes of the Pretender and his
minions, or, at worst, hypocrites who employed the language of country
radicalism and even republicanism to conceal their real intentions of
enslaving the English people by restoring the Papist Stuart Pretender. The
editor of the ministry sponsored *Daily Gazetteer* enquired thus into the
intentions of Caleb D'Anvers of the *Craftsman*:

> Is it to Restore the Rump that have been in their Graves three of four score
> Years; or the *pretended Stuarts*, that are alive and lusty in the *Pope's*
> Bosom, on the other side of the Water? Is it to erect a Commonwealth made
> up of Tories, Papists, High Church, and Libertines, or to make another
> annual Holiday by another Restoration, the Blessings of which, may be in
> part guess'd by the Blessings of the last, with the sweet Improvements of
> Inquisitions, Fire and Faggot?[110]

This criticism was made all the more telling when infamous Tories and
acknowledged Jacobites like Bolingbroke were among the government's
most virulent critics. Anti-government editors of papers and journals like
The Craftsman and *Common Sense* claimed that they, rather than the
ministry's presses, were the "true Whigs" and thus represented the interests
of the freeholders and people of England against the machinations of
politicians who were set upon enslaving both the king and his subjects. As
one writer put it, "the Interests of the King and People are inseparable:
Whoever is a Friend to either is so consequently to both."[111]

Opposition writers stressed the danger of the absolutism that would,
they believed, naturally accrue from the corruption of Parliament by the
ministry. They argued that the powers of the king to do good for his people
were held in check by his corrupt and self-interested ministers, who
employed the royal prerogatives to their own ends rather than for the
benefit of the people. These "country" critics offered a prescriptive analysis

of Whig government that was couched in the terms of the Age of Coke and the Long Parliament, and also of the Glorious Revolution and *Declaration of Rights*.[112] What Court Whigs found the most worrisome about this country-dominated opposition rhetoric was that it offered a reasoned, coherent critique of their measures that was well grounded in the English Whig constitutional tradition. It was loyal to the Hanover dynasty, it presumed the power of the legislature to oversee and restrain the executive, and it employed as its basis an interpretation, albeit more libertarian, of the same fundamental precepts of government that the Court Whigs employed. It was, in short, the flip side of the Whig ideological coin. The only real defense that Court Whigs could offer was that their country opponents disguised their actual intentions behind the mask of Whig rhetoric; that:

> whoever would aspire to *Tyranny* must cry *Liberty*, . . . [and] there are not a few, who in wishing for the Pretender, fancy that they wish well to Liberty; and believe that whatever thwarts his Interest promotes Slavery; and, that, therefore, they are now in a State of Slavery.[113]

Until the end of the American Revolution, Country opposition rhetoric offered a compelling vehicle for criticism against the Whig oligarchy by those outside of the ministry.

The prominent feature of English government under the first two Hanoverian kings was its domination by Whigs. After 1720 both the government leadership and the opposition came from the same party, so that government Whigs faced a Whig opposition across the aisle of the House of Commons. This nascent opposition coalesced around the Prince of Wales, the future King George II, and, in the same fashion, in the "court" of Prince Frederick after George II ascended the throne in 1727. There were always a few independent backbenchers who consisted primarily of country squires and Tories from the rural fringes of the kingdom whose constituencies had become all but hereditary, but even these gentlemen had largely accepted the premises of Whig government—the Protestant succession vested in the Hanover family, Parliamentary oversight and the supremacy of Commons, the preservation of order, and national prosperity. Although his power as a ruler dwindled under the Whig primacy, the king, at least in theory, held prerogative powers that enabled the executive to act as a check on the legislative branch of government. In practice, however, by the reign of George II most of the prerogative powers had atrophied from disuse. No ruler exercised his right to refuse assent to legislation after 1708.[114] In George III's reign,

Henry Fox informed the king that his veto, "like all his other prerogatives, should only be exercised upon the advice of his responsible servants," which indicates that the king's cabinet, rather than the king, himself, held control of the royal negative by that date.[115] Since the king was thus prevented from exercising a negative over new legislation by custom, and from dispensing with laws by the conventions of the *Declaration of Rights,* he had few actual means at his disposal to redress the grievances of his subjects. In actuality, most of the ruler's prerogative powers lay with the ministry or the collective executive institution of the Crown rather than with the king. From the point of view of the Whigs, the king's greatest importance lay in his nominating power to choose his ministers and to grant honors, create peers, nominate bishops and lesser church officials, and grant high military offices. He was the wellspring of patronage from which his supporters eagerly filled their buckets.

Since the argument over the constitution had essentially been won by the Whigs by 1722, there no longer existed two competing ideologies of governance in England. In general, the opposition agreed with the ministry on all essentials, and thus contention over particulars became difficult. Over the years, however, a political language had evolved that was well suited to the criticism of the English system of government. The "Country" language of opposition could be used by critics of government with reasonable safety because it contained within it the spirit of the *Declaration of Rights.* The political viewpoint, the "country ideology" upon which the language rested, offered an analysis of power and of English political life that was critical of ministerial influence and the effects that it had both on the king above and the legislature below. It encouraged parliamentary scrutiny of the ministry in order to weed out or restrain potentially corrupt or wicked advisors who might lead the king into error. It recommended limitations on the patronage that the ministry used to enhance its power. In order to restrain the corrupting influence of the executive over the legislature, country critics recommended frequent Parliaments and bills to preclude members of the legislature from appointive places in government. Country Whig critics also decried large standing armies in times of peace, both because the army might be used against the people by a corrupt ministry and because large armies required large numbers of officers (more placemen) to lead them. They feared that the traditional leaders of the nation, the landed gentry, might be superseded by a new breed of politician who derived his power from his office rather than from the land and who understood his duty and interest to lie with the masters from whom he had derived his power and position.[116] Under such courtiers, government could only exist to serve the interests of those who governed and not the people of the nation. In an age of consolidation and centralization of English government, country ideology offered both a traditional and an acceptable language of opposition. It gave those who opposed the government a means of criticism that resonated in the political consciousness of the English listener wherever they lived under the English Crown.

In essence, then two languages developed in the political climate of England between the Glorious Revolution of 1688 and the accession of George II. Both were based on the Whig understanding of the English constitution. Both assumed that the best government was a mixed monarchical republic and that the first order of governance could be summed up in the ancient adage *"salus populi, suprema lex esto."* The language of the court Whigs, those who governed, was a language of loyalty meant to foster support of the king and his government. It stressed the primacy of law and order, and, while acknowledging that government existed for the good of the people, it denied that the constitution was based entirely upon popular government. It emphasized that the people were best protected under a benign authoritarian regime that prevented domestic unrest, protected property, and promoted prosperity through a strong national defense. In opposition to the court view, the country opposition stressed that the interests of the nation were best served when the people were consulted. It strictly interpreted the provisions of the *Declaration of Rights* in a prescriptive analysis of the constitution and criticized the government for employing its powers to corrupt the constitution.

Most colonists far across the Atlantic Ocean in His Majesty's possessions in North America received both of these views of government, and interpreted both to fit their own circumstances. Colonists were, after all, Britons, and thus shared all of the basic assumptions about government with their English cousins. Where they differed was that they did not share the more recent history of England. American colonists had a history and political viewpoint of their own, or rather a set of histories and viewpoints, at once shared to a degree because of their symbiotic relationship with the mother country, and different because of the peculiarities of their different little commonwealths. The Glorious Revolution provided both an historical and ideological link between England and her American provinces; it was perhaps the most important shared event, in terms of molding the political culture of American Britons of the eighteenth century.

Notes

1. For an enlightening short commentary on the consequences of printing scandalous or seditious libel in a newspaper, see R.M. Wiles, *Freshest Advices: Early Provincial Newspapers in England* (Columbus, Ohio: Ohio State University Press, 1965), 281-292. For the various means that Hanover government employed to control the English press, see Jeremy Black, *The English Press in the Eighteenth Century* (London: Croom Helm, Ltd., 1987), 135-196. For seditious libel as applied to pamphlets, see Hebert Atherton, *Political Prints in the Age of Hogarth: A Study of the Ideographic Representation of Politics* (Oxford: Clarendon Press, 1974), 68-74. For Parliament's claim that its actions were immune to criticism in print, and Parliament's response to such material, see Atherton, *Political Prints*, 74-75, on the ministry and criticism in pamphlets and broadsides, Atherton, *Political Prints*, 75-83.

2. Charles E. Clark, *The Public Prints: The Newspaper in Anglo-American Culture, 1665-1740* (New York: Oxford University Press, 1994), 88-90.

3. Paul Langford, "British Correspondence in the Colonial Press, 1763-1775: A Study in Anglo-American Misunderstanding Before the American Revolution," in *The Press and the American Revolution,* Bernard Bailyn and John Hench, eds. (Boston: Northeastern University Press, 1980), 273.

4. *Daily Gazetteer*, August 25, 1737. English newspapers cited in this chapter were published in London, and may be found in the *Early English Newspapers* series, Research Publications, Inc. All dates are cited as they appear in the sources. If the Julian year is given in the source, but the context is lost without clarification, the Gregorian year is placed in brackets (i.e. January 6, 1688[/89]).

5. B.W. Hill, *The Growth of Parliamentary Parties, 1689-1742* (Hamden, Conn.: The Shoestring Press, 1976), 19.

6. Clark, *The Public Prints,* 41-43.

7. For literacy rates in England in the middle of the eighteenth century, see John Brewer, *Party Ideology and Popular Politics at the Accession of George III* (Cambridge: Cambridge University Press, 1976), 141-142, and for more extensive studies, see Lawrence Stone, "Literacy and Education in England, 1640-1900," *Past and Present* 42 (1969); Wyn Ford, "The Problem of Literacy in Early Modern England," *History* 78:1 (1993), 22-37; David Vincent, *Literacy and Popular Culture: England, 1750-1914* (New York: Cambridge University Press, 1989).

8. Clark, *The Public Prints,* 6-7.

9. Clark, *The Public Prints,* 259.

10. Lord Macaulay, *The History of England*, edited and abridged by Hugh Trevor-Roper (New York: Penguin Books, 1968), 279.

11. The ideological processes that led to this understanding of the Revolution are among the topics of discussion in this chapter. For a more complete analysis of the development of the English Whig interpretation of the Revolution during

reign of William and Mary, see Lois Schwoerer, ed., *The Revolution of 1688-1689: Changing Perspectives* (Cambridge: Cambridge University Press, 1992). She also offers an excellent historiographical study of the Revolution in the introduction. The historian who did the most to fix the Williamite understanding of the Glorious Revolution in the minds of his antecedents was Lord Macaulay. Whig historians from G.M. Trevelyan to William Speck have argued more subtly that James was a would be absolutist, and William a deliverer. Revisionist views of the Revolution may be found in the works of J.P. Kenyon, H.T. Dickinson, and J.R. Jones, and John Brewer, among others. Revisionists generally argue that the results of the Revolution achieved little change in government, representing a political compromise between Tories and Whigs to preserve the political status quo while ridding themselves of James II. Brewer makes the case that it was not the Revolution that changed the constitution, but the necessities of war and finance during the reigns of William and Mary, and Anne. See W.A. Speck, *Reluctant Revolutionaries: Englishmen and the Revolution of 1688* (Oxford: Oxford University Press, 1988); J.P. Kenyon, *Revolution Principles: The Politics of Party, 1689-1720* (Cambridge: Cambridge University Press, 1977); Dickinson, *Liberty and Property;* J.R. Jones, *The Revolution of 1688 in England* (New York: Norton, 1973); Brewer, *The Sinews of Power: War Money and the English State, 1688-1783* (Cambridge, Massachusetts: Harvard Press, 1990).

Since the 1960s several historians, of whom the most notable is Lois Schwoerer, and called, for lack of a better term, "Neo-Whigs," offered a rebuttal to the revisionist analysis of the Revolution. "Neo-Whigs" argue that while James' acts were less unconstitutional than earlier Whigs contended, the Revolution nevertheless wrought changes upon the English constitution that were fundamental and far-reaching, and that the Revolutionary settlement, as dictated by the Bill of Rights, went a long way toward redefining the "ancient constitution," and placed new constraints upon the Crown. For Neo-Whigs like Schwoerer and Corinne Weston, the settlement brought about a new, if not very radical, conception of kingship. See Lois Schwoerer, *The Declaration of Rights, 1689* (Baltimore: Johns Hopkins University Press, 1981); Corinne Weston, *English Constitutional Theory and the House of Lords, 1556-1832* (New York: Columbia University Press, 1965).

Other scholars, among them Mark Goldie and Marie McMahon, argue that radical ideas in the press and the Convention promoted by a small minority had an effect on the outcome of the constitutional settlement, creating the notion of kingship constrained by Parliament, thus permanently transferring the lion's share of the power of government from the executive to the Commons. See Marie P. McMahon, *The Radical Whigs, John Trenchard and Thomas Gordon: Libertarian Loyalists to the House of Hanover* (Lanham, Maryland: University Press of America, 1990); Mark Goldie, "Obligations, Utopias, and their Historical Context," *The Historical Journal* 26:3 (1983), 727-746.

12. *Declaration of Reasons*... Cited in Lois G. Schwoerer, "Propaganda in the Revolution of 1688-89," *American Historical Review* 82:4 (1977), 855. On the

propaganda of the counterfeit birth of the Prince of Wales, see Rachel J. Weil, "The Politics of Legitimacy: Women and the Warming-Pan Scandal," in *The Revolution of 1688-1689: Changing Perspectives*, 65-82.

13. Schwoerer, "Propaganda," 853.

14. *Character of His Royal Highness William Henry Prince of Orange* (London, 1689), 7. For a few other works that characterize William in heroic terms, both during and after the Revolution, see Francis Carswell, *England's Restoration Parallel'd in Judah's: or, The Primative Judge and Counsellor. In a Sermon Before the Honourable Judge at Abingdon Assizes, for the County of Berks. Aug. 6, 1689* (London: 1689), 30-32; Henry Parker, *The True Portraiture of the Kings of England* (London, 1688); [anon,] *The Abdicated Prince: or, The Adventures of Four Years. A Tragi-Comedy, as It Was Lately Acted at the Court of ALBA REGALIS, by Several Persons of Great Quality* . . . (London: 1690); "Poems on the Reign of William III (1690, 1696, 1699, 1702)," *The Augustan Reprint Society No. 166* (Los Angeles: University of California Press, 1974); [John Whittel,] *A Short Review of the Remarkable Providences; Attending Our Gracious Sovereign William the IIId* . . . (London, 1699); Edmund Waller, *Poems &c. Written Upon Several Occasions, and to Several Persons*. 6th ed. (London: H. Herrington & Thomas Bennes, 1693), 4, 16, 17; Thomas Hughes, *The Court of Neptune: A Poem Address'd to the Right Honourable Charles Montague, Esq.* (London: 1700); Gilbert Burnet, *An Abridgement of Bishop Burnet's history of His Own Times* (London, 1724),402; John Banks, *The History of the Life and Reign of William III, King of England, Prince of Orange, and Hereditary Stadtholder of the United Provinces* . . . (London, 1744); [anon,] *A Short Review of the Remarkable Providences Attending Our Gracious Sovereign William the IIId Continued from the Year 1693, Down to This Day.* (London, 1799).

15. For a few examples of works that employ specific themes (Papism, arbitrary rule, sexual impotence and sterility, cowardice, evil advisors, and, of course, the introduction of a counterfeit Prince of Wales) to vilify James, see *The Amours of Messalina. Late Queen of Albion* . . ., *by A Woman of Quality.*, 4 vols. (London: John Lyford, 1689); [Anon.,] *A Rara Show, A Rara Shight! A Strange Monster (The Likes Not in Europe)* . . . (London: R. Janeway, 1689); [Anon.,] *The Confession of Mrs. Judith Wilks the Queen's Midwife, With a Full Account of Her Running Away by Night; and Going into France I* (London[?], 1689); [Anon.,] *A Suppliment to the Muses Farewell to Popery and Slavery, Or a Collection of Miscellany Poems, Satyrs, Songs, &c, Made by the Most Eminent Wits of the Nation, as the Shams, Intreagues, and Plots of Priests and Jesuits Gave Occasion.* (London, 1690); J. Fraser, *A Friendly Letter to Father Petre, Concerning His Part in the Late King's Government: Published for His Defence and Justification* (London, 1690); [Anon.,] *The Pagan Prince: Or a Comical History of the Heroick Achievements of the Palatine of Eboracum. By the Author of the Secret History of King Charles II and King James II* (Amsterdam, 1690); John Shute, Viscount Barrington, *A Dissuasive from Jacobitism: Shewing in General What the Nation*

is to Expect form a Popish King; and in Particular, from the Pretender . . .
(London, 1713), (went through three editions in 1713-1714); Gilbert Burnet, *An
Abridgement of Bishop Burnet's History of His Own Times*, 326-397, 416-424;
[Anon.,] *A Brief Account of the Moral and Political Acts of the Kings and Queens
of England* (London, 1793), 240-249.

16. The best discussion of the propaganda of the Glorious Revolution (and
stereotyping of both William and James II) is Lois Schwoerer, "Propaganda in the
Revolution of 1688-89." For some examples of the vilification of James in satirists'
cartoons see plates on pages 863-867, and explanatory text. See also Stephen B.
Baxter, "William III as Hercules: The Political Implications of Court Culture;"
Steven N. Zwicker, "Representing the Revolution: Politics and High Culture in
1689;" and Lois Potter, "Politics and Popular Culture: The Theatrical Response to
the Revolution," all in *The Revolution of 1688-1689: Changing Perspectives*. For
an older, and less comprehensive view, but one that indicates the *international*
flavor of William's propaganda and characterizations, see M. Dorothy George,
English Political Caricature to 1792: A Study of Opinion and Propaganda, 2 vols.
(Oxford: Clarendon Press, 1959), 1:62-64. George's long study also stresses the
permanence of the stereotypical motifs in English political literature and art.

17. J.P. Kenyon, *Stuart England*. 2nd ed. (London: Penguin Books, Ltd.,
1990), 272.

18. Thomas Hobbes, *Leviathan*. C.B. MacPherson, ed. (London: Penguin
Books, 1985), 255. Significantly, John Locke agreed with Hobbes, writing that the
victor in a just war "has an absolute power over the lives of those, who, by putting
themselves in a state of war, have forfeited them." Locke argued that the despot
had no right to their possessions, however.   An interesting caveat.   Locke
apparently believed that the despot could kill his subjects with relative impunity,
but could not take their property. See John Locke, *Two Treatises of Government,
by John Locke. With a Supplement Patriarchia by Robert Filmer*, Thomas I. Cook,
ed. (New York: Hafner Press, 1947), 180. The question of whether or not William
ruled by right of conquest while the legitimate King "languished" in exile at St.
Germain became a subject for contention between Jacobites and Williamites even
after William's accession. Thomas Comber argued against the accusation of
usurpation by Jacobites, that James' flight was a voluntary act, and thus, William
filled the vacuum left by James' voluntary abdication. Comber assured his readers,
however, that William did so only at the request, and with the full submission, of
the people of England (Comber, *The Protestant Mask Taken off . . .*, 7-8, 25).

19. Lucile Pinkham, *William III and the Respectable Revolution: The Part
Played by William of Orange in the Revolution of 1688* (Cambridge,
Massachusetts: Harvard University Press, 1954), 202-203.

20. See Henry Parker, *The True Portrait of the Kings of England* (London,
1688), 35-38. Also *The British Mercury*, June 23, 1714, 1; "Those of the British
Kings Who Aimed at Despotic Power, or the Oppression of the Subject," *New York
Weekly Journal*, January 17, 173$^{7}/_{8}$; [Anon.,] *A Brief Account of the Moral and*

Political Acts of the Kings and Queens of England (London, 1793), 132-139

21. The idea of a regency was promoted primarily by supporters of James II as a means of avoiding a deposition, and keeping his claim alive. See Speck, *Reluctant Revolutionaries*, 99. See also Howard Nenner, *The Right to be King: The Succession of the Crown of England, 1603-1714* (Chapel Hill: University of North Carolina Press, 1995), 161, 163; Henry Horwitz, "Parliament and the Glorious Revolution," *Bulletin of the Institute of Historical Research*, 47 (1974), 44; Eveline Cruickshanks, et. al, "Division in the House of Lords on the Transfer of the Crown and Other Issues, 1689-1694: Ten New Lists," *Bulletin of the Institute of Historical Research* 53 (1980), 59.

22. Kenyon, *Stuart England*, 271-2; Maurice Ashley, *The Glorious Revolution of 1688* (New York: Charles Scribner's Sons, 1966), 179.

23. See Nenner, *The Right to Be King*, 163; Ashley, *The Glorious Revolution*, 179; Speck, *Reluctant Revolutionaries*, 102.

24. Speck, *Reluctant Revolutionaries*, 99-100.

25. J. Jones to A. Charlett, 21 January, 1689. Cited in Speck, *Reluctant Revolutionaries*, 95.

26. Speck, *Reluctant Revolutionaries*, 103.

27. Speck, *Reluctant Revolutionaries*, 105.

28. Schwoerer, *The Declaration of Rights*, 190-191.

29. Schwoerer, *The Declaration of Rights*, 184-185.

30. *The Declaration of Rights*, printed in Schwoerer, *The Declaration of Rights*, 295.

31. Schwoerer, *The Declaration of Rights*, 295-296.

32. Schwoerer, *The Declaration of Rights*, 296. Both the Convention and William took advantage of the long tradition of anti-Romanism in England. For a few relevant works that explore the English political and literary tradition, see Ethan Howard Shagan, "Constructing Discord: Ideology, Propaganda, and the English Responses to the Irish Rebellion of 1641," *Journal of British Studies* 36:1 (1997), 4-34; Alexandra Walsham, "'The Fatall Vesper': Providentialism and Anti-Popery in Late Jacobean London," *Past and Present* 144:2 (1994), 36-84; Peter Lake, "Deeds Against Nature: Cheap Print, Protestantism and Murder in Early Seventeenth-Century England," in *Culture and Politics in Early Stuart England*, Kevin Sharpe and Peter Lake, eds. (Stanford, California: Stanford University Press, 1993), 283, passim; James Morgan Reed, "Atrocity Propaganda and the Irish Rebellion," *Public Opinion Quarterly* 2:2 (1938), 229-244; Caroline Hibbard, *Charles I and the Popish Plot* (Chapel Hill: University of North Carolina Press, 1983); J.P. Kenyon, *The Popish Plot* (London: Heinemann, 1972).

33. Schwoerer, *The Declaration of Rights*, 296.

34. Schwoerer, *The Declaration of Rights*, 296.

35. See [Sir James Tyrell,] *A Brief Enquiry into the Ancient Constitution and Government of England, as Well in Respect to the Administration, as Succession thereof. Set Forth in a Dialogue, and Fitted for Men of Ordinary Learning and*

Capacities. By a True Lover of His Country (London, 1695), 11, 29-31, *passim.*; [Anon.,] *A Short Account Touching the Succession of the Crown* (London[?], 1689[?]); [Anon.,] *A Letter Writ by a Clergy-Man to his Neighbour. Concerning the Present Circumstances of the Kingdom, and the Allegiance that is Due to the King and Queen* (London, 1689), 8-9; Comber, *The Protestant Mask Taken Off,* 25. Both Schwoerer and Speck studied the extent to which the charges against James were constitutionally fair, and concluded that, in the words of the former, "not all the grievances were violations of known law, and not all of the rights were 'ancient' and 'undoubted,'" and that the *Declaration of Rights* was "intrinsically, a document that embodies the principles of Whigs who wanted to change the kingship as well as the king." See Schwoerer, *Declaration of Rights*, 100-101, and Speck, *Reluctant Revolutionaries*, 152-163.

36. "A *Defence* of the CONSTITUTION, against some LATE DOCTRINES, and ONE LATE ATTEMPT," *London Journal*, February 9, 1734.

37. F.W. Maitland, *Constitutional History of England* (Cambridge: Cambridge University Press, 1963), 388.

38. Lois G. Schwoerer, "The Coronation of William and Mary, April 11, 1689," in *The Revolution of 1688-1689: Changing Perspectives,* 114-115.

39. Schwoerer, "The Coronation of William and Mary, April 11, 1689," 115.

40. II Sam. 23:3.

41. Schwoerer, "The Coronation of William and Mary, April 11, 1689," 123.

42. Speck, *Reluctant Revolutionaries*, 164-165.

43. Steven N. Zwicker, "Representing the Revolution: Politics and High Culture in 1689," in *The Revolution of 1688-1689: Changing Perspectives*, 165-183.

44. For a discussion of the stereotypes in plays, poetry and ballads, see Lois Potter, "Politics and Popular Culture: The Theatrical response to the Revolution," in *The Revolution of 1688-1689: Changing Perspectives*, 184-197.

45. *The Abdicated Prince: or the Adventures of Four Years. A Tragi-Comedy, As It was Acted at the Court of ALBA REGALIS, by Several Persons of Great Quality* (London, 1690), 60. Cited in Potter, "Politics and Popular Culture," 190.

46. For an historiographical summary of Queen Anne's reign, see Geoffrey Holmes, *British Politics in the Age of Anne* (New York: St. Martin's Press, 1967), 1-9. Among the fairly recent studies of Anne's reign that display her in a more favorable light are (besides Holmes) Robert Walcott, *English Politics in the Early Eighteenth Century* (Oxford: Oxford University Press, 1956) and Edward Gregg, *Queen Anne* (London: Routledge & Kegan Paul, 1980). Holmes remarks with justice that Anne's historical stature has actually decreased in the last two decades, as Namierites like Walcott focus on the politics that surrounded the Queen, almost to the exclusion of the Queen herself (Holmes, *British Politics in the Age of Anne*, 2).

47. Brewer, *The Sinews of Power*, 110.

48. Kenyon, *Stuart England*, 317.

49. Kenyon, *Stuart England*, 316.

50. Gregg, *Queen Anne*, 135-136.

51. Ragnhild Hatton, *George I, Elector and King* (Cambridge, Mass.: Harvard University Press, 1978), 173.

52. George's reputation for tolerance, see Cotton Mather, *The Glorious Throne* . . . (Boston: B. Green, 1714), 35; Joseph Addison, "Freeholder No. 2," *The Works of Joseph Addison* . . ., 6 vols., George Washington Greene, ed. (Philadelphia: J.B. Lippincott & Co., 1880), 3:8-9. For the Schism Act and persecution, see Kenyon, *Stuart England*, 348, and Hatton, *George I*, 173.

53. Hatton, *George I*, 120.

54. Hatton, *George I*, 127.

55. Nicholas Rogers, *Whigs and Cities: Popular Politics in the Age of Walpole and Pitt* (Oxford: Clarendon Press, 1989), 25-26.

56. *The Flying-Post, or the Post-Master*, 21 June, 1715.

57. For various accounts of mob activities see *The Flying Post* issues from June through September, 1715.

58. Rogers, *Whigs and Cities*, 30.

59. Carl Stephenson and Frederick George Marcham, *Sources of English Constitutional History: A selection of the Documents from the Interregnum to the Present*. 2 vols. (New York: Harper and Row Publishers, Inc., 1972), 2:617-618.

60. Hatton, *George I*, 179-180.

61. *The Patriot*, September 23, 1714.

62. For a few examples, see *The Patriot*, August 7, 1714; "Letter From Warwickshire," *The Flying-Post, or the Post-Master*, August 13, 1715; "The Humble Address of the Mayor and Burgesses of the Borough of Truro in the County of Cornwall to His Majesty . . .," *The Flying-Post, or the Post-Master*, November 1, 1715; "Humble Address of the Knights, Citizens and Burgesses in Parliament Assembled . . ., November 18, 1715," *The Evening Post*, November 26, 1715; Joseph Addison, "Freeholder, No. 1," 3:6, "Freeholder, No. 2," 3:9, "Freeholder, No. 46," 3:225-228, *passim, The Works of Joseph Addison*.

63. *The Patriot*, August 12, 1714. See also *The Flying-Post; or the Post-Master*, June 4, 1715; "Humble Address of the Knights, Citizens and Burgesses in Parliament Assembled," *The Evening Post*, November 26, 1715.

64. Joseph Addison. "Freeholder No. IX, Friday, January 20, 1716," in *The Works of Joseph Addison*, 3:44.

65. "A Seasonable Admonition by the Provincial Synod of *Lothian* and *Tweeddale*, to the People in those Bounds, with respect to the Present Rebellion," *The Flying-Post*, November 15, 1715. For a few other examples, see *Flying-Post* April 26, 1715, "Humble Address . . . from the Mayor, Jurats, Common-Council . . . of the Corporation of *Gravesend* and *Milton* in the County of Kent," August 16, 1715; "The Humble Address of the Mayor and Burgesses of the Burough of *Truro* in the County of Cornwall . . .," November 1, 1715; "The

Humble Address of the Turkey, Russia, East-Country, Hamburgh, Dutch, Italian, Portugal, West-India, Virginia, and other Traders, &c., of the City of London . . .," *London Gazette*, October 15, 1715; "Humble Address of the Protestant Dissenting Ministers of Several Denominations, In and About the Cities of London and Westminister, August 18, 1715," *The Evening Post*, August 18, 1715; "Humble Address of the Mayor, Recorder, Bayliffs, and Burgesses of Your Majesty's Ancient Borough of Leicester in the County of Leicester, August 26, 1715," *The Evening Post*, August 30, 1715.

66. Hatton, *George I*, 178-180. See also Rogers, *Whigs and Cities*, 30.

67. J.H. Plumb, *England in the Eighteenth Century* (London: Penguin Books, 1963), 58; also John B. Owen, *The Eighteenth Century, 1714-1825* (New York: W.W. Norton & Co., 1974), 11-12.

68. "Considerations upon the Reports Relating to THE PEERAGE, by a Member of the House of Commons," *The Plebian* (London: S. Popping, 1719), 6.

69. Lewis B. Namier, *The Structure of Politics at the Accession of George III.* 2 vols. (London: Macmillan & Co., 1929), 1:9.

70. Owen, *The Eighteenth Century,* 12-14.

71. Marie P. McMahon, *The Radical Whigs, John Trenchard and Thomas Gordon: Libertarian Loyalists to the New House of Hanover* (Lanham, Maryland: University Press of America, 1990), 170, 172-173, *passim*.

72. *St. James Journal*, May 10, 1722.

73. *St. James Journal*, May 17, 1722, 13-14; May 24, 1722, 19-20.

74. *St. James Journal*, May 3, 1722, 1. "They only are professed of the popular Authority, who are intitled to it from the Property they enjoy: Power is ever naturally and rightfully founded there."

75. *St. James Journal*, August 2, 1722, 80.

76. *The Plebian*, No. 1, 1719, 6.

77. Jonathan Swift, *The Prose Works of Jonathan Swift*, H. Davis, ed. (Oxford: Clarendon Press, 1939-62), 3:66.

78. Joseph Addison, *The Freeholder*, James Leheny, ed. (Oxford: Clarendon Press, 1979), 2-8.

79. Addison, *Freeholder* No. 1, Friday, December 23, 1715, 40.

80. For a discussion of popular instructions and representatives' responses to the notion in both England and America, see Edmund S. Morgan, *Inventing the People: The Rise of Popular Sovereignty in England and America* (New York: W.W. Norton, 1988), 209-223, *passim*.

81. Dickinson, *Liberty and Property*, 157.

82. *London Journal*, May 26, 1733, cited in Dickinson, *Liberty and Property*, 158-159.

83. H.T. Dickinson, "Whiggism in the Eighteenth Century," in *The Whig Ascendancy: Colloquies in Hanoverian England*, John Cannon, ed. (New York: St. Martin's Press, 1981), 41.

84. *London Journal*, May 26, 1733, cited in Dickinson, *Liberty and Property*, 158.

85. Dickinson, *Liberty and Property*, 158.

86. Dickinson, *Liberty and Property*, 296, 305-306.

87. *St. James Journal*, May 3, 1722, 1. The extent to which Commons was a representative body, and who, or what, it represented is taken up at length in J.R. Pole, *Political Representation in England and the Origins of the American Republic* (New York: St. Martin's Press, 1966), 23-26, 388-456. For the impreciseness of Locke's theories of representation, see 17-26. For the relationship between the Whig political ascendency, the Septennial Act, and the increase in Whig assertions that the people were "tacitly" or "virtually" represented, see 407-414. Edmund Morgan notes that "representatives in England and America have never been legally or constitutionally bound to follow the instructions, advice, or expressed wishes of their constituents." He reviews the Whig arguments against the practice in Edmund Morgan, *Inventing the People*, 217-229.

88. *St. James Journal*, August 16, 1722, 91-92; August 23, 1722, 97-99.

89. *St. James Journal*, August 30, 1722, 103.

90. Owen, *The Eighteenth Century*, 26.

91. *St. James Journal*, August 30, 1722, 104.

92. "The Declaration of Right was not intended to introduce any new Form of Government, but only to claim and assert the Rights, Liberties and Privileges of the Subject under the Old, which had been notoriously violated and infringed by King James, . . . nor [was] any Diminution required of the just Prerogatives of the Crown, but only to reduce them within the Bounds prescribed by the Laws and Constitution of England." *Daily Gazetteer*, Feb. 10, 1737. See Dickinson, "Whiggism in the Eighteenth Century," 38. W.A. Speck offers a very good explanation of this Whig interpretation of the constitutional results of the Glorious Revolution in *Reluctant Revolutionaries*, 1-2, along with a brief historiographical review. See also J.R. Pole, *Political Representation*, 438-440; Lois Schwoerer, *Declaration of Rights*, 283.

93. Dickinson, "Whiggism in the Eighteenth Century," 33-36, 38.

94. Dickinson, *Liberty and Property*, 99.

95. Owen, *The Eighteenth Century*, 100.

96. Owen, *The Eighteenth Century*, 103.

97. Dickinson, "Whiggism in the Eighteenth Century," 36.

98. See Thompson, *Whigs and Hunters*, 21-24, 197-198, *passim*.

99. *Fog's Weekly Journal*, January 20, 1733. See also Brewer, *The Sinews of Power*, 203-204; Rogers, *Whigs and Cities*, 48-55.

100. Namier, *The Structure of Politics*, 1:7-10.

101. Namier, *The Structure of Politics*, 1:7-10.

102. Namier, *The Structure of Politics*, 9.

103. Lord Chesterfield to Bubb Doddington, September 8, 1741, cited in Namier, *The Structure of Politics*, 1:10. The following from Sir Edward Turner

illustrates the frustration that Parliamentary leaders who desired support from the country members experienced. He asked: "Are you still a Country Gentleman and can you make any Enquiry after Taxes? Persons of that Denomination seem to have forgot Public affairs. Few of their Representatives have appeared at the House this Session." Sir Edward Turner to Sanderson Miller, December 6, 1746. *An Eighteenth-Century Correspondence*, Lilian Dickens and Mary Stanton, eds. (London: John Murray, 1910), 124.

104. Paul A. Rahe, *Republics Ancient and Modern: Classical Republicanism and the American Revolution* (Chapel Hill: University of North Carolina Press, 1992), 527.

105. John Brewer, *Party Ideology*, 4-5.

106. J.H. Plumb, *The Growth of Stability in England, 1675-1725* (London: Macmillan & Co., 1967), 115; and Brewer, *Party Ideology*, 4-5.

107. Dickinson, "Whiggism in the Eighteenth Century," 37.

108. SOLON, "General View of Civil Liberty, its Extent, and Restraints," *Daily Gazetteer*, May 2, 1737.

109. *The Flying-Post or Post-Master*, June 4, 1715.

110. *Daily Gazetteer*, April 20, 1737.

111. *Common Sense*, August 16, 1740.

112. See Brewer, *Sinews of Power*, 155-166.

113. *Daily Gazetteer*, May 23, 1737.

114. Maitland, *Constitutional History*, 423.

115. Richard Pares, *King George and the Politicians: The Ford Lectures Delivered in the University of Oxford, 1951-2* (Oxford: Oxford University Press, 1953), 132. See also Maitland, *Constitutional History*, 423.

116. Brewer, *Sinews of Power*, 116.

2

Revolution in Massachusetts

It would require a long Summers-Day to Relate the Miseries which were come, and coming in upon poore *New-England*, by reason of the *Arbitrary Government* then imposed on them; a *Government* wherein, as old *Wendover* says of the Time when *Strangers* were domineering over *Subjects* in *England*, *Judicia committebantur Injustis*, *Leges Exlegibus*, *Pax Discordantibus*, *Justicia Injuriosis*; and Foxes were made the Administrators of Justice to the Poultrey. — Cotton Mather, *Magnalia Christi Americana.*[1]

There are a sort of men, who call those that are for *English* Liberties, and that rejoyce in the Government of Their present Majesties King *William* and Queen *Mary*, by the name of *Republicans*, and represent all such as Enemies of Monarchy and the Church. It is not our single Opinion only, but we can speak it on behalf of the generality of Their Majesties Subjects in New England, that they believe (without any diminution to the Glory of our former Princes) the *English* Nation was never so happy in a *King*, or in a *Queen*, as at this day. And the God of Heaven, who has set them on the Throne of these Kingdoms, grant them long and prosperously to Reign. — E.R. & S.S. *The Revolution in New England Justified, and the People there Vindicated . . .*[2]

On 4 April 1689, a vessel from Nevis arrived in Boston. Its captain hurried off to report news from England to Governor Andros, news that he and his associates apparently hoped to keep from the people of the Dominion of New England for as long as possible. A passenger on board the ship, one John Winslow, a Boston merchant, provided the town with the information instead, and was arrested for his trouble.[3] He brought copies of the Prince of Orange's *Declaration of Reasons*, and it was soon printed and circulated throughout Massachusetts. Although the manifesto was not specifically addressed to the colonies, but to England, it resonated among the people of Massachusetts who thought that the Prince's message applied equally to their own province.[4] William's declaration that "magistrates who had been unjustly turned out" should resume their old offices provided them with the stimulus that they needed to revolt.[5] To that end, the "principal Gentlemen of *Boston* met with Mr. MATHER" (among them the Governor and several of the magistrates of 1686) and produced their own document modeled on Prince William's, the *Boston Declaration of Grievances*, in which they listed their reasons for ousting the Andros regime.[6]

All of the North American colonies received the news of the Revolution by the end of April. Colonists were quick to interpret the message of William's declaration and to respond to the news of the invasion and accession of the new rulers within the context of their own circumstances. Maryland and New York, like Massachusetts, erupted with revolutions of their own. Plymouth and Rhode Island waited, allowing their big sister, Massachusetts, to take the lead. Virginia, apart from a short and easily quashed disturbance in Stafford County, responded by celebrating the accession of the new rulers with festivities similar to those that the colony had staged a few months earlier to commemorate the birth of James Stuart, the Prince of Wales. In each case colonists' responses to the news of the events in England depended upon the peculiar circumstances of each colony. In general, where the policies of Charles II and James II had had negative consequences for the colony, and where the governing regime was despised by at least a sizeable segment of the colonists, conflict followed. Where the government was stable, the Governor trusted, and the hands of the last two Stuart monarchs had touched only lightly, the transition of power across the sea caused little disturbance. Despite the fact that reaction in each province was dictated by local circumstances, by the end of the Glorious Revolution American colonists everywhere had reached a broad ideological consensus on what the Revolution meant. They agreed with William's conceptions of Protestant kingship and the Stuart conspiracy, as promoted by the Prince's propaganda and in the *Declaration of Right*. The legacy of this development had a profound effect upon colonial political thought.[7]

Massachusetts' controversy before the Glorious Revolution rested less with James II than with the King's choice of governor, Sir Edmund Andros, who arrived at Boston on 19 December, 1686, scandalously dressed in a scarlet coat and periwig. According to Thomas Hutchinson, the new Governor's reputation preceded him; "he was known to be of an arbitrary disposition," and those who read his letters written as Governor of New

York "discovered much of the dictator" in him.[8] Andros quickly surrounded himself with a set of "his creatures to say yes to everything he proposed."[9] What he proposed shocked the people of Massachusetts. Andros levied taxes without representation. He attempted to reform the land tenures of the Massachusetts colony and to require quitrents on the new titles. He remodeled the colony's judicial system in a way that, while reasonably consistent with English Common Law, was at odds with the traditional usage of the Congregationalist Commonwealth. He employed English regular officers to command local militiamen who were not accustomed to the hard treatment English troops received as a matter of course from their commanders. Worst of all, Andros was a cavalier and an Anglican whose demeanor and religion were repugnant to most of the Saints of Massachusetts. In short, the Governor of the Dominion of New England and his regime embodied all of the qualities of government, religion and manners that the Puritan Fathers had forsaken when they left Old England to plant God's Vineyard in the New World some two generations before his arrival.[10]

Massachusetts had already lost its charter when Charles II established it as a royal colony in 1684. The Dominion of New England created by James II dissolved its assembly. The Dominion extended from Maine to New Jersey. The composition of its governing council, haphazardly comprised of members from all of those provinces, could only be viewed by Massachusetts men to contain "such Men as were Strangers to and Haters of the People."[11] Taxes were imposed by the Royal Governor in Council. When several towns complained that the imposition of taxation without representation violated the liberties of English freeholders and refused to pay, their leaders were arrested. An official at their trial informed them that the rights of Englishmen did not follow them "to the Ends of the Earth" and that they had "no more Privileges left, but this, that you are not bought and sold for Slaves."[12]

The right of Englishmen to be taxed only by their own consent was considered to be among those ancient rights guaranteed by the Magna Carta and substantiated by long tradition. As early as 1610, the House of Commons in England carried a bill that no impositions might be set by the Crown without its consent. In the Short Parliament of 1614, Commons unanimously voted to deny the King's right to levy taxes without first consulting Parliament and refused to grant him any subsidies until the matter was settled.[13] That no one ought to be compelled to pay "any tax, tallage, aid, or other like charge not *set by common consent* in Parliament" was one of the sticking points that brought about the English Civil War.[14]

By the 1680s, the doctrine was generally accepted by English jurors as settled law. The right was even extended to the colonies. In 1685, at the request of the Lords of Trade, the Attorney General for England ruled that it was illegal to govern New England without an assembly.[15] Hence, when Massachusetts was deprived of its assembly and Andros levied taxes upon the colonists with no more support than the consent of a council partly comprised of members whose homes were far away in New York, or even England, the Bay Colonists reasoned that they had been deprived of a basic liberty. According to Edward Rawson and Samuel Sewall, Andros and his council "made what Laws they pleased *without any consent of the People, either by themselves or by representatives*, which is indeed to *destroy the Fundamentals* of the *English*, and to *Erect* a *French Government*."[16]

In the spring of 1687, Andros began to levy a series of taxes on Massachusetts, including land taxes, excises on various goods, and import duties.[17] In July the government sent out warrants to the sheriffs ordering that the taxes be collected. The Boston Selectmen questioned the legality of the policy, and the town of Taunton sent an angry complaint to John Usher, the Dominion tax collector. The people of Essex county, led by the Reverend John Wise of Chebacco, revolted against the new impositions.[18] In a town meeting, the people of Ipswich were quickly persuaded by Wise that "raising money without an Assembly did abridge them their liberty as Englishmen." They agreed not to pay any taxes until "it be appoynted by a gen^ll. Assembly Concurring with the Govern^r. And Councill."[19] Andros responded to the Ipswich mutiny by arresting twenty-eight citizens for tax evasion and sedition.[20] Taxation without representation, and the government's swift and ruthless response to complaint, gave the people of the colony more evidence that the Dominion government was arbitrary and unconstitutional, and its policies little more than "a Treasonable Invasion of the Rights which the whole *English* Nation lays claim unto."[21]

New Englanders became convinced that their property as well as their liberty was at stake when the new government attempted to reform Massachusetts land patents to make property titles originate with the King and thus conform to traditional practice of land tenure in England. Andros informed the freeholders that their titles became void when the charter was vacated, and that, in any case, old land titles had not been made under the seal of the colony, "a notable defect, which possession and improvement could not heal."[22] Land owners were required to petition for new titles and pay taxes and fees to have their ownership confirmed. Colonists were angered both at the prospect of paying for their own property and at the intimation that the legitimacy of titles issued by their own past government should be questioned by Andros and his bevy of "Strangers." Additionally, the colonists were convinced that the Governor's "favorites looked with an envious eye upon some of the best estates," eagerly waiting for them to fall into arrears so that they could employ the colonial courts to snatch them up.[23]

The laws and judicial system of Massachusetts before Andros' arrival represented a synthesis of the laws of God, as interpreted by the Calvinist Congregationalist traditions of Massachusetts, and the laws and liberties that the colonists understood to be their birthright as Englishmen. "It was," according to Edmund Morgan, "a blueprint of the whole Puritan experiment, an attempt to spell out the dimensions of the New England way."[24] Before Andros, Massachusetts freemen were, with very few exceptions, Congregational Church members, and chose juries from among their number. Jurors were thus church members, as well as neighbors and peers. Most defendants were tried in the locality where the crime was committed by judges and juries who were local residents and parishioners. Although the Word of God might decide what acts were criminal and how those acts should be punished, the Common Law protections of a local trial by a freeholder jury and the limitations of *habeas corpus* generally protected the liberty of the accused against arbitrary acts of the colonial government in Boston. Andros considered the Massachusetts system of justice untidy and inefficient. Armed with a commission from London that directed him to remodel the legal system, the new Governor set to work shortly after his arrival to centralize and reform it. Under the new system, defendants were often brought to Boston to be examined and were even tried there, not before their peers in their own towns and counties, but before the officials of the Dominion government whom they considered their oppressors.[25] The judges levied fines that were frequently, by colonial standards, arbitrary and extortionate. Many colonists became convinced that if the Governor's "Officers wanted money, it was but Seizing and Imprisoning the best Men in the Countrey for no fault in the World, and the greedy Officers would thereby have Grist for their Mill."[26]

Nor might defendants expect the legal protections to which they were accustomed in their own communities, because Andros changed the composition of juries in local courts as well. Under the new scheme, sheriffs appointed by the Governor instead of the freemen of the county or township chose local juries. The Governor changed the jury qualifications so that sheriffs were free to choose any colonists who had a freehold valued at thirty pounds. They need not be freemen, as the term had been employed by Bay Colonists in the past, since Congregational Church membership was no longer a criterion for selection. The freemen of Massachusetts viewed these "packt and pickt Juries" as yet another example of "the most detestable Enormities" that their oppressors practiced against their liberties.[27]

Another complaint that Puritans had against the Governor was his requirement that oaths be taken on the Bible, a practice that had been banned in Massachusetts because it was considered idolatrous. Before the new government began to demand that the Bible be used, oaths were sworn by lifting the right hand and swearing in the name of God. Massachusetts men claimed that their practice was not in conflict with the law and traditions of England, and was practiced elsewhere under the English Crown, where the law "not only indulges, but even commands and enjoins the Rite of lifting the Hand in Swearing."[28] Several native born judges, among them the pious and respected William Stoughten, refused to institute the practice in their courts and were lectured like schoolboys for their obstinance by the frustrated Governor.[29] It appears that at least one of Andros' magistrates, Edward Randolph, realized the importance of following local custom in this matter. In January 1688 he allowed one Mr. Hale, who "pleaded he might not lay his hand on the Bible; must Swear by his Creator, not Creature," to take the oath in the traditional fashion.[30] Nevertheless, others were fined or imprisoned for "refusing to take the Oath as by Law is required."[31] Those who refused to swear in the new fashion were excluded from juries and other offices that required the oath. According to Boston leaders, this "one very comprehensive Abuse" angered and frustrated "Multitudes of pious and sober Men through the Land."[32]

The mode of worship of Andros and his favorites also vexed the people of Massachusetts. Within minutes after the new Governor was sworn in, he informed the Congregationalist ministers present that he required that they make a church available for Anglican services.[33] Andros was likely aware, either through the King himself or from his communication with the Lords of Trade, that James was in the process of instituting religious tolerance in both England and the colonies. In calling for a place of worship for Anglicans, it is reasonable to assume that Andros was, in fact, complying with the King's wishes by giving Anglicans in Boston the opportunity to exercise their consciences by worshiping in their own way. This interpretation was certainly promoted by those who supported the Governor in the pamphlet war that followed the revolution of April of 1689.[34] On the other hand, he may have decided, possibly under the influence of Edward Randolph, that it was to his political advantage to champion the cause of the growing number of moderate and prosperous Anglicans against the established Congregationalist majority.[35] At any rate, this impolitic request by the new Governor, made so recently after his arrival and installation, was met with stiff resistance from the Congregationalist ministers and leaders of Boston. Cotton Mather and Simon Willard informed Andros two days later that none of the Boston congregations were willing to host Anglican services in their buildings.[36] The Governor let the issue lie until 23 March, when he sent Edward Randolph to demand the keys to the Third (South) Church so that the Anglicans might hold their Easter services there.[37] A delegation of the members of that church met with Andros and asserted that the building belonged to them and produced a deed as proof. They declared that they would not "consent to part with it to such use."[38] Andros prevailed, however, and the church hosted Anglican services thereafter to the dismay of the regular Congregational parishioners, who were, according to member Samuel Sewall, often forced to wait for the Anglican service to finish before they had their own Sunday meeting.[39] The very existence and use of the vestments, Prayer Book, and paraphernalia of the Church of England, those "filthy stinking thing[s]," were repugnant to the Boston Congregationalists who "came from England to avoid such things."[40] In their cavalier use of religion to antagonize the citizens of Boston, as in their threat to land titles and judicial meddling, Andros and his servants helped convince New Englanders that they were governed by a tyrant who threatened their liberty, religion and property. The religious controversy only added weight to the people's complaints against the Governor and his entourage.

Curiously, there is little evidence that the people of Massachusetts had any grievances against the King. They must certainly have known that James II was a practicing Roman Catholic, which in itself should have prejudiced them against him. But there is little evidence from sources written *before* the news of the Revolution in England to indicate that they suspected the King's own complicity in the oppression of the colony. All of the blame was assigned to Andros and his creatures. In fact, many Bay colonists were heartened by "[t]he sight of his Majestyes Declarations for Liberty of Conscience," which was published in Boston in the summer of 1687.[41] In his declaration dated 4 April 1687, James announced that, "though heartily wishing all the people of his dominions were members of the Catholic Church," he desired that his subjects should be granted free exercise of their own religion. He suspended the tests and oaths that had been required to guarantee that government officials and military officers be Anglican Church members, and he granted pardons and indemnities to all who were subject to prosecution or imprisonment for violations of the ecclesiastical laws.[42]

Increase Mather celebrated the declaration in his sermon of 25 August. Preaching from the fifth verse of Jude, he "Praised God for the Liberty good People enjoy in England. Said 'tis marvellous in our Eyes."[43] Colonial writers later wrote, in agreement with William's propagandists, that the declaration was only a ruse used by the King to dupe English Dissenters into supporting his government, and only of benefit to Catholics. Most Massachusetts colonists, like their dissenting brethren in England, however, received it with heartfelt gratitude in the summer of 1687.[44] Increase Mather wrote an address of thanks to the King in the name of his congregation. Cotton Mather noted that "Protestant Dissenters had abundance of reason to be thankful for" the King's favor, even though "it assumed an illegal power of dispensing with laws." He argued that the King should not be faulted since the test laws were "contrary to the laws of God, and the rights and claims of human nature."[45] The ministers of Boston, acting on the younger Mather's motion, wrote addresses of thanks to the King for his declaration and designated a day of thanksgiving to celebrate the event. Andros appears not to have shared their elation over the King's declaration, for he "with many menaces, forbade their proceedings, and particularly threatened that he would set guards of soldiers on their church doors, if they attempted what they pretended to."[46]

Increase Mather went to England in the Spring of 1688, ostensibly to present the addresses of thanks from the various Boston churches to the King, but also to present a case to the King and Lords of Trade against Andros and to attempt to get the Massachusetts colony charter restored. There he read at least five addresses to the King in June of 1688. James responded that he hoped that he might "by a Parliament . . . obtain a *Magna Charta* for *Liberty of Conscience*."[47] The King also asked Mather whether the people of the colony were happy with Andros, and the Boston minister took the opportunity to rehearse some of the complaints of his fellow colonists. The Governor, he replied, ignored the King's Declaration of Indulgence. Andros and his council took pains to discourage the Massachusetts churches from thanking his Majesty for his declaration, and when the congregations of Boston had set aside a day to thank God for their King and his wisdom, Sir Edmund threatened to use troops to prevent them from doing so. He also complained that Andros' judges imprisoned and fined those who scrupled to swear on the Book.[48]

Increase Mather gauged the monarch well. He neither claimed the rights of Englishmen for his fellow colonists, nor complained of unlawful taxation, loss of representation, or threats to the property of his Majesty's subjects in the Dominion. He focused instead on complaints of religious persecution. Here he knew the ground was firm. Neither James nor his court might be predisposed to worry about the rights of colonists who resided so far from London, but James appeared to be keenly, and, despite later Whig allegations to the contrary, genuinely concerned about religious toleration within his realms.

James, like his brother and predecessor Charles II, exhibited a tolerance for religious diversity that was uncharacteristic of the era. Charles' tolerance of heterodox faiths (including, with reservations, Catholicism) placed him at odds with the conservative Anglican gentry who had supported the Stuart Restoration in 1660. Charles evidently felt that religious tolerance, if confirmed by law and adhered to by English government and society, would help to insure stability within his realm.[49] Although James feared Presbyterians primarily because he associated them with republicanism, he exhibited tolerance for religious sects in general and was more solicitous toward his fellow Roman Catholics than his brother had been. According to historian John Miller, "James claimed very consistently that he was against persecution for conscience's sake."[50] The King felt that once universal toleration was effected in his realm, most Englishmen would voluntarily choose to convert to Roman Catholicism; thus, he did not feel the need to force his own beliefs on others. If, however, Britons did not convert, he felt that his realm was still better off if its subjects were left unhindered to worship as their consciences dictated.[51]

Mather might have understood James better than the Anglican Whigs who were already plotting that ruler's end. In fact, Mather found that those who were the most supportive of his aims and most influential at the court in London were often individuals whom he was least inclined to trust. As might be expected, dissenting ministers supported him, and during his stay in England he showed his appreciation by preaching in their churches. But Calvinist Dissenters could offer him little support at the center of government. He obtained more telling support from William Penn, the Quaker leader who disliked Andros, Randolph and other members of the Dominion government and who had the King's ear. A number of Catholics at court were civil to him and may have solicited the King on his behalf. While he did not trust any of them, he gave Penn some praise and appears to have accepted the support of most Catholics who were inclined to give it to him. His acceptance of Catholic support had limits, however, for he avoided the aid of the infamous Father Petre, James' confessor and Privy

Councillor.[52] While Mather was soliciting the King and the great ones at court, however, events were unfolding that made his efforts moot.

William's accession and James' flight required Mather to begin his work in London anew. Slipping into rhetoric that more clearly reflected the ideology of the recent Revolution, Mather argued before the new ruler that the colonies, oppressed under the previous reign, ought to share in the liberation that William had brought to England and have their ancient privileges restored to them. Mather and his ally Sir William Phips asserted that the revocation of the colonial charters that comprised the Dominion was illegal and unconstitutional, and that they should be restored. William turned the question over to the Lords of Trade for review. They concluded that the revocations and the creation of the Dominion were legal because the colonies in question, especially Massachusetts, had repeatedly violated both their charters and the trust that resided between the Crown and its subjects. So Mather and Phips were unable to achieve their primary objective expeditiously. They did, however, succeed in convincing William to omit confirmation instructions to Andros, thus depriving the Governor of authoritative support from London. With neither instructions from the Crown nor any confirmation of his authority under the new regime at home, Andros' position in Boston became precarious.[53] While Mather continued to lobby and publish tracts in London that aimed at swaying the government to his point of view, the scene of action shifted to the colonies themselves, and especially to Massachusetts.

When William's declaration arrived in Boston and was printed, disseminated and studied, leaders began to reinterpret the Andros regime in the light of the Prince's rationale for his invasion of England. New Englanders' understanding of the treatment that they had received under the Dominion government acquired a new dimension. Now it was not simply the work of a few renegade petty tyrants bent on filling their pockets at the expense of colonists, and in contravention to the trust that the King had placed in them. The Dominion administration had become a part of the greater and more sinister conspiracy of James II and his Popish advisors to deprive Englishmen everywhere of their liberty, property, and Protestant religion. Then, according to Samuel Mather, "a Strange Disposition entred in the Body of the People to assert their *Liberties* against the Arbitrary Rulers that were fleecing them."[54] When the Boston leadership framed their *Declaration of Grievances* against the Dominion, they prefaced it with an historical interpretation that pitted Protestantism against Papism as a rationale for the actions of both the Andros government and their own revolutionary response to it. Their complaints were no longer couched simply in the libertarian issues of property rights and representative government. Now, this constitutional oppression made sense to them within the wider context of the great struggle between English Protestantism and European Catholicism. As the Boston leaders observed in their own declaration:

> We have seen more than a decad of Years rolled away since the English World had the Discovery of an horrid Popish Plot; wherein the bloody Devotoes of Rome had in their Design and Prospect no less than the Extinction of the Protestant Religion: which mighty Work they called the utter subduing of a Pestilent Heresy; wherein (they said) there never were such Hopes of Success since the Death of Queen Mary, as in our Days. And we were of all Men the most insensible, if we should apprehend a Countrey so remarkable for the true Profession and pure Exercise of the Protestant Religion as New-England is, wholly unconcerned in the Infamous Plot.[55]

In fact, the assertion that Andros was involved in a plot to Romanize New England was something of a problem for the Governor's critics in the Bay Colony because there existed not the slightest indication that either he or any of his assistants in Massachusetts were Papists. Most of them were Anglican, and while the Congregationalists were not happy to see Anglicans worshiping in their midst, and worse, holding sway over them, they were sufficiently cognizant of both history and theology and lived in close enough proximity to the French to know the difference. Andros did not fit the pattern of the stereotypical Roman Catholic conspirator. He was not accompanied by Jesuits, he made no concerted effort to convert the Puritans, he closed no churches, and he imposed no liturgy. Bible swearing aside (which to Andros was probably a judicial rather than a religious matter), no one was imprisoned for their faith, and the government forced neither the Prayer Book nor the Roman mass, down the throats of the Saints of Massachusetts. Even the annalists of the period tacitly admitted as much by omission. If Andros had employed his authority and his troops to that end, surely such staunch Puritan souls as Samuel Sewall, William Stoughten, and the Mathers would have mentioned it.[56]

If Massachusetts' revolution was to be analogous to England's, however, a Popish Plot was a crucial ingredient in the mix. It was not sufficient merely to give lip service to the Popish Plot of 1679; some explicit evidence was required to show that the Andros regime conspired with James to subvert the liberties and religion of the colonists. Where there was Popery, there was slavery, and *vice versa*. The two were so closely linked in English thought and so explicit to William's rationale for his invasion that Massachusetts leaders needed an analogous link in order to convince England that their rebellion against the authority of the Dominion government was legitimate. To that end they concentrated on the one series of events that offered the best evidence, albeit conjectural, that Andros had had a role in the greater conspiracy hatched by James and his Popish advisors to enslave and forcibly convert Englishmen to the Roman faith. That link was the Governor's Indian policy.

The New Englanders' relations with the Indians and the French in the period after King Philip's War were reasonably peaceful. Local tribes were loath to suffer the fate of the Wampanoags and so left the Englishmen alone. Indians allied to the French in upper Maine made occasional forays against settlers in the North country, but even these were rare. In part, peaceful relations between England and France contributed to the state of peace on the frontier. A fair amount of the credit, however, should also go to the Baron de Castine, a French trader whose harem of Indian wives made him an in-law to most of the tribes of the area and who controlled a small trading empire for himself in Canada and northern Maine. The Baron encouraged peace with the English among the Indians primarily because it was good for business, and the English settlers left Castine alone for the same reason. Besides, they feared the consequences of molesting so powerful a player in the affairs of the region.[57]

In May of 1688 Andros sailed up the Penobscot River to Castine's trading post. The Baron and his retinue took refuge in the forest while Andros' soldiers confiscated the trader's goods. Castine responded to this insult by encouraging his Indian allies to attack English settlers.[58] In the summer, Andros began a campaign to placate Indian tribes within the Dominion. He angered the Iroquois by ordering them to cease hostilities against the French and their Indian allies and to return their hostages. He gave gifts to local sachems in New England and New York. While the Governor was attempting to promote a policy of peace and conciliation, however, local officers and settlers, frightened by rumors of war with France, initiated hostilities against local Indians. At the same time, Indians on the northern frontier, incited by Castine and supplied by both the Baron and the Canadian French, prepared for war. Minor skirmishes took place in Maine, Massachusetts and New York. Settlers began to arm, supply and drill their militia companies and to fortify their communities in preparation for war. The Dominion Council raised an army to go to Maine without consulting the Governor. All of these preparations convinced the Indians that war was imminent. Andros found himself powerless to control the situation and complained that the colonists were sabotaging his attempts to promote peace.

In November of 1688 Andros returned from Albany to Boston. He was eager to forestall any actions on the part of the colonists that the Indians might construe as a threat. Along the way the Governor ordered watches and patrols to stand down and return to their homes. When he arrived at Boston, he found the jail filled with Indian prisoners and ordered their release. He then issued a proclamation that promised amnesty to Indians who had not actually killed any colonists if they would lay down their arms and release their captives.[59] New Englanders, whose attitude was simply that the best Indian policy was one of eradication, viewed the Governor's policy toward the Indians as incompetent meddling at best and, at worst, a treasonous secret alliance with the French. Rumors began to circulate between Albany and Boston that Andros had allied himself with the French and that he conspired with various tribes to wipe out the Bay colonists.[60]

By the end of November the Maine Frontier was in chaos. Militia units that the council had sent earlier in the fall had returned home, and the French and Castine were arming and supplying Indians to attack English settlements. Andros was forced to respond to the attacks. He began to make preparations for a winter campaign in the Maine wilderness. He ordered his regular units to Maine, leaving only the Frigate *Rose* and a small guard in Boston, and issued orders to raise 500 militiamen to accompany his regulars. The Governor chose Fitz-John Winthrop, the colony's ranking militia officer, to command the expedition. Winthrop declined, claiming that he was too ill to go on such a rigorous expedition. In the same letter he also explained that the government had not yet confirmed the titles to his properties in the colony.[61] So Andros decided to lead the expedition himself.

While Andros and his army tramped through the Maine snows in a vain attempt to locate Indians to fight, Boston simmered. The local leadership was loath to do anything that might complicate Increase Mather's diplomatic negotiations in London, but they were becoming increasingly anxious about his lack of success.[62] Mather's reports home indicated that James II would soon grant New England "a certain Magna Charta for a speedy Redress of many Things," but after months of negotiations no real results were forthcoming.[63] By mid-December, news from Europe began to enter the colony that hinted at a Dutch invasion of England. On 10 January, Andros issued a proclamation ordering the militia to be vigilant and ready to repel Dutch invaders. The confused Puritan leaders in Boston bided their time until events in England might become clearer.[64]

Throughout January and February rumors of William's landing and advance filtered into the colony. By March, Cotton Mather received a copy of a tract that his father had published in London. The tract, *A Narrative of the Miseries of New-England, By Reason of an Arbitrary Government Erected there Under Sir Edmund Andros*, listed the colonists' complaints and contained the details of the elder Mather's negotiations with James II along with two appendices. The first appendix was an address of the Bishop of London and the Anglican clergy of the city showing support for William's invasion "for the Deliverance, & Preservation of the Protestant Religion."[65] The second was a similar address of the dissenting ministers of London to the Prince, delivered to William at the Court of St. James. The significance of the tract was three-fold. First, it rehearsed the grievances of the Bay colonists in language that was tailored to the new regime's interests. It also reminded the colonists that in spite of the best efforts of the respected elder Mather, James had done no more than listen to their complaints. Finally, the appendices offered more substance to the rumors that William was present in London, and that, whatever the fate of James, the Prince of Orange held court at the capital. Richard Pierce, the official printer of the Dominion, agreed to publish the tract at some personal risk. At the same time, he printed a second edition of Increase Mather's anti-Anglican pamphlet, *A Testimony Against Several Profane and Superstitious Customs, Now Practised by Some in New England.*[66] The authorities responded to this attack by jailing a few minor trouble makers in the city, among them possibly Pierce; but without orders from the Governor, and in as much confusion about affairs in London as anyone else, they hesitated to do more.[67]

Andros remained in the North. He had received news of the coup in London but did not yet know his own status. Whitehall had issued instructions on 12 January to all colonial governors ordering them to proclaim the new rulers and continuing all Protestant officials in their offices.[68] Andros had received no official instructions, however, because Mather and Phips had been able to prevent the government from sending him any. In March, the militiamen in Maine received the news that James had escaped to France and been welcomed by their enemy, King Louis XIV. This, combined with the fact that Andros had yet to confirm William and Mary, revived the rumors of the previous fall that the Governor was in league with the French. Now, however, the rumor was embellished by the addition of the late King as an active participant in the conspiracy. A local Indian, one John James, appeared at Sudbury and announced that Andros had hired Indians to massacre the English.[69] Shortly thereafter the Governor sent an officer to Canada to arrange a truce, and militiamen speculated that the meeting was a further proof of Andros' complicity with James and the French.[70] On 10 April, amid a storm of rumor and innuendo, angry militiamen shouldered their weapons, ignored their officers' commands, and returned to their homes. They brought with them all of the gossip that had circulated in Maine as well as stories of the brutal treatment that they had received from the British regular officers under whom they had served during the futile winter campaign. They were joined by other militia companies that fell in with them during their march to Boston, and they, together with some of the townspeople, began to accumulate in the streets, angry, armed, and ready to rebel against the Andros government.

At this point the Boston leaders decided to take control of the situation. "Then," wrote Samuel Mather forty years later, "to prevent the Shedding of *Blood* by an ungoverned Multitude, some of the Gentlemen present would appear in the Head of what Action should be done; and a Declaration was prepared accordingly."[71] The authors of *The Declaration of the Gentlemen, Merchants and Inhabitants of Boston and the Country Adjacent* were comprised of William Bradstreet, the former Governor of the colony, "with several magistrates chosen in 1686, and some of the principal merchants and other principal inhabitants" of the town of Boston.[72] In keeping with the Prince of Orange's declaration which was published the previous month in Boston, these "illegally turned out" magistrates printed their own declaration as part of their preparations to resume control of the colony from the mob in Boston. At the same time they wanted to justify their actions in a way that was analogous to William's stated reasons for his seizure of the English government.

The preamble of the declaration consisted of a rehearsal of the history of Romanism in Protestant England from the reign of Mary Tudor through the Popish Plot of 1679. The first actual grievance that the Bay elders listed was the loss of the Massachusetts Bay Charter under Charles II. They stated that their charter was vacated because of the "slanderous Accusations" of one man (presumably Edward Randolph) in order to "get us within reach of the Desolation desired for us." From the context of the document, the tacit implication is that the charter had been revoked with the intent of introducing Papism (implied in the preamble) and arbitrary government into the colony, just as James had tried to introduce Popery and tyranny into England. The declaration went on to itemize the colony's grievances against Andros' government, much as William's declaration had itemized complaints against James. The Governor exercised his powers in an arbitrary manner by raising taxes, levying troops, and creating laws as he pleased with only the consent of his Council (hence without a representative assembly). Andros was accompanied by an army "now brought from Europe to support what was imposed upon us." Andros loaded "Preferments principally upon such men as were Strangers to and Haters of the People," especially "a Crew of abject Persons fetched from New York," who extorted and oppressed the people of Massachusetts "without any rules but those of their own insatiable Avarice and Beggery." The people were treated like slaves "with multiplied Contradictions to Magna Charta, the Rights to which we laid claim to." Deprived of their Assembly, judged by unqualified juries and corrupt judges and often punished without benefit of jury or habeas corpus, "it was now plainly affirmed . . . that the People in New England were all Slaves." The Bay leaders complained of Andros' land schemes and taxes that they claimed were promoted to enrich the strangers placed over them and "to impoverish a land already Peeled, meeted out and Trodden down." The authors of the declaration stated that, while the good people of the colony "bore all these, and many more such Things, without making any Attempt for any Relief," Increase Mather undertook to represent them before King James. The King "more than once or twice" promised relief but did nothing more. The leaders then moved to the issue of the Indian wars. They alleged that "in the Army, as well as in the Council, Papists are in Commission" and that these men were instrumental in bringing about the failure of the Maine expedition, and had even conspired to give New England over "to a Forreign power." For all these reasons, the Boston leaders wrote, "we do therefore seize upon the Persons of these few men which have been (next to our Sins) the Grand Authors of our Miseries" in order to secure them for whatever justice the government in England saw fit to visit upon them.[73]

Historians, pondering the vagueness of the Declaration, have theorized that those who wrote it were unsure as to events in London. Hall and Leder write that "it seems certain that on April 18 Boston did not know definitely that William had been successful and was already installed on the throne of England . . . otherwise the Declaration would have been specific on that point."[74] Although the Boston leaders might not have been clear as to the details of William's accession, they were certainly aware that a change of government had been effected in England and that the new government was hostile to the old. Increase Mather's tract with its appendices had reached Boston and been published in the previous month. Edward Randolph believed that Cotton Mather received frequent updates on the situation in England, and, if this was the case, the Boston leadership at least knew that James II no longer sat upon the throne and William held power in

London.[75] Additionally, John Winslow's arrival on 4 April with copies of the Prince's *Declaration of Reasons* confirmed the evidence of William's presence in England. It is more likely that the terms of the document were vague because its authors were at pains to publish it quickly before matters got out of hand in Boston and caused a bloody, and possibly politically embarrassing, confrontation. It was also vague because the Boston leadership wanted their accusations against the Andros regime to parallel those leveled by William against James II.

The two necessary ingredients of the Prince of Orange's *Declaration of Reasons* were arbitrary government *and* Popery, and while Andros and his creatures displayed ample evidence of the former, the Boston leaders had no concrete evidence that the Governor or any of his principal assistants in Massachusetts were Roman Catholic and certainly none that they had conspired to introduce Popery to New England. In fact, they had established, not Romanism, but Anglicanism in Massachusetts, a fact that the authors failed to mention in their declaration. So, with no real evidence of a Popish Plot hatched in Massachusetts and understanding the necessary connection between Popery and slavery, the authors of the declaration rehearsed past English history (the reign of "Bloody Mary" and the Popish Plot in England of 1679), and employed the gossip that had filtered from Maine to hint that Andros was in league with his master James, the French and their Indian allies, and left it at that.[76] To the modern reader these allegations seem vague indeed, but to the people of Boston who were nurtured on *Foxes' Martyrs* and recently reacquainted with the traditional Puritan arguments that there was little substantial difference between Anglicanism and Popery, and who were aware of James II's Catholicism, the allegations in the declaration had substance.[77] The declaration was sufficient for the accomplishment of its first purpose, to enable the "principal Gentlemen in *Boston*" to take control of the unruly mob, and for its second, as it acted as a warrant, of sorts, for the arrest of Andros and his officers in Boston on 18 April. As to how the government in London would respond to the revolution in Boston, they were willing to put their faith in God's providence, the new regime at Whitehall, and in the diplomatic abilities of their agents, friends and supporters in England.

The arrest of Andros and his most objectionable supporters amounted to little more than a day's work, but the Glorious Revolution in Massachusetts was not yet over. After Andros and other members of his administration were incarcerated and an interim government created, the battleground moved from the streets of Boston to the Court of St. James. There, various factions in the Bay Colony and members of the purged government competed with each other to influence the new King and the Lords of Trade, who would ultimately decide the fate of the Dominion leaders and the political future of the colony. What followed was a war of letters, addresses and pamphlets that lasted until 1691. The Lords of Trade were not enthusiastic about revolutions in the colonies, and the ex-Governor and some of his co-defendants had influential friends in England. In order to garner both public and private support for their cause, Andros, Randolph, Reverend Ratcliffe, and their allies wrote letters and pamphlets that cast the Dominion administration in a favorable light and criticized the colonists. Randolph began his own letter writing campaign shortly after his incarceration in "yᵉ Common Goal [sic] in Boston" and continued to solicit support from men of influence in this fashion into the next year.[78] Andros himself wrote an account of his tenure in which he stressed his faithfulness to his royal commission.[79] Others wrote pamphlets in which they praised the Governor and his administration, and characterized the leaders of the Revolution in Massachusetts as religious bigots, smugglers, pirates, and traitors. Andros and his co-defendants were acquitted of maladministration by the Lords of Trade in October, 1690.

The "Anglican faction" that supported the Andros regime argued that the rebel leaders of Boston consisted primarily of "Preachers and their Adherents," who "highly inraged the Minds of the People against the Governor."[80] To them, the Revolution in Boston was partially aimed at the Church of England.[81] It was not a supportive response to the Revolution in England, but a "long contriv'd piece of Wickedness" planned by a small group of influential Puritans in Boston and carefully instilled into the populace. According to the Anglican faction's interpretation of the events in Boston, William's landing only gave the theocrats an opportunity to put their conspiracy into action.[82] Andros' supporters argued that the New England rebels were not allied with William of Orange but with James II, and illustrated their point by describing Increase Mather's relationship with the Stuart king and his Catholic advisors. Mather, they claimed, had endeared himself "into the affections of F. Peters [Petre], Mr. Brunt, and Nevil Pain . . . to satisfie his own malice and prejudice (without any ground or reason) conceived against the then Government of New-England."[83] Randolph and others also alleged that before 1685 the Massachusetts colonists had become rich by ignoring the Acts of Trade and by providing safe (and lucrative) havens for pirates.[84] According to Randolph, "it is not the person of Sʳ. Edmund but the government itself, they designe to have removed, that they may freely trade . . . without ever touching at or paying the customes of England as the law requires." He further alleged that, before Andros governed the colony and enforced the laws of navigation and trade, "this place was the common receptacle of pyratts of all nations . . . who have been received and p'tected by some in the present government."[85]

The allegations that seem to have troubled the Boston rebels the most were those that centered around religion. Within weeks of the Revolution in Boston, Anglicans began to send complaints of mistreatment and discrimination to the government in London. In May, Edward Randolph complained to the Archbishop of Canterbury that "M'. Mather has published here a booke called 'the Idolatry of ye Common prayer worship' which renders all of us of that church obnoxious to the common people who account us popish & treat us accordingly."[86] Just after the April revolution, Anglicans sent an address to London.[87] In it they claimed that "such is the malice of our dissenting neighbours that wee are become the object of their scorn, and are forced to take many affronts and indignityes by them frequently offered to our persons and religion, which some of their principall Teachers have lately in a printed treaty [treatise] charged to be idolatry and Popery." The Boston Anglicans alleged that "our Church by their rage and fury having been greatly hurt and damnified" and was "daily threatened to be pulled down and destroyed." Their minister was "hindered and obstructed in the discharge of his duty." They were "put under the burden of most excessive rates and taxes to support the interest of a disloyal prevailing party amongst us who . . . designe nothing but ruin and destruction to us and the whole countrey."[88]

Pamphlets followed letters and addresses, each more critical of the new Puritan government than the last. In 1690 a tract by John Palmer was published in London. Palmer noted that the new government was comprised of *"New England* Reformers, . . . [who] now had the opportunity to make themselves Persecutors of the Church of *England,* as they had before been of all others that did not comply with their Independency." He claimed that the new government there could be expected to mete out the kinds of punishment—"Fines, Imprisonment, Stripes, Banishment, and Death"— to Anglicans that they had reserved in the past for others who did not conform to the New England Way.[89] The author of *A Particular Account* declared that one of the Puritan ministers "was for cutting the throats of all of the Established Church and then (said he religiously), wee shall never bee troubled with them again." Other Puritans allegedly replied "that it was no more a sin to kill such as they were, than to cut off a dog's neck."[90] C.D., an unknown Anglican writer, argued that it was not the government of Andros that galled the colonists but the Church of England men in positions of power there. He noted that:

at the time of the Revolution most of the Principal Officers in the
Government were of the Independent and Presbyterian Party, yet their
malice and fury was not shewn to any of them, but only used and exercised
against those of the Church of England, whom . . . they seized and
barbarously Imprisoned.[91]

The new Anglican chapel was defiled when angry Puritans, "stir[red] up to
Faction and Rebellion," broke its glass windows and daubed it "with dung,
and other filth, in the rudest and basest manner imaginable." The Anglican
minister, Rev. Ratcliffe, escaped the colony, his church, and his flock, C.D.
alleged, for his own safety. In short, Dominion supporters argued that the
new regime was dominated by religious fanatics, who were far more
tyrannical toward the property and religion of Anglicans than the Andros
regime had ever been toward the Congregationalists.[92]

   Mather and other supporters of the Boston Revolution responded to the
charges of their detractors through pamphlets and by collecting all of the
allegations and complaints against the Andros regime that they could find.
The latter did them little good in London. Their accusations came to nought
when the Dominion officers were acquitted by the Lords of Trade. The
pamphlets were important, however, both as a means of influencing the
Crown's decision to give the colony a new charter and because it offered
the colonists, as well as the government in London, a viable interpretation
of the Revolution in Boston. It is ever the case that the winners of
revolutions write the history for posterity, so it was with the winners of the
Glorious Revolution both in England and in Massachusetts.

   One problem that confronted the memorialists of the Revolution in the
Bay Colony, however, was that the comparison between Popery and the
Church of England, so useful in focusing the resentments of the colonists,
represented a political liability in London. It was one thing to accuse
Andros and his accomplices of treachery and conspiracy along with James
II. It carried little weight in London, but it was safe. It was quite another to
condemn the Church of England of being no more than Popery dressed in
English fashion. Increase Mather's statements that the Anglican service
consisted of "broken Responds and shreds of Prayer which the Priests and
People toss between them like Tennis Balls," that "a stinted Liturgy is
opposite to the Spirit of Prayer," and that the surplice and cross were "Idols
of Rome," could not help his cause in London.[93] Such comparisons were
not employed there. In fact, Increase Mather and his allies confronted a
very different problem in the capital. They and their co-religionists in

Massachusetts were accused of behaving toward Anglicans and other Dissenters like a Papist government.

The accusations of Anglicans against the Boston Puritans were particularly embarrassing. Massachusetts agents first tried to accuse the Boston Anglicans of treasonably applying to James II (or possibly even Louis XIV) for support against the Congregationalists in Massachusetts. In *The Humble Address of the Publicans of New-England, To which King You Please . . .*, an anonymous pamphlet published in London in 1691, the author claimed that the supposed members of the Church of England who had sent an Address to the King, were really men educated in "Debauchery and Depravation."[94] Mather and others characterized the Anglican faction in Boston as ardent supporters of James II, "Tools of Tyranny," who were confused without the Stuart King's guidance.[95]

Mather, himself, apparently decided that the best means of answering the Anglicans' allegations were both to dismiss them as inconsequential and to do all that he could to influence the government in Boston to adopt a policy of tolerance henceforth. To the first end he wrote that the accusations of the Boston Anglicans were mostly falsehoods. He admitted that a few windows were broken on the new Anglican chapel. The new church had been built next to a school yard, and who could fault the innocent accidents of the local lads playing at ball? "What?" he asked incredulously:

> must not a Boy in New England throw a Stone or a Ball amiss but the *King* shall hear of it? To a *Domitian* (who counted *Fly Catching* not below him) this might have been a proper Address: But for these Impurtinences to be laid before the High and Mighty *WILLIAM* the Greatest Prince now in *Europe*, . . . there was doubtless a *mistake in the delivery.*[96]

At about the same time, Mather called for religious tolerance in Massachusetts. He informed his friends at home that the "Archbishop of Canterbury that now is, and many of the present Bishops, are Friends to New-England," and he warned them that the new King and his Court were considering a charter in which "Liberty is granted to all Men to Worship God after that manner which in their Consciences they shall be perswaded is the most Scriptural way."[97] He implied that if the colonists wanted a new charter that guaranteed them their property, English liberties and a representative assembly, the price that they would have to pay was tolerance toward other Protestant denominations. Anglicans in Massachusetts had achieved the high ground early on the issue of religion, and their opponents were willing to surrender it to them and move on to constitutional considerations where they thought their arguments the strongest.[98]

In 1690, Increase Mather and other colonial agents answered Randolph's accusations that the colony ignored the trade laws and encouraged piracy. "The Government and Inhabitants in generall," they wrote, "have no advantage by irregular Trade but the Offenders only, whom they have been and will alwaies be ready and forward to find out and punish as the Acts direct." They argued that Randolph as commissioner of customs persecuted shippers with false charges of "irregular Trading" and engaged in further corrupt and illegal acts under Andros. They questioned Randolph's veracity and character. After all, they asserted, when the "Councill took upon them[selves] to make Laws and levy mony without an Assembly or any Consent of Their Ma[ts]. Subjects" to the destruction of English rights in Massachusetts, Randolph was one of the collaborators.[99] Pamphlet writers thereafter argued primarily that Andros and his regime had been arbitrary rulers who conspired with the tyrant James II against the people of New England and William. Each pamphlet contained a similar list of the New Englanders' allegations. Andros and his accomplices had governed without an assembly, had taken their property, including the South Church, without due process, had erected arbitrary courts, and had generally perpetrated "a treasonable invasion of all the Rights belonging to the English Nation" just as James II had to the people of England.[100]

In the meantime, while the pamphlet war and negotiations continued in England, the interim government in Massachusetts fared poorly. The Maine frontier was left undefended after the troops had deserted Andros and returned to their homes, and, since England and France were now at war, the French and their Indian allies ravaged Maine with impunity.[101] When the provisional government in Boston tried to levy troops throughout the colony to fight in Maine, they encountered stiff resistance from the smaller towns whose leaders claimed that they had contributed more than their fair share of both blood and treasure under Andros. In a sermon delivered in response to these complaints, Cotton Mather replied that the current war was just and necessary for the defense of the colony.[102] Probably at the suggestion of the colonial agents in London, Massachusetts embarked on an extravagant, and ultimately ruinous, expedition against French Canada, successfully taking Port Royal and then mounting an attack upon Quebec. The war was popular in the colony at first. Merchants, stung in the past by the attacks of French privateers and enthusiastic at the possibility of booty, supported it. The Puritans viewed the war as a crusade against French

Popery. The leaders of the Bay Colony, both in Boston and England, hoped that their expedition against the new rulers' enemies would convince the government in London of their loyalty and enthusiasm and thus hasten the creation of a more favorable charter. The Quebec expedition, poorly planned and manned from the start, failed, and Boston once again saw militia companies in its streets. This time, however, the unpaid soldiers turned out to protest against the provisional government.[103] To promote the war, the government in Boston was forced to levy taxes that were thirty-two times higher than those raised in 1660.[104]

The failure of King William's War, the increased taxation, and the resultant public disorder caused a rift between the moderate merchants of the colony and the more conservative Puritan leaders. These two parties, and the Andros supporters in the colony, bombarded their agents and friends in London with requests for a new charter and the restoration of legitimate and ordered government in Massachusetts.[105] Their appeals and prayers finally bore fruit when King William granted the colony a new charter on 17 October, 1691.[106]

The charter of 1691 itself became a bone of contention between conservative Puritans like Elisha Cooke and Thomas Oakes, "who trusted God more than Kings," and would not be satisfied with anything less than the full restoration of the old charter, and the majority of the Bay leadership who were reasonably happy with the new one and "were too intelligent to believe that the clock could be turned back."[107] Most colonists looked forward with optimism to the new charter and the stability they were convinced it would foster.

The new Massachusetts charter had a profound effect on both the colony's internal politics and its relationship to the mother country. The Massachusetts assembly was restored, but the Governor, who would henceforth be appointed by the king, had the power to veto legislation as did the Crown after him. The new Governor was to put the Crown's interest first and was thus given the power to control a popular assembly that had a reputation for ignoring imperial policy that it found inconvenient. The Governor also had the right to appoint all of the officials of the judiciary and military with the consent of his council.[108] His choices might be constrained by local interests, however, because the colonial council was chosen by the assembly rather than by the Crown—an innovation peculiar to Massachusetts among royal colonies. The colonial assembly, called the General Court, was to be elected annually in order to select councilors. While it was sitting it could legislate as it saw fit for the colony. Its annual election was fixed by royal charter rather than by the invitation of the governor, who could neither prevent it from sitting, nor guarantee its pliability. This, and the fact that the assembly chose the council gave it primacy over the executive. Its powers were comparable to those of the House of Commons in England. Indeed, a succession of governors would come to agree with William Shute, who reported to the King in 1723, "I found the House of Representatives, who are chosen annually, possessed of all the Powers of the House of Commons, and of much greater."[109]

While the form of government might have heartened the Puritan conservatives, the new charter's provisions for liberty of conscience and broader suffrage did not. Liberty of conscience was granted to all Protestants, and suffrage was secularized, so that all adult men who possessed a forty shilling freehold or property valued at forty pounds sterling had the right to vote. While this innovation over the old ways did not completely destroy the political power of the "theocrats," as Viola Barnes argues, it had the effect of widening the electorate and opening the doors of Massachusetts politics to the growing politically and religiously moderate urban merchant class of the colony.[110] In fact the charter and the legacy of the Glorious Revolution helped to create a new alliance between moderate Congregationalists, who were increasingly more tolerant of other Protestant faiths, and the growing merchant class. This new alliance was based on the imperial politics fostered by the new charter and the ideological legacy of the Glorious Revolution. The Andros regime and the struggle for the new charter had the effect of making Bay colonists, whatever their religious convictions, and whatever their calling, conscious of their relationship with the mother country, and conscious of a common devotion to liberty, property and Protestantism that spanned the Atlantic. In essence, Bay Colonists replaced their provincial Calvinist values for those traditional English values enunciated in William's revolutionary propaganda and in the more secular and libertarian English Whig ideology.

From its founding, Massachusetts had worked hard to earn its own way. It had not been founded or settled to promote economic prosperity or even to avoid political adversity, but "as a positive crusade for an idea."[111] The idea was Congregational utopianism, and the first generation of colonial leaders did all that was in their power to nurture it, including promoting separation between their colony and the tainted politics and established religion of their homeland. In order to "create in New England the kind of society that God demanded of all His servants but none had yet given Him," the founders removed the colonial charter from London to Boston, so that Massachusetts "could become in effect a self-governing commonwealth."[112] As a result, the Bay Colonists devoted their early years to insular concerns associated with utopia building and largely avoided entanglements in the controversies and events that took place in England from the 1630s until 1685. In Massachusetts before 1691, the social covenant was one made between the people, their God, and their colonial magistrates.[113]

The new ideas of the Glorious Revolution were not entirely inconsistent with the old covenant theology of the colony. Bay Colony leaders revised the old covenant idea to include the role of providential kings in the political and civil life of the colony. In 1689, Cotton Mather preached an election sermon in which he blamed Massachusetts' misfortunes, not on King James II or Andros, but on the apostasy of the colonists themselves.[114] Before the Glorious Revolution, Bay Colonists feared and distrusted English kings, whom they viewed as erroneous in their religion and arbitrary in their government.[115] William's rescue of the liberties and religion of Englishmen and his new charter for Massachusetts, in essence, created a new covenant for the Bay Colony between the people, their God, and their king. Perry Miller notes that "the humiliation of New England under Andros was a covenant affliction" in the eyes of Puritan colonists, "while William and Mary were a providential deliverance, according to the promise." In July of 1689, Increase Mather claimed that New England would have closer ties to the Crown, because the new rulers had restored and preserved the liberties and Protestant religion of all Englishmen by their "Happy REVOLUTION." Henceforth the King and the people were allies (as they had been in the Revolution of 1689) in the great undertaking of government and the preservation of the rights of Englishmen against the dark threats of Popery and slavery. Perry Miller notes that the "substance of the covenant" was "firmly attached to the Protestantism of the English Crown."[116] This theme became part of the stock in trade of New England Ministers from the late 1690s on. In 1700, Cotton Mather preached an election sermon that might best be classified as an anti-Jeremiad. In *A Pillar of Gratitude*, he praised Massachusetts, "the climate, the college, the government with its theocratic and democratic principles, the wise and good English king," and, although he commented on the absense of heresy in the colony and blasted Popery, he refrained from including Anglicanism on his list of unorthodox positions.[117] From 1701 through 1766, many election sermons in Massachusetts were to echo Mather's themes of a free people, ordered government, and good monarchs. Perry Miller argues that these Whig themes became an integral part of the post-Revolutionary social covenant idea. For Miller, "Protestantism was imperceptibly carried over into the new order, not by turning from religion to an absolutist state, but by translating Christian Liberty into those liberties guaranteed by statute."[118] In essence, for Miller the Puritans of New England made a gradual transition toward the ideology of post-Revolutionary English Whiggism with its consistent themes of liberty, good order, and support for the Protestant Whig monarchy. The transition was eased by the fact that Puritans had always believed that the people were ruled by their own consent, and the Settlement of the Glorious Revolution allowed them to transfer this idea to English monarchs as well as representative assemblies.[119]

Additionally ministers began to claim that good kings were not only the constitutional bulwark of the people's liberty, but also the moral arbiters of the Protestant English nation. As Soloman Stoddard declaimed in his election sermon of 1703:

> Rulers are to be keepers of both tables; and they must practice Religion and Morality themselves, so they must take care that the people do it; they must use all proper means, for the suppression of Heresy, Prophaness & Superstition & other Corruptions in Worship.[120]

New Englanders began their revolutionary journey with the loss of their charter and hence their autonomy under Charles II, and it continued with the deprivation of their rights and property and their enforced Calvinist homogeneity under James II and his servant Sir Edmund Andros. The price that they were willing to pay for the restoration of their rights and property, and some degree of autonomy vested in a new colonial constitution, was Protestant religious tolerance and the acceptance of monarchical government. Although the threat of Popery resonated in the minds of the people of Massachusetts, it was both less substantive and less important in stimulating the Revolution in New England than it would be in New York and Maryland. That is not to say that Bay Colonists' preoccupation with an imagined Popish Plot in their midst is not significant. The fact that New Englanders made so much of a Catholic Conspiracy from so little evidence should inform contemporary historians that religious considerations were still a focus of concern and anxiety among them and still represented a powerful symbolic rallying cry in seventeenth-century America, just as it did in England. Perhaps the discovery of a Popish Plot in New England also supplied colonists there with a reasonable explanation for the arbitrary rule of Andros and the Dominion government, for, as Englishmen everywhere understood politics, arbitrary government and the Catholic religion went hand in hand. Massachusetts colonists employed a tautological interpretation of the events of their recent history. Where there was tyranny, one should look for Popery. Once the colonists understood that the actions of Andros and his master, James II, were motivated by Popery, the arbitrary government that they had experienced since 1685 could better be explained. In turn Andros' past political transgressions further confirmed the evidence of a Popish conspiracy in the Bay Colony.

Ultimately, Massachusetts kept its covenant with God by admitting into it both the Revolutionary principles of 1688 and the enthusiastic acceptance of English Protestant limited monarchy. Just over a half-century later, in 1746, Charles Chauncy summed up the Revolutionary covenant of Massachusetts at a time when England was once again under the twin threats of Stuart tyranny and Romanism:

> Let us, my *Brethren* . . . express our Love, and Gratitude, and Loyalty, to our Sovereign, and Concern for the Safety of his Kingdom. Let us be constant and importunate in our Supplications to god, that he would preserve the *Person*, and protect the *Crown* of our rightful and Lawful King; . . . that he would mercifully save his people from *Popery* and *Slavery*; perpetuating to them the Enjoyment of their *Rights* and *Liberties*, which distinguish them from the other Nations of the Earth.[121]

Notes

1. Cotton Mather, *Magnalia Christi Americana: Books I and II,* Kenneth B. Murdock, ed. (Cambridge, Massachusetts: Belknap Press, 1977), 289. The Latin phrase states, "Judgements were entrusted to the unjust, laws to outlaws, peace to quarrelers, and justice to wrongdoers."

2. E.R. & S.S [Edward Rawson and Samuel Sewall], *The Revolution in New England Justified, and the People there Vindicated from the Aspersions Cast upon them by Mr. Joseph Palmer, in his Pretended Answer to the Declaration, Published by the Inhabitants of Boston, and the Country Adjacent . . .* (Boston, 1691), iv.

3. Thomas Hutchinson, *The History of the Colony and Province of Massachusetts Bay*, 2 vols. Lawrence Shaw, ed. (Boston: Harvard University Press, 1936), 1:317. See also E.R. & S.S, *The Revolution in New England Justified . . .*, 4-6.

4. Winslow's news only corroborated rumors that had spread throughout the colony for a few weeks. See Theodore Burnham Lewis, "Massachusetts and the Glorious Revolution, 1660-1692" (Ph.D. diss., University of Wisconsin, 1967),

300. See also John Gorham Palfrey, *History of New England*, 3 vols. (Boston: Little, Brown & Co., 1882), 3:574.

5. Lewis, "Massachusetts," 300.

6. "Samuel Mather's Account of the Preliminary to Revolt, April 1690," in Michael G. Hall et al., ed., *The Glorious Revolution in America, Documents on the Colonial Crisis of 1689* (Chapel Hill: University of North Carolina Press, 1964), 39.

7. See Lewis, "Massachusetts," 370-371, 382-386; Hall, *Glorious Revolution*, 212-214.

8. Hutchinson, *History*, 1:300.

9. Hutchinson, *History*, 1:301.

10. Useful secondary narrative sources for a study of the Revolution in Massachusetts include Viola Florence Barnes, *The Dominion of New England: A Study in British Colonial Policy* (New Haven: Yale University Press, 1923), Lewis, "Massachusetts" and David S. Lovejoy, *The Glorious Revolution in America* (New York: Harper & Row, 1972). Barnes is generally more sympathetic toward Andros. She states that the Dominion was created in order to defend the colonies in the north, and to "offer greater opportunities for the development of a constructive commercial program" that would benefit both the colonies and the mother country (30). Additionally, she argues that Massachusetts was included in the Dominion in order to "break the power of the theocracy there, and free that region from Puritan domination" (42), a prospect that the author appears to have relished. For Barnes, the Glorious Revolution in New England was prompted by "the fanaticism of the Puritan theocrats, who were more Hebrew than English in their thought and government" (250-252). T.H. Breen counters that the revolution in Massachusetts "had little or nothing to do with religion" and that colonists based their critique of Andros' government "in terms of life, liberty, and property." See (T.H. Breen, *The Character of a Good Ruler: A Study in Puritan Ideas in New England, 1630-1730* (New Haven: Yale University Press, 1970), 152). In fact, both historians err in carrying their arguments too far in one direction. While Barnes makes far too much of the theocratic nature of the revolt against Andros, Breen underestimates the significance of the Anglican presence, and anxiety over Popery in the colony.

Lewis's narrative of the Andros government and the development of the revolt itself provides an excellent blow-by-blow description of the events from the Restoration to 1692. Lewis argues that the Revolution in Massachusetts was brought about and succeeded because of the cooperation of contending factions (Puritan conservatives and economically mobile moderates) who ceased their twenty-year-old political feud to concert their efforts to regain control of the colony from a government that worked against their various interests. Lovejoy's view that the Glorious Revolution in America represented a response to a renewed effort by the Crown to make the colonies profitable, implies that the Revolution should have taken place in much the same way and with much the same complaints in all of the colonies, which was not the case. Frustrated (and often incarcerated) English officials, like Edward Randolph, would certainly have agreed with Lovejoy (and, for that matter, Barnes), when they argued that the chief reason for the Revolution in America was the vigor of the trade laws. (Randolph to the Lords of Trade, May 29, 1689, *Edward Randolph, Including His Letters and Official Papers From the New England, Middle, and Southern Colonies in America . . .*, Robert N. Toppan, ed., *Publications of the Prince Society*, XXVII (New York: Burt Franklin, 1967), 279-280. (Henceforth referred to as *Randolph Papers.*) Few, if any, supporters of the revolt in Massachusetts argued thus, as they would in the 1760s. Additional secondary material is included in Hall and Leder's *The Glorious Revolution in America,* as well as some very useful primary documents.

11. "The Boston Declaration of Grievances, April 18, 1698," Hall, 42. The original title of this document is *The Declaration of the Gentlemen, Merchants and Inhabitants of Boston, and the Country Adjacent.* (see *Narratives of the Insurrections, 1675-1690,* Charles M. Andrews, ed. [New York: Charles Scribner's Sons, 1915], 175). I have used the title that Hall and Leder assign to it here and in all references that follow.

12. Cited in Breen, *The Character of a Good Ruler,* 145. See also Lovejoy, *Glorious Revolution,* 182-186; the "Boston Declaration of Grievances," Hall, *Glorious Revolution,* 43; William Stoughten, *A Narrative of the Proceedings of Sir Edmund Androsse and His Accomplices, Who Acted by an Illegal and Arbitrary Commission from the Late King James . . .* (Boston, 1691), 9-10; and E.R. & S.S., *The Revolution in New England Justified . . .*, 8.

13. F.W. Maitland, *Constitutional History of England* (Cambridge: Cambridge University Press, 1963), 259. In 1610 the House of Lords rejected Commons' claim. In 1614 James I dissolved Parliament in response. For a discussion of the "consent to taxation" doctrine in English constitutional history and its transatlantic scope, see John Phillip Reid, *Constitutional History of the American Revolution: The Authority to Tax* (Madison, Wisconsin: University of Wisconsin Press, 1987), 139-146, 275-277.

14. "The Petition of Right," Stephenson and Marcham, *Sources of English Constitutional History,* 1:450. See also Maitland *Constitutional History,* 307-308.

15. Barnes, *Dominion,* 90.

16. E.R. & S.S., *The Revolution in New England Justified . . .*, 6. See also Stoughten, *A Narrative of the Proceedings of Sir Edmund Androsse,* 6-7.

17. Barnes, *Dominion,* 84-86. Barnes notes that the writ issued to raise the taxes was irregular as it was not issued in the king's name, and argues that this fact rather than the constitutional irregularity of levying taxes without representation provided the stimulus to resist the taxes. It is more probable that the omission of the King's name gave grounds for complaint against the import tariffs, which, like tonnage and poundage and other duties raised in England, were customary royal revenues usually raised for the life of the monarch and thus considered as a different legal category from domestic impositions. See Maitland, *Constitutional History,* 182-

183, 307, 435; Reid, *The Authority to Tax*, 162-163.

18. Barnes, *Dominion*, 86-87; Lewis, "Massachusetts," 227-237.

19. *Massachusetts Archives*, 127:101, cited in Lewis, "Massachusetts," 230.

20. Barnes, *Dominion*, 87-88.

21. "An Account of the Late Revolution in New England by A.B," Hall, *Glorious Revolution*, 48.

22. Hutchinson, *History*, 1:305. For a discussion of the origins and constitutional legitimacy of quitrents in Massachusetts, see Barnes, *Dominion*, 174-211.

23. Hutchinson, *History*, 1:305-306. See also the *Diary of Samuel Sewall, 1674-1729*. 3 vols. *Collections of the Massachusetts Historical Society*, Vol. V, Fifth Series. (Cambridge, Massachusetts: University Press, 1878), 1:220-221; 1:231-232, passim; "Grievances Against the Governor, 1687-89," Hall, 33-34; Stoughten, *A Narrative of the Proceedings of Sir Edmund Androsse*, 8-9; E.R. & S.S., *The Revolution in New England Justified . . .*, 12-13.

24. Edmund Morgan. *The Puritan Dilemma: The Story of John Winthrop* (Boston: Little, Brown & Co., 1958), 170.

25. "The Boston Declaration of Grievances," Hall, 44. Far from being an ancient right of Britons enshrined in the Magna Carta, as was claimed by some of those accused in Massachusetts, the statutory protection of *habeas corpus* was quite new, having only been passed into statute in 1679 (31 Car. II, c. 2). See Maitland, *Constitutional History*, 314-315. The act itself is vague as to whether it might actually apply to subjects residing in the colonies. For the Act, see Stephenson and Marcham, *Sources*, 2:557-558. Lewis, however, indicates that although the English statute may not have applied to the colonies, "it had been the practice in Massachusetts to grant bail for offenses which were unbailable under English law" (Lewis, "Massachusetts," 235); thus, *habeas corpus* writs, or their equivalent, had a legal tradition in that colony. Maitland observes that *habeas corpus* writs were part of the English legal tradition before the reign of Elizabeth. (Maitland, *Constitutional History*, 313).

26. E.R. & S.S., *The Revolution in New England Justified . . .*, 35. See also "The Boston Declaration of Grievances," Hall, *Glorious Revolution*, 44; A.B., *An Account of the Late Revolution*, Hall, *Glorious Revolution*, 48; Stoughten, *A Narrative of the Proceedings of Sir Edmund Androsse*, 10.

27. "Boston Declaration of Grievances," Hall, *Glorious Revolution*, 43-44.

28. Hall, *Glorious Revolution*, 44.

29. Lovejoy, *Glorious Revolution*, 189.

30. Sewall, *Diary*, 1:201.

31. Sewall, *Diary*, 1:208.

32. "The Boston Declaration of Grievances," Hall, *Glorious Revolution*, 44.

33. Sewall, *Diary*, 1:162; Edward Randolph to the Committee for Trade and Foreign Plantations, March 25, 1687, in *Randolph Papers*, 4:152. See also Hamilton Andrews Hill, *History of the Old South Church (Third Church), Boston,*

1669-1884, 2 vols. (Boston: Houghton, Mifflin and Co., 1890), 1:265.

34. "Andros' Report of His Administration, 1690," Andrews, *Narratives*, 230; C.D. *New England's Faction Discovered*, in Andrews, *Narratives*, 258.

35. According to Edward Randolph (who probably overcounted), "Wee have at present 400 persons who are daily frequenters of our church [presumably meaning Anglican Communicants], and as many more would come over to us, but some being tradesmen, others of mechanick professions, are threatened by the congregationall men to be arrested by their creditors, or to be turned out of their work, if they offer to come to our church." Randolph to the Archbishop of Canterbury, Boston, October 27, 1686, *Randolph Papers*, 4:131. See also Lewis, 214; Henry Wilder Foote, *Annals of King's Chapel From the Puritan Age of New England to the Present Day*, 2 vols., (Boston: Little, Brown, & Co., 1882), 1:88-94.

36. Sewall, *Diary*, 1:162-163.

37. Randolph to the Committee, Boston, March 25, 1687, *Randolph Papers*, 4:152; Sewall, *Diary*, 1:171.

38. Sewall, *Diary*, 1:171.

39. Sewall, *Diary*, 1:172, 177, 217-18, *passim.*

40. Sewall, *Diary*, 1:218.

41. Samuel Sewall to John Storke, August 8, 1687. *Letter Book of Samuel Sewall. Collections of the Massachusetts Historical Society*, Vol. I, Sixth Series. (Cambridge, Massachusetts: University Press, 1886), 52.

42. Sewall, *Letter Book*, fn. 1, 52-53.

43. Sewall, *Diary*, 1:186. "I will therefore put you in remembrance, though you once knew this, how that the Lord, having saved the people out of the land of Egypt, afterward destroyed them that believed not." Jude 5.

44. Hutchinson, *History*, 1:304. For the immediate response of Dissenters in England and Massachusetts, see Sewall, *Letter Book*, fn. 1, 54-55.

45. Sewall, *Letter Book*, fn. 1, 56. At least one Puritan minister, Thomas Danforth of Cambridge, was less than sanguine about James' proclamation. He explained to Mather in a letter of 8 November, 1687, "For my own part, I do more dread the consequences thereof [universal tolerance] than the execution of those penal laws the only wall against Popery . . ., We may, without a breach of charity, conclude that Popish Counsels are laid deep: time will show more." Sewall, *Letter Book*, fn. 1, 57.

46. Sewall, *Letter Book*, fn. 1, 57.

47. Sewall, *Letter Book*, 58. Mather and the other Congregationalist leaders undoubtedly felt that the King's declaration of tolerance put them in a dilemma. While they hoped that they could use it to claim that they had been wronged by Andros and his Anglican supporters who had violated their civil rights because of their religion, they must have worried about the difficulties that they would certainly encounter if, upon the restoration of their old charter, *they* had to abide by the letter of the proclamation and tolerate Anglicans, Quakers, and even Roman

Catholics. Mather and his supporters were willing to cross that bridge when they came to it if they could get their old charter restored and free themselves from Andros' government.

48. Lovejoy, *Glorious Revolution,* 223.

49. See Paul Seaward, *The Cavalier Parliament and the Restoration of the Old Regime, 1661-1667* (Cambridge: Cambridge University Press, 1989), 162, *passim.*

50. John Miller, *James II: A Study in Kingship* (London: Methuen, 1989), 126. Miller argues that James was more concerned with advancing the cause of Catholicism than with strengthening the monarchy and that James was less concerned with restoring a Catholic hierarchy in England than with the practice of religion (admittedly, for preference, the Catholic religion) according to the dictates of individual consciences. This contrasts with the Whig view, as promulgated by Williamite and Hanover propaganda and transmitted by Macaulay and his predecessors, that James intended to set up an arbitrary and Catholic nation in England. It also goes a long way to explain the problems in J.P. Kenyon's account of James. Kenyon argues that James wanted to make Catholicism the religion of the English state, but his cynical and inept attempts at it alienated English lay Catholics as well as the Pope. (Kenyon, *Stuart England,* 246-250) Miller agrees that James' statecraft was often inept, that the monarch was "so obsessed with his own rightness that he showed virtually no interest in the views of others," and that his policies often ran hard against the Anglican ruling elite and the traditional prejudices of the average Englishman "who equated 'Popery' with 'arbitrary government.'" (Miller, *James II,* viii, 128) Employing exhaustive research of James' personal papers, Miller argues convincingly that James religious tolerance was heartfelt and sincere, even if impolitic, and that he had no plans to convert England into a Roman Catholic state by force. For a more recent study of James II as "Catholic zealot and political reformer," see Mark Kishlansky, *A Monarchy Transformed: Britain, 1603-1714* (London: The Penguin Press, 1996), 265-269.

51. Miller, *James II,* 126-127, *passim.*

52. Increase Mather, "Autobiography," cited in Lovejoy, *Glorious Revolution,* 224.

53. Lovejoy, *Glorious Revolution,* 227-228.

54. "Samuel Mather's Account of the Preliminary to Revolt, April 1689," Hall, *Glorious Revolution,* 39.

55. "The Boston Declaration of Grievances," Hall, *Glorious Revolution,* 42.

56. Sewall does mention that some of the people of Boston *voluntarily* joined in the Anglican services at the South Church. References are scattered about in his *Dairy* (see 1:171). Edward Lilley was probably an Anglican convert. He apparently requested an Anglican funeral. For a short synopsis of the scandal (ultimately blamed on Andros) that took place when his executors decided on a Puritan service but the Anglican Rev. Mr. Ratcliffe appeared to perform the funeral rites, see H.A. Hill, *History of the Old South Church,* 1:279-280.

57. Barnes, *Dominion*, 223; Lewis, "Massachusetts," 270.

58. Lewis, "Massachusetts," 269-270. Most of the Narrative which follows is from Lewis, 269-300. For an account of the Dominion's Indian problems that is more forgiving of Andros, placing most of the blame for the conflict on the Puritans whose "faith in God's protection was substituted for the building of expensive forts and training skilled soldiers," see Barnes, 213-230. Lewis offers a fairly balanced view of the conflict. He argues that Andros' handling of the Indians was less than adroit, and the colonists preference in Indian policy ran to extermination rather than negotiation. Lewis, "Massachusetts," 273, *passim*.

59. Lewis, "Massachusetts," 273-274.

60. Lewis, "Massachusetts," 274. See also "Boston Declaration of Grievances," Hall, 45; "An Account of the Late Revolutions in New England, by A.B.," Hall, 49; "The Charges Against Sir Edmund Andros, Governor," Hall, 57; Hutchinson, 1:314.

61. Lewis, "Massachusetts," 276. Richard Dunn remarks that "Fitz frequently fell sick on such occasions" and was not so ill that he could not return to New London in Mid-November. See Richard S. Dunn, *Puritans and Yankees: The Winthrop Dynasty of New England, 1630-1717* (New York: W.W. Norton & Co., 1971), 251-252.

62. Moody to Increase Mather, 4 October, 1688. *Massachusetts Historical Society Collections*, ser. 4, 8:365-368.

63. Rumors circulated in the fall of 1688 that Mather had already been successful in his negotiations. Samuel Sewall wrote on 20 September, "Eldridge comes in, who sais the Amsterdam Gazett reported that Mr. Mather's Petition is granted . . .," Sewall, *Diary*, 1:226; see also Samuel Sewall to Increase Mather, 8 October, 1688, in note 1, 1:229. These rumors undoubtedly raised false hopes among people of Massachusetts that were dimmed as time passed with no change in the government of the colony, and as further reports from London indicated the fruitlessness of the elder Mather's mission.

64. Lewis, "Massachusetts," 278. See also Sewall, *Diary*, 30 December, 1688, 1:214, 1 January, 168$^8/_9$,1:242; and Hutchinson, 1:317.

65. *Andros Tracts II*, cited in Lewis, *Glorious Revolution*, 294. See also Lovejoy, *Glorious Revolution*, 228.

66. Lewis, "Massachusetts," 295. Evidently, at about the same time other attacks against the Church of England were published in the Bay Colony. Edward Randolph complained in May that "M^r. Mathers book ag^t. Y^e Common Prayer" was in circulation at the time of the Revolution in Boston (Randolph to the Bishop of London, *Randolph Papers*, 4:305-306).

67. Lewis,"Massachusetts," 295.

68. Lovejoy, *Glorious Revolution*, 228; Lewis, "Massachusetts," 295-296.

69. Lewis, "Massachusetts," 298-299.

70. Lewis, "Massachusetts," 299.

71. Samuel Mather, *The Life of the Very Reverend and Learned Cotton Mather* . . . (Boston, 1729), 42.

72. Hutchinson, *History*, 1:321.

73. "The Boston Declaration of Grievances," in Hall, *Glorious Revolution*, 42-44.

74. Hall, *Glorious Revolution*, 39. See also Lewis, "Massachusetts," 308-309, and Hutchinson, *History*, 1:323. Barnes argues that the document was "inconsistent" because it contained "two different points of view," those of the moderates whose complaints were primarily legal and secular, and those of the "theocrats," who presumably inserted the religious material (*Dominion*, 242-243). I agree with Lovejoy, who argues that the declaration was a "carefully written and eloquent document" that juxtaposed vague threats of a Papist conspiracy with real complaints of arbitrary government and was meant primarily to influence the people assembled in Boston. See Lovejoy, *Glorious Revolution*, 241.

75. Randolph to the Governor of Barbados, May 16, 1689, *Randolph Papers*, 4:265.

76. "Boston Declaration of Grievances," Hall, 45-46. The Declaration states, "The whole War hath been so managed, that we cannot but suspect in it a Branch of the Plot to bring us low . . . we secure them [Andros and his officers] lest, ere we are aware, we find . . . ourselves to be by them given away to a Forreign Power" Hall, *Glorious Revolution*, 45-46.

77. Richard Dunn assumes that "the more credulous Puritans" among Boston's leaders honestly believed that "Andros was betraying the militia to the Popish French" (Dunn, *Puritans and Yankees*, 252).

Other publications were circulated in Boston in April that carried anti-Catholic and anti-Anglican sentiment. In addition to Mather's *A Testimony Against Several Profane Practices,* published in February, the most important of these was Increase Mather's *A Brief Discourse Concerning the Unlawfulness of the Common-Prayer Worship.* See Randolph to Dr. William Sancroft, Archbishop of Canterbury, May 28, 1689, *Randolph Papers,* 4:270, and Foote, *Annals,* 96. Apparently the Congregationalist ministers also did their part to promote anti-Anglicanism as well. Randolph notes that "Mr. Mathers booke ag[t]. y[e] Common Prayer" and "y[e] Ministers has perswaded the people that wee were Idolaters & therefore not fitt to be intrusted longer wth y[e] Gom[t]." (Randolph to the Bishop of London, October 25, 1698, *Randolph Papers*, 4:305).

78. See *Randolph Papers,* Randolph to the Governor of Barbados, Boston, May 16, 1689, 4:264; Randolph to Dr. William Sancroft, Archbishop of Canterbury, Boston, May 28, 1689, 4:268; Randolph to the Lords of Trade, May 29, 1689, 4:271; Randolph to Blathwayt, from Gaol, July 22, 1689, 4:283; Randolph to my Lord Privie Seale, July 23, 1689, 4:284; Randolph to the Com[tee], September 5, 1689, 4:292; Randolph to the Com[tee], October 15, 1689, 4:297; Randolph to the Bishop of London, October 25, 1689, 4:305; Randolph to the Bishop of London, October 26, 1689, 4:309; Randolph to Mr. Chaplain, October 28, 1689, 5:20;

Randolph to the Committee, January 10, 1689/90, 5:28; "Randolph's Answer to Matters Objected Against Him, April 24, 1690," 5:31.

79. "Andros' Report of his Administration to the Right Hon'ble Lords of the Committee for Trade and Plantations . . .," in Andrews, *Narratives*, 229-236.

80. [Robert Ratcliffe?], *A Particular Account of the Late Revolution at Boston in the Colony and Province of Massachusetts*, in Andrews, *Narratives*, 196, 199. See also C.D., *New England's Faction Discovered; or A Brief and True Account of their Persecution of the Church of England; the Beginning and Progress of the War with the Indians; and other Late Proceedings there, in a Letter from a Gentleman of Quality. Being an Answer to a False and Scandalous Pamphlet Lately Published; Intituled, News from New England, etc.*, in Andrews, *Narratives*, 258; Randolph to the Lords of Trade, May 29, 1689, *Randolph Papers*, 4:280, Randolph to my Lord Privie Seale, July 23, 1689, *Randolph Papers*, 4:285.

81. *Humble Address of Your Majesty's most loyal and dutiful Subjects of the Church of England in Boston in Your Majesty's Territory and Dominion of New England*, Foote, *Annals*, 1:101; Randolph to Dr. William Sancroft, Archbishop of Canterbury, Boston, May 28, 1689, *Randolph Papers*, 4:268; Randolph to the Bishop of London, October 25, 1689, *Randolph Papers*, 4:305, 4:307-308; *A Particular Account*, Andrews, *Narratives*, 207; *Faction Discovered*, Andrews, *Narratives*, 258-259.

82. *Particular Account*, Andrews, *Narratives*, 196. See also "Mr. Randolph's Pet^n. To be Restored to his Employment, May 22, 1690," *Randolph Papers*, 5:34.

83. *Faction Discovered*, Andrews, *Narratives*, 253-254. See also Randolph to the Lords of Trade, May 29, 1689, *Randolph Papers*, 4:272; Randolph to the Lords of Trade, May 29, 1689, 4:271. Brunt was well known Catholic advisor to James and, according to Andros, solicitor to Fr. Petre. For Brunt and Payne, see Andrews, *Narratives*, fn. 2-4, 254. Fr. Petre was the King's personal chaplain and confessor.

84. Randolph to the Governor of Barbados, Boston, May 16, 1689, *Randolph Papers*, 4:267; Randolph to Dr. William Sancroft, Archbishop of Canterbury, May 28, 1689, *Randolph Papers*, 4:269; Randolph to the Lords of Trade, May 29, 1689, *Randolph Papers*, 4:273; [Edward Randolph?] *Considerations Humbly Offered to the Parliament, Randolph Papers*, 5:11-13; *Mr. Randolph's Acco^t of Irregular Trade in New England since ye Revolution*, 1690, *Randolph Papers*, 5:35-37; *Particular Account*, Andrews, *Narratives*, 209, "Letter of Captain George to Pepys, 1689," Andrews, *Narratives*, 219.

85. Randolph to the Lords of Trade, May 29, 1689, *Randolph Papers*, 4:278-279.

86. Randolph to Dr. William Sancroft, Archbishop of Canterbury, May 28, 1689, *Randolph Papers*, 4:270. See also Randolph to the Bishop of London, October 25, 1689, *Randolph Papers*, 4:305.

87. Although Mather and other rebel pamphlet writers alleged that this address was written to James, and not to William and Mary because only one ruler is

mentioned in the title, it is more probable that the Anglicans who wrote it, like the authors of the "Declaration of Grievances," knew only that William presided over the government at London but were not yet aware that William was to rule in partnership with Mary. See Foote, *Annals*, fn. 2, 1:100.

88. *Humble Address of Your Majesty's most loyal and dutiful Subjects of the Church of England in Boston in Your Majesty's Territory and Dominion of New England*, Foote, *Annals*, 1:101-102.

89. John Palmer, *And Impartial Account of the State of New England, etc.*, cited in Foote, *Annals*, fn. 2, 1:106.

90. *A Particular Account*, Andrews, *Narratives*, 207.

91. *Faction Discovered*, Andrews, *Narratives*, 259.

92. *Faction Discovered*, Andrews, *Narratives*, 259.

93. Increase Mather, *A Brief Discourse Concerning the Unlawfulness of the Common Prayer Worship . . .*, cited in Foote, *Annals*, 1:96.

94. [Anon.], *The Humble Address of the Publicans of New-England, To Which King You Please, with Remarks upon it. (A Publican is a Creature that Lives Upon the Common-Wealth)* (London, 1691), 10. At least one pamphleteer reported to London readers that the Revolution in Boston was supported by Anglicans as well as Congregationalists. A.B. wrote, "even some of that [Anglican] Communion did appear in their Arms to assist the enterprize." "An Account of the Late Revolution," Hall, *Glorious Revolution*, 51. Some Anglicans did indeed take sides against the Dominion government. Henry Wilder Foote noted that "Mr. John Nelson," an Anglican, "but a lover of liberty, took command of the impatient militia and led them against the fort just in time to intercept the Governor's escape." Foote, *Annals*, 1:85-86.

95. *Humble Address of the Publicans*, 7, 9.

96. Increase Mather, *A Vindication of New-England, From the Vile Aspersions Cast upon that Country By a Late ADDRESS of a Faction there, Who Denominate Themselves of the Church of England in Boston* (Boston, 1690?), 20.

97. Increase Mather, *A Brief Account Concerning Several of the Agents of New-England, their Negotiation at the Court of England . . .*, Andrews, *Narratives*, 288-289. See also [Cotton Mather?], *A Letter of Advice to the Churches of the Non-Conformists in the English Nation . . .*, (London, 1700), *passim.*

98. T.H. Breen argues that the justification for the Massachusetts Revolution represented a turnabout in New England political writing. He writes that in these works we see the transformation of Massachusetts political thought from religious to secular as New Englanders argued that Andros threatened their liberty and property, but not their religion. Breen claims that the accusation of Popery "was a minor theme in the protests agains [sic] his [Andros'] administration" (T.H. Breen, *The Character of a Good Ruler*, 153). Perhaps such accusations were omitted in the pamphlet war in London and gradually diminished in Massachusetts primarily because they were less credible to London readers and thus were not productive in the propaganda battle for the new charter.

99. *An Answer to M'. Randolph's Acco'. Touching Irregular Trade Since y' late Revolution, 1690*, Randolph Papers, 5:45-46.

100. *A Vindication of New-England*, 13. A few other pamphlets, each of which feature approximately the same allegations include Nathaniel Byfield, *An Account of the Late Revolution in New England* . . .(London, 1689), Andrews, *Narratives*, 170-182; [Anon.], *The Plain Case Stated* (Boston, 1689); [Anon], *An Appeal to the Men of New-England* (Boston, 1689); A.B., *An Account of the Late Revolutions in New England* (London, 1689), Hill, 48-53; E.R. & S.S., *The Revolution in New England Justified*; William Stoughten, *A Narrative of The Proceedings of Sir Edmund Androsse and his Complices, Who Acted by an Illegal and Arbitrary Commission from the Late K. James, during his government in New England. By Several Gentlemen who were of his Council* (Boston and London, 1691), Andrews, *Narratives*, 239-249; [Anon.], *The Humble Address of the Publicans of New-England*.

101. Hall, *Glorious Revolution*, 55; Barnes, *Dominion*, 257; Lewis, "Massachusetts," 337-338.

102. Cotton Mather, *Souldiers Counselled and Comforted: A Discourse unto Some Part of the Forces Engaged in the Just War of New-England Against the Northern and Eastern Indians* (Boston: Samuel Green, 1689).

103. Barnes, *Dominion*, 259.

104. Hall, *Glorious Revolution*, 55.

105. Hall, *Glorious Revolution*, 55.

106. Lewis, "Massachusetts," 353.

107. Lovejoy, *Glorious Revolution*, 371; Lewis, "Massachusetts," 356.

108. In theory, the governor's position was powerful because of his patronage rights and his veto. The Crown's rights were theoretically greater still, but the Crown, for both practical and ideological reasons, rarely exercised a prerogative over the colonies that, in effect, had not changed since Charles II. See Jack P. Greene, "The Glorious Revolution and the British Empire, 1688-1783," in *Negotiated Authorities: Essays in Colonial Political and Constitutional History* (Charlottesville: University of Virginia Press, 1994), 84-86.

109. "Memorial of Governor Shute to the King, 1723," cited in Lewis, "Massachusetts," 355. For a description of the charter of 1691 see Barnes, *Dominion*, 269-271.

110. Barnes, *Dominion*, 272; Lewis, "Massachusetts," 356.

111. Perry Miller, *The New England Mind: The Seventeenth Century* (New York: Macmillan, 1939; reprint, Boston: Beacon Press, 1961), 433.

112. Morgan, *Puritan Dilemma*, 46.

113. Miller, *Seventeenth Century*, 409. Some general works that touch upon the politics of Massachusetts before 1676, see Perry Miller, *Orthodoxy in Massachusetts* (Boston: Beacon Press, 1959), 144-145, *passim*; Perry Miller, *The Seventeenth Century*, 414-418, 423-431, *passim.*; Perry Miller, *The New England Mind: From Colony to Province* (Cambridge, Massachusetts: Harvard University,

96 Chapter 2

1953; reprint, Boston: Beacon Press, 1961), 119-129, 410-420, *passim*; Edmund Morgan, *The Puritan Dilemma;* T.H. Breen, *The Character of a Good Ruler*, 35-41, *passim.*

114. Cotton Mather, *The Way to Prosperity . . ., May 23, 1689,* in A.W. Plumstead, *The Wall and the Garden: Selected Massachusetts Sermons, 1670-1775* (Minneapolis: University of Minnesota Press, 1968), 109-139.

115. Miller, *The Seventeenth Century*, 410-413.

116. Miller, *From Colony to Province,* 158-163.

117. Plumstead, *The Wall and the Garden,* 144.

118. Miller, *From Colony to Province,* 159-172, *passim.*

119. Both Miller and John Dunn claim that the Puritans anticipated and informed Locke's political theory of consent in his *Two Treatises.* See Miller, *From Colony to Province*, 296; and John Dunn, "Consent in the Political Theory of John Locke," *The Historical Journal* 10:1 (1967), 153-182. T.H. Breen offers a different interpretation that is worthy of mention, if less convincing. Breen claims that the aftermath of the Glorious Revolution split colonists into ideological factions based on a Court and Country dichotomy. Breen argues that the new monarchical tone of sermons in New England was symptomatic of the Court persuasion that was largely undemocratic and elitist. Breen contends that "the clergymen in New England tended to favor the Court's philosophy" (Breen, *The Character of a Good Ruler*, fn. 12, 210), but the people of the colony were, in fact, becoming increasingly democratic (211). The Court party, he argues, "would just have soon forgotten the Glorious Revolution" with its troubling democratic underpinnings and challenge to authority (213), a difficult assertion in the face of a wealth of sermon material from the 1690s into the 1760s that incorporated praise for the king and for ordered, authoritative government *and* emphasized the importance of English popular rights that included representative government, and the preservation of personal property, and the Protestant religion. Although the politics of the colony contained Country and Court factions by the middle of the eighteenth century, Breen's claim to see such pronounced ideological differences before the 1720s is rather difficult to support from the evidence of the sources.

120. Soloman Stoddard, cited in Perry Miller, *From Colony to Province,* 176. See also Benjamin Coleman, *A Sermon for the Reformation of Manners . . .* (Boston: Fleet & Crump, 1716) 2, passim; Ebenezer Gay, *The Duty of a People to Pray for and Praise their Rulers . . .* (Boston: Thomas Fleet, 1730), 18-19.

121. Charles Chauncey, *The Council of two Confederate Kings to set the Son of Tabeal on the Throne Represented as Evil . . . A Sermon Occasion'd by the present Rebellion in Favour of the Pretender. Preached in Boston . . . February 6ᵗʰ, 1745.* (Boston: D. Gookin, 1746), 43. See also Cotton Mather, *The Glorious Throne . . .* (Boston, B. Green 1714), 30, 35; Benjamin Coleman, *A Sermon Preach'd at Boston in New England, on Thursday the 23ʳᵈ of August, 1716 . . .* (Boston: Fleet and Crump, 1716), 6-7, 17.

3

The Duke's Province and the Glorious Revolution

This French Government being thus (by Commission) introduced, it was natural that Papists should be employed in the highest Trusts; such as the Council, the Revenue, and the Military Forces; . . . since no Law was left alive to make them unqualifyed, therefore this obedient Governor admitted . . . professed Papists to assist in making Arbitrary Placats, and forcing obedience to them from a Protestant Free People . . . This was the condition of New York, the Slavery and Popery that lay under it, until the Hand of Heaven sent the glorious King William to break those chains, which would otherwise have fetter'd all Europe. And these were the reasons that moved the Gentlemen concerned with the Revolution of New York to be early in shaking off their Tyrants, and declaring for their Deliverer. — *Loyalty Vindicated*, 1698[1]

News of William's invasion of England, James' flight, and the Revolution in Boston trickled into the New York colony in April and May of 1689 and was welcomed by most colonists. New Yorkers had numerous grievances against James Stuart that extended back more than two decades. As the Duke of York, James had been the proprietor of the colony from 1664 until 1685, when he became King James II and ruled New York as a Royal colony. In 1688 New York was made part of the Dominion of New England. From the start, James governed his province like a highly centralized feudal state, eschewing representative government there in favor of a governor and council, making laws and levying taxes as he pleased, and meddling in local political and religious affairs when it suited him. Whereas New Englanders had to search diligently and imaginatively to find evidence of Romanist influence in their government under the Dominion, New Yorkers had no such difficulties. James had filled some of the highest civilian and military positions in the province with Catholic appointees, and the trappings of Romanism were apparent there in the form of chapels, roving Catholic missionaries, and even a Jesuit school in the colonial capital. There was much justice in a pamphleteer's claim that in New York, James "at one jump leapt over all the bounds, and Laws of English Right and Government."[2]

At the time of its occupation by the English in 1664, New York's population was the most diverse of any colony in North America. As early as 1644, a visiting Jesuit, Father Jogues, found that eighteen languages were spoken in the province whose residents already included Dutch, Walloons, English, Swedes, Danes, Norwegians, French, Germans, Scotch-Irish, Portuguese Jews and Africans.[3] In 1666, Col. Richard Nicholls, the first English governor of New York, estimated that three quarters of the population of the colony were Dutch, and they remained in the majority throughout the century.[4] Peter Stuyvesant noted in 1667 that "the most considerable Inhabitants of these parts" were "composed of the Dutch nations," and Governor Andros reported eleven years later that while there were "some few of all Nations," most of the two thousand inhabitants able to bear arms were Dutch.[5]

Dutch residents had increasing reason to chafe at the English occupation of New York. The surrender agreement between the Dutch colonists and the English had seemed more than equitable.[6] Any Dutch inhabitants who wished to leave and return to the Netherlands might do so. Those who stayed were guaranteed liberty of conscience.[7] Their laws, property, contracts, debts, and inheritance practices were preserved, and their local magistrates were allowed to continue in their offices "til the customary time of a new election." No Dutch inhabitant or Dutch ship might be pressed into service in war against any other nation. Article Six of the agreement stated that Dutch settlers were allowed to move into the colony in the future, and "Dutch vessels may freely come hither, and any of the Dutch may freely return home, or send any sort of merchandise home in vessels of their own country." Article Seven, in an apparent contradiction to the former, stated that Dutch trade should only continue for six months.[8]

The trade articles of the agreement created confusion and frustration among the Dutch merchants for some time to come. Article Six appeared on its face to exempt New York from the strictures of the Navigation Acts in respect to trade with the Netherlands. It was, however, unclear as to whether it opened the colony to Dutch trade or only enabled Dutch citizens to carry their property with them when they entered or left New York. If the former, an interpretation preferred by the Dutch merchants, then Article Seven presented a clear contradiction. Did Article Seven refer to Dutch ships that only engaged in the carrying trade, or did it also apply to ships carrying settlers to and from New York, thus, essentially limiting intercourse with the Netherlands, apparently guaranteed by Article Six, to six months? If the latter were the case, then Article Six was moot, as England and Holland were currently at war, and no Dutch ships (at least commercial ones) might be expected in New York until the war ended.[9] These questions caused contention between the colony and the government in England until the Glorious Revolution.

Within a few months of the conclusion of peace between England and Holland, city officials and Dutch merchants had begun to petition the Governor and the Duke of York to allow the continuation of the Dutch trade for at least five years with exemptions from various duties.[10] Governor Nicholls himself allowed some of the New York merchants to trade with Holland, thus creating a precedent of sorts for reviving the trade.[11] The English government, in fact, gave permission to the colony to engage in limited trade with Holland in 1667. To encourage trade and commerce in New York, the Privy Council granted the Dutch inhabitants "temporary permission for seven years" to trade with Holland "with three shipps onely" per year.[12] The next year, the Lords of Trade sent a notice to King Charles requesting that the policy be stopped. They claimed that it was detrimental to English trade and industry, and that, since the Dutch did not allow English vessels to trade at any of their ports or colonies, they should not be allowed to trade with an English colony. Finally, they argued that, once in the American colonies, Dutch goods "will not only suply the consumption of your maj^ties afors^d Plantation in New York," but would be traded throughout English North America, from New England to Barbados. In response to the Lords of Trade, the Royal Council reversed its earlier decision and issued an order prohibiting Dutch trade with New York altogether, even withdrawing the passes that they had already granted to three ships for the current year.[13] Although they kept their thoughts to themselves, New York merchants were undoubtedly frustrated and probably angry at what must have seemed to them little less than calculated duplicity on the part of the Crown.

Dutch merchants had already gone to some expense to outfit and load ships for Holland when the news that the King had revoked his permission arrived in New York. The merchants petitioned Charles II that the trade be allowed for at least one ship, ironically named the *King Charles*, that already stood, fully laden, in New York Harbor.[14] In December 1668, the Council authorized one pass allowing the *King Charles* to sail for Holland but stipulated that it could only make one such voyage. The Council added that the King and Duke "do not for the future grant any other Passe or Passes to any Dutch Shipp or Shipps whatsoever to trade to New Yorke."[15]

The Holland trade was, to a great extent, the life's blood of the various merchant communities of the New York colony in the mid-seventeenth century. Dutch goods, far less encumbered with taxes and duties than English merchandise, were more profitable to those who retailed them in New York and elsewhere in North America. Some Dutch goods, especially farming implements, were either of a better quality than their English counterparts, or were simply preferred by the Dutch farmers of New York, or perhaps both. Stuyvesant noted that the Dutch "manner of agriculture is wholly different from that way practiced by the English," and thus the English could not supply them with the necessary "utensills relating to the cultivating of the Land" upon which Dutch farmers depended.[16] In addition, Indians prized the sturdy Dutch cloth, called duffel, and preferred to trade their furs for it over French exchange goods that they could get for their pelts in Canada or English goods in New England. This fact gave the Albany fur traders a distinct advantage over their competitors in neighboring colonies, but the cloth was only obtainable from Holland, so the fur merchants also had an interest in the Dutch trade.[17] Another reason that the merchants favored the Holland trade was simply that it was dependable. The English trade was established in the older English colonies, but few ships of that nationality put in at the port of New York during the first few years of English occupation. According, again, to Peter Stuyvesant in 1667, it was "most certainly evident noe shipps from England are resolv'd to visit those parts this season, soe that unlesse the Inhabitants be supply'd before spring with all necessaryes from Holland, It will be not onely impossible for them to subsist, but they must be constrained to forsake their Tillage and seeke out a Livelyhood elsewhere."[18]

The change in trade status from a Dutch to an English colony retarded New York's economic growth for years to come. When Sir Edmond Andros arrived after the Dutch reoccupation ended in 1674, Dutch residents once more requested that trade be reopened with Holland.[19] Some of the leaders of the merchant community went so far as to request that they be allowed to depart the colony and return to the Netherlands if the trade could not be reopened. Governor Andros was annoyed by the request and had eight of the petitioners arrested and jailed. At the advice of the Duke of York that "whosoever pleased might withdraw" to Holland and that Andros go lightly with the offenders, the Governor released them.[20]

The merchants of New York, no matter what their ethnicity, probably realized that their return to English possession boded lean times ahead, and they were correct. Andros reported in 1678 that between ten and fifteen ships totaling some one hundred tons traded with New York in the previous year, and about half of the shipping was accounted for by coastal traders.[21] Some evidence indicates that Sir Edmund may have decided, along with the merchant community, that trade with Holland was in the best interest of both the Duke and the colony and turned a blind eye on clandestine Dutch trade, at least until he was rebuked for his inattention by his superiors in London.[22] The tone of Governor Dongan's report of 1684 indicates that he also thought that trade in New York fell well short of expectations. Dongan reported that "a thousand ships may ride here safe from Winds and weather," but admitted that the previous year had seen only about ten "three masted ships of eighty or a Hundred Tuns burthen," and some coastal traders. Dongan also admitted that some of the colony's annual trade went to Holland.[23] The decline of trade in New York both increased the frustration of English and Dutch merchants and induced James to look to other methods of raising revenues from his colony. Those means most often chosen by the Duke and his resident governors were land taxes, quitrents and excise taxes. Unfortunately, so long as the colony lacked a representative assembly, these particular methods of garnering revenue angered the other sizeable ethnic population in New York, the Long Island Puritans. These English settlers from Connecticut resisted James' authority throughout the proprietary period and beyond, generally because the constitution of the province lacked the protection afforded by a representative assembly.

New York had a much longer experience with James Stuart's style of governing than any of the other colonies. James, the Duke of York, became its proprietor in 1664 when the English wrested the colony from the Dutch. James chose to rule his province like a feudal principality.[24] He appointed a governor who, with the assistance of a council chosen by the Duke, administered the colony's affairs. In addition to an administration, James established a court system that included lower courts modeled after the English Shire Courts and an annual Court of Assizes that had appellate jurisdiction over the lower courts, heard cases in equity, and heard petitions of grievance from the colonists. Cases from any of the provincial courts might be appealed to the Crown.[25] The Duke might pass what laws he wished so long as they were "not contrary to but as conveniently may be agreeable to the Laws, Statutes & Government . . . of England."[26] The Duke's grant and his instructions to the governor and council were, in essence, the constitution of New York.

The notable absence of an assembly in the Province's constitution reflected the Stuart distrust of representative bodies. Additionally, James probably assumed that no assembly was required because the colony had never had one under Dutch administration.[27] The omission of a colonial assembly in the New York constitution provided colonists, especially those who were of English extraction, with a bone of contention from the very beginning of James' proprietorship. The first governor of the province, Richard Nicholls, promised the English inhabitants of Long Island that he would call an assembly and that they would receive "equall (if not greater Freedomes & immunityes) than any of his Mat[ies] Colonies in New England" but did nothing to bring his promise to immediate fruition.[28] Under fairly constant pressure from Long Island residents, Nicholls did call an assembly to meet at the town of Hempstead in 1665, but he only empowered its representatives to approve a code of laws that had already been prepared by the Duke in advance of the meeting. The representatives, realizing that they had been hoodwinked into giving what amounted to popular consent to the new constitution, gritted their teeth, and "publickly and unanimously declare[d]" their "cheerfull submission to all such Lawes, Statutes and Ordinances which shall be made" by the Duke and his heirs forever.[29] The new code, called the Duke's Laws, went into effect immediately. Having done its duty, the assembly was dissolved, and its members returned home, each undoubtedly reflecting on how he would explain his behavior and that of New York's first representative assembly to his constituents. Governor Nicholls was positively self-congratulatory at the results of the Hempstead Assembly. He wrote to his master the Duke, "My endevours have not been wanting to put the whole Government into one frame and policy, and now the most refractory Republicans cannot but acknowledge themselves fully satisfied with the method and way they are in."[30] Here the Governor underestimated his subjects. The continued lack of a colonial assembly aroused protest from colonists, especially Long Islanders, from 1665 to 1691.

The people of Long Island vented their anger and frustration by castigating the returned assembly members and by refusing to appoint the local magistrates required by the Duke's Laws. Although the representatives claimed that they had shown their loyalty to the Duke in order to influence him to liberalize the charter and create a permanent assembly, irate townsfolk apparently behaved so badly toward their erstwhile representatives that Nicholls found it necessary to pass an ordinance that made it a crime to "reproach or defame any person . . . who shall act in any publick Employment . . . or speak against any of the

Deputyes" who had confirmed the Duke's Laws. Towns all over Long Island refused to appoint new officials, and, where magistrates were appointed, so many prominent colonists refused to serve that the Council decided to fine anyone who shirked his civic duty and refused to hold a magistracy. The "seditious practices" of the Long Islanders continued to anger Nicholls, especially when they took every opportunity to remind the Governor of his unkept promise to give the people of New York "freedoms and Immunityes" consistent with English government. In 1667, the people of Flushing took their frustration over the government to the streets, and Nicholls became so concerned with the popular disturbance that he decided to disband and disarm the local militia. Shortly thereafter, a Setauket citizen was tried for publicly stating "that the King was none of his King, an ye Govern'r none of his Governour." In Jamaica several townsmen were tried and convicted of seditious speech, but pardoned by Nicholls.[31]

New Yorkers, especially those who were culturally English, argued repeatedly that, since there was no assembly in the colony, the Duke and his representatives had no right to levy taxes. From 1665 on, the government fought an uphill battle to collect various taxes and duties from irate subjects. Not only did colonists refuse to pay taxes, but on occasion officials even refused to collect them.[32] When Francis Lovelace, who succeeded Nicholls in 1670, levied a new tax on the colony for the much needed repair of Fort James on Manhattan Island, he encountered stiff resistence to the measure. A town meeting of Huntington claimed that the tax ran counter to the "Liberties of Englishmen" because it was levied without an assembly and also because the town received no direct benefit from the tax.[33] The people of Jamaica, Long Island, agreed to pay the tax only if the King insisted on its payment but nevertheless complained that the tax was "contrary to the Liberties his Majesties subjects enjoyes in all his territories."[34] Other town meetings issued similar protests. The new Governor pronounced the petitions seditious and ordered that they be publicly burned and their authors investigated.[35]

Innovations in the taxation of the colony meant to bolster James' revenues caused a series of governors grief.[36] Nicholls attempted to reform the New York land patents during his tenure, both as a means of settling disputes between colonists and Indians and so that the lands might be assessed and quitrents charged to the landowners. Most of the counties reluctantly complied, but the New Englanders of Long Island balked at the notion. In 1665 Nicholls reminded them of their responsibilities, and was still doing so in 1667. Governor Lovelace, who succeeded Nicholls, threatened court action to compel the recalcitrant Long Islanders to renew their patents, to no avail. The residents gave a number of reasons for their failure to comply with the new land policy, but in every case the absence of a representative assembly was a key element of their grievances. For the people of Oyster Bay, it was the only reason; they claimed that they would submit their patents only when the colony received an assembly.[37]

After a brief interlude of Dutch occupation from 1673 to 1674, Long Islanders continued to protest the absence of a popular assembly in the colonial constitution. In fact, during the occupation, Long Islanders petitioned both the Dutch and English governments, claiming that they were really part of Connecticut and should be governed by that colony. If that was not possible, they argued, then the New York colony, whether English or Dutch, should at least be granted an assembly comparable to those of other colonies.[38] When the Duke of York recovered his province in 1674, he appointed Sir Edmund Andros to govern it. Andros, like his predecessors, did all that he could to disabuse colonists of the notion of an assembly. His master, James, was pleased that Andros had "done well to discourage any motion" toward the creation of an assembly "wch ye people there seeme desirous of in imitacon of their neighbor Colonies."[39] In his correspondence with the Duke and Lords of Trade, however, Andros appears to have espoused the idea that New York might be better governed if it were allowed a representative assembly.[40]

James was not easily convinced. He responding that he suspected such an innovation "would be of dangerous consequence, nothing being more known than the aptness of such bodies to assume to themselves many privileges wch prove destructive to, or very oft disturb, the peace of ye governm^t wherein they are allowed."[41] James informed Andros that an assembly was unnecessary and redundant in New York, as well as "inconsistent wth ye form of governmt already established" in the colony.[42] The Duke argued that the people had the right to redress their grievances by means of addresses to the governor and jurists at the annual Assizes and that the Assize justices were men of such prestige in their localities that "in all probability [they] would be theire Representatives if any other constitucon were allowed."[43] Nevertheless, James told Andros that he would consider future arguments and proposals that the Governor might make in favor of a colonial assembly.[44] Here again, James betrayed his own distaste at representative government and his fundamental misunderstanding of English colonists' desire for a representative body in their colonial constitution. To them, as to all Englishmen, an assembly was an ingredient necessary for good, free, and equitable government, not only so that the people might air their grievances, but also so that they might make their own laws and have a vote in the creation of taxes for the upkeep of the colony and the enrichment of the proprietor.

In order to increase his master's revenues, Edmund Andros instituted a new land patent and quitrent policy. In response to Sir Edmund's command that New Yorkers once more renew their land patents, many Long Island Town meetings claimed that they were still part of Connecticut.[45] Andros quickly wearied of the Long Island claims. He ordered the leading trouble makers to come to New York City and explain themselves before the Council. Several leaders were punished for "writing & signing seditious Letters . . . against ye Governm^t."[46] The Long Island towns ultimately settled their patents when Andros, his patience at its limit, threatened to confiscate their land. Even after the settlement, however, Long Island towns tried, generally without success, to evade their annual rents.[47]

The quitrent controversy between the colonial governors and the towns of Long Island increased in vehemence during the tenure of Thomas Dongan (1683-1688). Using a legal technicality as an excuse, Dongan recalled the patents that Andros had issued and required that landowners renew them. "The people," he informed the Lords of Trade, "for their own ease & quiet & that of their Posterity . . . have renewed their Patents, with a reservation of a certain Quit-Rent to the King to no small advancement to his Revenue." He added, either too hastily or rather ingenuously that "none will in the least complain but on the contrary express themselves thankful for it."[48] It may be that Dongan had some success in his land policies because he had established the colony's first genuine, albeit shortlived, assembly, and colonists hoped that he might call it again if they complied with his demands with only minimal complaint. If this was the case, the colonists must have felt that they had been ill-used again, because the assembly was not recalled, and the "Charter of Libertyes and Privileges," the chief measure promulgated by that body, was vetoed in 1686 by James Stuart, now King James II. The Lords of Trade notified the Governor in his instructions for that year that the "Bill or Charter passed in ye late Assembly of New York" was "forthwith repealed and disallowed," but that the duties, impositions and other taxes levied by the body should be kept on the books and collected.[49] Thus, for the second time, New Yorkers saw an assembly created and destroyed after one sitting that benefitted only their ruler, and saw themselves taxed without the representation that they understood to be their right as Englishmen.

It was not only quitrents over which New Yorkers evinced dissatisfaction. In the summer of 1680, Andros returned to England. He had neglected to renew the triennial levy of customs and duties for the colony that expired in November. Without the governor to raise them, many New Yorkers claimed that the rates could not be renewed. Ships entered and cleared cargoes in the colony's ports without paying duties, and the Lieutenant Governor, Anthony Brockholls, and the Council watched impotently as customs revenues dried up. When William Dyer, the Duke's Collector of Customs, tried to collect the duties he was accused of treason. In a bill against the Collector, the city judge of New York alleged that Dyer "severall times . . . trayterously, maliciously and advisedly used and exercised Regall Power and Authority over the King's Subjects." The Judge also alleged that, in attempting to collect the duties for which no current law obtained, the Collector had "contrived Innovacons in Government" and subverted "the known Ancient and Fundamentall Lawes of the Realme of England . . . contrary to the great charter of Libertyes [Magna Charta], Contrary to the Peticon of Right." The Court claimed that Dyer's acts offended "the honour and peace of our most Sovereign Lord the King that now is, his Crowne and Dignity."[50] Dyer argued that the court had no right to try him because both he and the judges held their commissions from the same source, the Duke of York. The court, eager to pass the case elsewhere, agreed, and the unfortunate collector was shipped to England for trial.[51] The Duke hastily sent instructions to Brockholls, informing him that, in the Governor's absence, the Lieutenant Governor could make "temporary ord[rs]" to continue the customs statutes for the province and should do so posthaste.[52]

The controversy over duties led to increased demands for a colonial assembly. Even the grand jury that indicted Collector Dyer complained that their job would be easier if New York, "like their fellow Brethern and subjects of the Realm of England in our neighboring Plantations," had an assembly.[53] If the government of the colony were "settled in the hands of a Governor and Assembly," the grand jury claimed, "wee may enjoy the Benefit of the Good and wholsome Laws of the Realm of England." They argued that the addition of an assembly to the New York constitution would "bring forth the fruites of a Prosperous and fflourishing Government for want of which wee have been (and yett are) in a most wythering and Decaying Condicon."[54] The Court of Assizes in New York City agreed with the grand jury and sent a memorial to the Duke of York. It informed James that for many years the colony had:

Grond [groaned] under unexpressable Burdens by having an Arbitrary and Absolute power Used and Exercised over us by which yearly Revenue is

Exacted from us against o^r Wills . . . and the inhabitants wholly shutt out and Deprived of any share Vote or Interest in the Government to their Greate Discouragement and Contrary to the Laws, Rights, Liberties and Privileges of the [English] Subject.[55]

In 1681 the Collector for Albany, Robert Livingston, arraigned John De Lavall for refusing to pay the excise on the sale of 510 gallons of rum. In stating his defense, De Lavall asked the court a number of questions. What right, De Lavall asked, did Livingston have to collect the excise? If it was by order of the governor, what power did the governor have to levy taxes? Had the power been given to the chief executive of the colony by the king, Lords and Commons? If so, what statute granted it? Were the king's subjects in New York free born English subjects with all the rights that pertained thereto? If not, by what statute, in the reign of what king, were their liberties taken away, and they enslaved?[56] The jury was shocked at De Lavall's rather novel defense but nevertheless struggled to come to terms with his questions. It was forced to admit that it could find no statute that authorized the excise or any that empowered the governor to raise taxes by what amounted to arbitrary means. The Jury was faced with the frustrating realization that New York not only lacked a representative assembly of its own to raise taxes with the consent of the freeholders, but, as a proprietary colony under the rule of James, the Duke of York and what assistants that he chose to dwell among them, New Yorkers were also denied the protections afforded other English subjects by the government in London as well.

One protection that James did afford residents of his colony from the start was religious tolerance. This was not only appropriate, given the incredible diversity of religious sects present in the colony, but was in keeping with the spirit of Dutch colonial policy after about 1650.[57] New York was as heterodox in its worship as it was diverse in its ethnicity. By the 1680s, a host of religions were represented. In the main, colonists were Calvinists, the largest group being Dutch Reformed church members and the second largest being the Congregationalists of Long Island. The colony also contained some French Huguenots and German Calvinists (like Jacob Leisler). Dutch and French Lutherans were also present in fairly large numbers but these sects were certainly not alone. Governor Andros noted in 1678 that the colony hosted "Religions of all sorts."[58] Governor Dongan reported in 1685 that:

Here be not many of the Church of England; a few Roman Catholics; abundance of Quaker preachers men and women especially; singing Quakers; ranting Quakers; Sabbatarians; Antisabbatarians; Some Anabaptists; some Independants; some Jews; in short of all sorts of opinions there are some, and the most part of none at all.[59]

The Governor was well off the mark in his assumption that a diversity of religious sects in the colony indicated weakness in religious principles or passions among New York colonists. The colony's heterogeneity prevented any one religious group from employing a policy of persecution comparable to that of Massachusetts Puritans. Still, religious tensions in the colony were always evident. Tensions between Calvinists and Lutherans had begun under Dutch rule and continued to be a problem among the Dutch throughout the century. One commentator noted that Dutch Calvinists and Lutherans "behaved themselves so shilly and uncharitably as if *Luther* and *Calvin* had bequeathed and entailed their virulent Spirits upon them and their heirs forever."[60] Both Dutch and English Calvinists opposed the growing number of newer dissenting sects in the colony that included Quakers, Anabaptists and Mennonites.[61] Additionally, New York, like New England, proved fertile ground for schism within the ranks of the Calvinists. Like their brethren in New England, New York Calvinist congregations occasionally strayed from the fold into the heresies of Arminianism, Brownism, and Antimonianism. The theological doctrines that had the most influence on both Dutch and English Calvinists, however, were the orthodox pietist teachings of Gysbertus Voetius and Jacobus Koelman. These two Dutch church leaders taught an uncompromising Calvinist creed and promoted the purification of the church by the elimination of all lingering Roman Catholic influences from the Dutch Reformed services and traditions.[62] Like the Mathers and other conservative New England Puritans, Voetian Calvinists viewed the Church of England as little more than an English brand of Catholicism.[63] They also considered any meddling by the secular state in the affairs of the local churches an intolerable and tyrannical imposition.

James Stuart violated that principle when he placed appointments to vacant ministries within the purview of his resident colonial governor. Probably out of political considerations rather than religious ones, to create more patronage within his colony, James authorized Governor Dongan to fill vacancies in any "churches, chapells, or other Ecclesiastical Benefices . . . as often as any of them shall happen to be void."[64] In fact, James' orders to Dongan only systemized the haphazard meddling that the

Duke and his governors had exercised in church matters for just over a decade. In 1675, James appointed Nicholas Van Renselaer, an ordained Anglican priest, to the pulpit of the Dutch Reformed Church in Albany. The senior minister of the community, Domine Schaets, and many prominent parishioners resented the imposition on both doctrinal and sectarian grounds.[65] At the behest of Domine Newenhuysen of New York City and the elders of the Church, Van Renselaer was forbidden to perform his duties. The controversy appeared settled after Governor Andros called a convocation, of sorts, comprised of Domine Newenhysen, and a number of influential New York City Reformed ministers and elders. After a long debate (and some pressure from Andros) the ministers agreed that Van Renselaer should be restored to his position. Van Renselaer, for his part, agreed that he would perform his religious functions in strict conformity to the doctrines, rites and traditions of the Dutch Reformed Church. The next year, two Reformed visitors from New York City, Jacob Leisler and Jacob Milbourne, complained against Van Renselaer after hearing him preach, alleging that his performance was heretical, and that he should thus be removed.[66] Andros had had enough of the controversy. He told the magistrates of Albany that he was fed up with the dispute and ordered them to use their "utmost indeavour to asuage and prevent all animosity whatever and to stop all disputes . . . or arguing over the mater."[67] In spite of the Governor's warnings, the dispute continued until Van Renselaer's death in 1677.

Two years later, Andros meddled in the affairs of the Dutch Reformed Church once again. Parishioners of a congregation on the Delaware River requested that the New York elders ordain their interim preacher, one Peter Tesschenmaker, so that his ministry there might be made permanent. Tesschenmaker held the necessary degree of Bachelor in Divinity, but the elders declined to ordain him, explaining that they had no authority to do so. They said that only the Classis of Amsterdam could give the necessary examinations required for ordination. Andros entered into the controversy and ordered that the minister be ordained. His heavy-handed behavior in the matter offended both the traditions of the Dutch Church and the sensibilities of the New York Calvinist community.[68] In 1686, the Roman Catholic Lieutenant Governor, Anthony Brockholls appointed an Anglican priest to a multi-ethnic Calvinist congregation on Staten Island, only to find that the congregation adamantly refused to support their new minister.[69] Both English and Dutch congregations resented the meddling of James and his officials in the affairs of their churches.

Regardless of the denomination or doctrines of the Protestant Churches in New York, all were united in their hatred of Roman Catholicism. From the late 1670s on, James Stuart used his policy of religious toleration in the colony to allow Catholics to practice their religion there. Catholic priests traveled freely in the province. James not only gave tacit support to Catholic missionaries in his colony, he appears to have been planning to promote them more energetically. Edward Randolph noted in March, 1688, that James intended to "send over some priests to New York" and worried about the Protestants response to the policy.[70] Catholic churches were built and the mass celebrated openly in the colony—Governor Thomas Dongan even created a Catholic chapel for himself in the fort.[71] During Dongan's administration, a Jesuit school was built in New York City, and many of the town's most important merchants and officials sent their sons there.[72] James also began to use New York as a source of patronage for his co-religionists whose faith excluded them from lucrative positions in England and other colonies.

In 1681 James appointed Anthony Brockholls, a Roman Catholic, to the position of commander of New York's military forces. The next year he commissioned the Irish Catholic, Colonel Thomas Dongan, to the governorship. Dongan increased local anxiety when he arrived with his personal chaplain, Father Thomas Harvey, S.J., in tow.[73] During his tenure, Dongan filled a number of important and lucrative posts with fellow Catholics. He began circumspectly enough, appointing co-religionists to fairly humble occupations. In 1684, for example, he appointed Irish Catholic James Cooley to be the blacksmith of the city fort. In 1687 Dongan began to fill more important positions with Catholics. In the spring of that year, he granted the manor lordship of Cassiltowne, an estate of twenty-five thousand acres, to John Palmer, an English Catholic, whom Dongan also hired to be his agent to England. The same year, the Governor appointed Catholics to several important colonial offices, including commands of the Albany garrison and Fort James, and places on the customs commissions and the provincial granary. Residents of the colony hoped that once Dongan had gone and the colony became subsumed within the Dominion of New England under Anglicans Edmund Andros and Francis Nicholson, the placing of Catholics in positions of power and trust would be reversed, or at least stopped. Their hopes were frustrated, however, when King James continued to employ Catholic friends in colonial offices. In 1688, the King appointed his co-religionist, Matthew Plowman, to the lucrative post of customs collector for the port of New York City.[74]

As New York Protestants watched with increasing anxiety, some of the most important civilian and military posts in the colony were filled, either by the governor or the King, with Roman Catholics. Dutch and English Calvinists and other Protestants viewed the process as one more indication that the colony was being moved toward a "French" tyranny. They were governed by a Catholic king by means of an autocratic constitution without the traditional English safeguard of a representative assembly. Their property had been periodically alienated from them, reassessed, and sold back to them, burdened with new taxes that the freeholders had no voice in raising. Their Protestant magistrates and rulers were being gradually replaced with Papists. New York Protestants began to look at these signs and compare their own plight, and that of Englishmen everywhere, with that of Huguenots in France under Louis XIV.

French Protestants had been protected, at least from official persecution, by the Edict of Nantes of 1598. In 1685, Louis XIV repealed the settlement with the Edict of Revocation which banned Protestantism in his realm, banished Protestant ministers, and commanded that all French children be baptized into the Catholic faith. Although the Edict stated that Protestants should not be molested "while awaiting the time when it may please God to enlighten them," in fact, the Revocation began a period of persecution against Protestants unparalleled even in European history. Thousands died, and historians estimate that as many as a million Huguenots fled France.[75] James II, a co-religionist and ally of Louis XIV, provided ample evidence to anti-Catholic observers that he was bent on replicating a French Papist tyranny in his own realm. James' policy of employing religious toleration to relax sanctions against Catholics in England and the colonies, especially New York, became suspect to his Protestant subjects as more and more Roman Catholics were given important positions in the government and military. There also existed ample printed material in the colony to help readers make the connection. In the mid-1680s, William of Orange exploited the situation in France and England to promote his own European territorial ambitions. The Dutch press published a vast number of pamphlets that portrayed Louis XIV's policy toward Protestants in the most graphic terms and warned readers that England under James II was headed in the same direction. Despite James' attempts to ban the publications in England, at least 230 anti-Catholic tracts were in circulation there between 1685 and 1688.[76] These works were written in both English and Dutch and appeared in the American colonies in both languages by 1687.[77] By the time that William of Orange's *Declaration of Reasons* appeared in New

York in the spring of 1689, New Yorkers were well prepared to accept the Prince's rationale for his invasion.

When Lieutenant Governor Francis Nicholson first received word that William and Mary had landed with an army at Torbay, he was shocked, but he quickly regained his composure and assured himself that if the rumor was true, the Dutch invasion would have no better success than the ill-fated Monmouth Rebellion. Nicholson asked "Hath he [William] not an example from Monmouth?" He responded to his own question that "there [is] burrying place enough for him and his people with him . . . the very prentice boys of London will drive him out again."[78] Nicholson forbade those who knew about the invasion to tell anyone else in the colony, but the news spread through the city within a few days anyway. Jacob Leisler received information about the Orange landing from a friend in Maryland, and more news arrived in letters and by word of mouth as several ships arrived in New York in March.[79] On 1 March, Nicholson received confirmation of the news of James' flight and capture in a letter from Pennsylvania Governor John Blackwell.[80] The news had been received in Albany by March, when Robert Livingston wrote to Edward Randolph to tell him that "there is a total Revolution at home."[81] Nicholson and the Council decided to consult with Andros (who was in Maine at the time) and await his orders, but did little else.

On 26 April, Nicholson received news of the revolt and subsequent arrest of Andros and several Dominion Council members in Boston. He met with the four remaining Council members, and they resolved to assemble with the Mayor and aldermen of New York City to decide what should be done.[82] The aldermen complained that the fort was inadequately manned and should be reinforced. They suggested that militia companies from the surrounding counties be employed for the purpose.[83]

As word of the events in England spread, anti-Jacobite and anti-Catholic agitation increased throughout the New York province. On 3 May, 1689, the freeholders of Suffolk County, Long Island, in a town meeting, declared their readiness to join their brethren in Boston and the Orangist cause to secure "our English Liberties and propertyes from Popery and Slavery, and from the Intended invasion of a forraign French design and more than Turkish cruelties." The Suffolk freeholders claimed that it was the "bounden duty" of New York Protestants to secure the colony's fortifications against Papists and Jacobites until they received further instructions from Parliament.[84] A few days later the Council received word that the Queens County militia were "all in armes and the whole country in an uproar."[85]

The trained bands and militia were among the most important members of the Orangist movement in the colony. According to the account of Joost Stol, an ensign in the New York City trained band, virtually every militia company in the colony had some members who worked together "to bring the Gouvernment without threat of bloodsheding under obedience of King William and Queen Mary." Stol reported that the Militia companies tried to convince the provincial Council to disarm Papists and fortify the city against a possible French invasion. The Council replied that "wee deserved, that six or seven persons of our assembly should be hanged for our paines." When word arrived that William and Mary were on the throne and James in France, Stol noted that the bearer of the news to the Council was "turned out the doore with hard threatenings and scoldings," and that the Lieutenant Governor and Council declined to proclaim the new monarchs. Since the Jacobite government refrained from announcing the new rulers, the Orangist militiamen "resolved for the behoofe of theire Majesties King William and Queen Mary and for the security of the inhabitants, to make ourselves masters of the Fort or castle . . . as we happily did."[86]

On 30 May, Nicholson and a militia officer quarreled about the placement of guards at the fort. Nicholson, in frustrated rage, threatened to shoot him. Betraying fear of his current predicament, Nicholson stated that he was in constant fear for his life, and "before it would go longer in this manner he would set the town in fyre."[87] Nicholson's rash statement circulated throughout the city over the next few hours, and by the next day New York residents were shocked to hear that the Lieutenant Governor and his Council, with the aid of numerous Papists, were preparing to burn the city to the ground and massacre those Protestant residents who escaped the flames.[88] Rumors flew as they had in Boston in the previous month. On Staten Island it was reported that Catholics planned to massacre Protestants and burn New York City. The English troops in the fort, it was said, were all Papists, and were daily reinforced with co-religionists from all over New England. Ex-Governor Dongan was said to be outfitting a warship to plunder the New York coast.[89] Nicholson had turned the guns of the fort on the city and only awaited more Catholic reinforcements before opening fire and massacring the Protestant inhabitants.[90] All of the rumors shared a common theme, an unholy alliance of Catholics and Jacobite government officials.

In the midst of the panic, the colonial militia seized the fort at New York City, declaring themselves the allies of Prince William and promising to preserve the city from Papists and Jacobites—the Prince's enemies and their own. They stated that they would only surrender the fort to "the person of the Protestant religion that shall be nominated" by the English government.[91] On 1 June, the militia asked Dominion Councilor Nicholas Bayard to lead them, and, when he refused, they turned for leadership to militia captain Jacob Leisler, who was then commander of the fort. On 8 June, five militia captains and some 400 freeholders elected a Committee of Safety which, in turn, confirmed Leisler's leadership.[92] At about the same time, the city learned that William and Mary occupied the throne.[93] On 22 June, Leisler and his militia companies proclaimed the new rulers in front of the fort and then again at the City Hall.[94] Two days later Governor Nicholson took ship for England, leaving behind him two governments in the province, one comprised of the few remaining Dominion Council members, the New York City mayor, and a few aldermen, and the other, a Committee of Safety presided over by Captain Jacob Leisler.[95]

The composition of the New York Committee of Safety was almost as diverse as the province itself, but its makeup did not reflect the ethnic demography of the colony. Five members were English, four were descendants of French Huguenots, and only one was Dutch. As might be expected, all of the members were either wealthy merchants, like Leisler himself, or substantial husbandmen. The common tie that bound the members together was their fervent Calvinism. All of the Committee Members held prominence in either a Voetian Reformed Dutch congregation or an English Congregationalist church.[96] Under the Committee of Safety the political Revolution in New York quickly became a spiritual reformation as well. Leisler and the Committee began early to purge the colony of Catholic influences and to try to enforce their own brand of Calvinism. Leisler reported in July that "I hope before two days [come] to an end . . . to have some Papists disarmed & also those Idolls destroyed which we heare are daily still worshipped."[97] By September, the Committee had begun to collect affidavits against Roman Catholics and their "fellow travelers" in the province.[98] The reformers displayed their Voetian zeal, targeting for harassment and persecution not only Roman Catholics, but also Quakers, Anglicans, and even some non-Voetian Calvinist clergymen who displayed a conciliatory attitude toward Anglicans and even Roman Catholics.[99]

While Voetian reform and anti-Catholic ferver in New York provided, what William Smith called, "the leaven of opposition," colonists had a wealth of complaints against James Stuart and his policies of governance that stretched nearly thirty years and a variety of reasons to support the Dutch Protestant Prince William of Orange.[100] William's allegations that

James and his minions had ruled arbitrarily and unconstitutionally and were part of a Catholic conspiracy to deprive English Protestants of their liberty, property and religion, validated the grievances and suspicions of Protestant New Yorkers whatever their ethnicity. Residents of the Duke's Province could justly claim that they had "groaned under the heavy burdens" of James Stuart's preferred methods of government longer than any other English subjects.[101] For English subjects at home, the new monarchs offered a sort of tonic, a preventative from the worst excesses of arbitrary government yet to come. To the inhabitants of New England, James' innovations were recent since barely four years had passed since the New England colonies had been brought under his domination. But New York had seen more than two decades of James Stuart's rule. Their taxes and laws had been created by James or his officials without consultation with a representative assembly since 1664. On the two occasions when assemblies had been convened, they had been manipulated to benefit only the Duke and to the perceived detriment of his subjects. Since 1673 positions of trust in the colony had been filled with Roman Catholics as the Protestant New Yorkers watched impotently. Thus William and Mary's promise to restore the liberties and privileges of English subjects, to preserve the Protestant religion, and to purge the nation of Catholics who held high office had a particular resonance among the people of New York. Additionally, the Dutch citizens of the colony held William of Orange in very high regard, looking upon the Prince and his family as national heroes.

The Dutch viewed the House of Nassau as special defenders and protectors of the Dutch nation and of Dutch Protestantism. New York Reformed clergymen noted that the magistrates of New York were bound to support the Prince of Orange whose "forefathers liberated our ancestors from the Spanish yoke and his royal highness had now again come to deliver the Kingdom of England from Popery and Tyranny."[102] Patriotism was not, however, the only factor that motivated the Dutch to support the new rulers of England. The mercantile interests in the colony likely viewed the accession of the Dutch Prince as the answer to their prayers for more practical reasons. If Stadholder William ruled both England and Holland, it was probable that the Dutch trade might be resumed. To New York merchants a combination of English colonial status and Dutch trading privileges was an excellent prospect because, although they wanted to trade with Holland, they had no desire to see New York revert to a Dutch colony. Return to Dutch control would mean that the colony would be placed under the auspices of the Dutch West India Company or some similar concern, in "which case, the colonists would be squeezed to fill the coffers of the commercial oligarchy in the United Provinces."[103] The New York merchants had no desire to reopen the lucrative Holland trade only to see their profits fall into someone else's pockets. The merchants' prayers were answered and trade between New York and Holland was resumed. By 1720, they "conducted an extensive and lucrative business between New York and Amsterdam."[104]

That the Dutch merchants supported William and Mary in no way implied that they supported Jacob Leisler. Indeed, they may have viewed the Leislerian coup as an impediment rather than a blessing. In May of 1690, the New York Merchants sent an address to the King and Queen in which they pledged their loyalty but complained of Leisler and the "ill men amongst us who have assumed your Ma[tys] Authority over us . . . assisted by some whom we can give no better name than Rable."[105] Opposition to Leisler was especially fierce in Albany, where those involved in the Indian trade feared that Leisler and his government would do harm to the lucrative enterprise.[106] The city government there proclaimed William and Mary in July of 1689 with "y[e] ringing of y[e] bell, bone fyres, fyre works and all other demonstrations of joy."[107] The next month city officials and some remnants of the Dominion regime, employing the wording of a royal proclamation that Protestant magistrates and officials should retain their offices, established a government that they called a "convention" over the Albany area until further instructions should arrive from England.[108]

English New Yorkers also had good reason to welcome William and Mary to the throne. The monarchs had taken full advantage of English anti-Catholic sentiment in both their *Declaration of Reasons* and in their communications with the colonies, and New Yorkers, especially the Long Island Puritans, viewed the new rulers as their liberators from the chains of Popery, but colonists rarely praised them solely for their anti-Romanism. Instead they invoked the English constitutional trinity of liberty, property and religion together, thanking the new rulers for restoring all three to England and delivering English subjects from the opposite conditions, tyranny, Popery and slavery. The New York militia made the comparison eloquently when they gave thanks to God for their delivery:

> blessing the great god of heaven and earth who has pleased to make your majesty so happy an instrument in our deliverance from Tyranny, popery and slavery, and to put into your Royall breasts to undertake the glorious work towards the reestablishment and preservation of the true Protestant religion, liberty and property, had we tho in so remote a part of the world, presumed to hope to be partakers of that blessing, we having also long groaned under the same oppression, having been governed of late, most

part, by papists, who had in a most arbitrary way subverted our ancient priviledges making us in effect slaves to their will contrary to the laws of England; and this was chiefly effected by those who are known enemies to our Religion and liberty.[109]

In the wake of the revolution neither Leisler's government nor the Albany Convention rushed to create a colonial assembly. This fact proved less of a detriment to the Convention than to the Committee of Safety in New York City. Since the former was comprised of the aldermen of the city, as well as remnants of the Dominion Council, and held authority only over the city of Albany and the surrounding countryside, its members could argue with some justice that it represented the "Burghers and Inhabitants" of the area.[110] Leisler's government did claim authority over the whole colony, and was faced with the need to raise revenues for its defense and upkeep. To that end the Committee of Safety renamed itself the Royal Council and gave the title of Lieutenant Governor to Leisler. The new regime revived the acts of the 1683 Assembly "for defraying the expenses of the Government" by proclamation in December of 1689.[111] That Leisler proclaimed the 1683 taxes, created by the short lived Assembly of that year, rather than simply continuing the taxes of the previous year probably indicates that he and his council wanted the legitimacy that statutes created by a representative body, even an extinct one, conveyed, but feared the possible outcome of actually seating a new assembly before his regime could exert more complete influence over the whole colony.[112]

The Council's authority to raise taxes without representation met with immediate resistence not only in those areas like Long Island, that had always resisted taxation without an assembly, but even in New York City itself. Wherever tax proclamations were posted, people tore them down and replaced them with a broadside written by the "English Freemen" of New York. These broadsides declared that the government had no right to levy taxes without representation. They forced Leisler and his Council to counter them with the response that the taxes were necessary for the support of the colony and were constitutional, having been created by the "supreme legislative Authority" of New York that "reside[d] in the Governor, Council & the People met in general Assembly."[113] By the spring of 1690 the Leisler regime's existence was less precarious, in part because Albany had surrendered its authority to New York City in exchange for aid against the French and Indians. The Lieutenant Governor then issued writs in King William's name for the election of a new assembly to meet in April.[114] The New York Assembly met twice that year, and after 1692 met almost continuously until the American Revolution.

The Glorious Revolution in New York remolded the character of the province, making it both more democratic than it had ever been, and at the same time, drawing it closer to the Crown—fostering loyalty and devotion to the ruling monarch from the participants in New York politics and government. The first two Governors appointed by the Crown after the Revolution allied themselves with members of the old Jacobite regime. When Leisler and the militia surrendered the fort to the new Royal Governor in May of 1691, the militia leader was promptly arrested along with some of his chief supporters for high treason. The New Yorkers were given a quick trial, condemned and attainted, and executed.[115] In the aftermath of Leisler's execution and the resumption of royal control under Governors Sloughter and Fletcher, both Leislerians and Anti-Leislerians sought support from the Crown not only to advance their political aspirations but also to validate their past acts. In 1692, Leisler's widow and son began to petition the government in England in order to clear the names of the Leislerians and have the attainder lifted from their estates.[116] Leisler's petitions initiated a flurry of claims and counter-claims in London between Leislerians and anti-Leislerians. The latter feared that if Leisler and his supporters were cleared and the English government agreed that the New York militiamen and their leaders had acted out of loyalty to William and Mary and in support of the principles of the Revolution in England, then those responsible for their prosecution had committed treason, and were themselves liable to trial, execution and confiscations.

For almost the rest of the century, Leisler's supporters worked to gain support from London for their contention that the New York City regime had been legitimate, and the Leislerians' punishment at the hands of their enemies, primarily members of the old Dominion Regime, had amounted to treason. At the same time, Anti-Leislerians contended before the Crown and Parliament that Leisler had usurped power from a legitimate government in the colony without cause. Both sides claimed that they had participated in the Glorious Revolution on the winning side, and both factions accused their opponents of disloyalty to William and Mary and to the principles of the Glorious Revolution.[117]

Anti-Leislerians, especially Colonel Bayard and other members of the old Dominion regime, claimed that they represented the legitimate governing authority in the province before and after the Revolution and had always been supported by "every man of Sence, Reputation, or Estate" in New York.[118] They argued that they had recognized the accession of the new rulers as soon as they were required to do so by Whitehall and had complied with their command to purge the government of Roman Catholics. Leisler, and his accomplices, they argued, were usurpers, demagogues who had taken advantage of the distraction of the Revolution in England and the Boston rebellion to set up an arbitrary "Olliverian" state in New York.[119] Anti-Leislerians claimed that Leisler became a tyrant, that he ignored the "Laws and Liberties of the English Nation" and that he found "the sweetness of arbitrary Power agreeable."[120] Leisler's detractors alleged that the new regime in New York City ruled arbitrarily, levying taxes without Crown authority, imprisoning their Majesties subjects "without and Warrant of Commitment . . . as the Law directs," and ruling the colony "according to [the] maxim, The Sword must rule and not the Laws."[121] Bayard and his supporters also claimed that Leisler, "that incorrigeable brutish coxcomb," had stirred up the "ignorant and innocent" people of the city, the rabble, with "lyes and falcityes" in order to take power purely for selfish motives.[122] Worse still, they stated that Leisler and his accomplices ruled without the authority of the Crown "in violation of the s[ai]d Prerogative and in Contempt of their May[ties]."[123]

Members of the old regime claimed that they had complied with William and Mary's command that Catholics be put out of their offices and cited the dismissal of Collector of Customs Mathew Plowman. The Collector had been a scapegoat, however, for Anthony Brockholls, Major Baxter, and other known Catholics remained in positions of authority for some time after Plowman was dismissed.[124] Although the old regime made frequent protestations of loyalty and devotion to the King and Queen in their petitions and pamphlets after 1691, the evidence indicates that they had done nothing formally to proclaim the accession of the new rulers until forced to do so by the militia on 22 June 1689.[125] The remnants of the Dominion Council still seemed rather tentative in respect to the new political order in England even after the new monarchs had been proclaimed, as for some time later, they still had not taken the oath of loyalty required of Crown magistrates, nor changed the letter "J" for James to "W" on the coat of arms in the council chamber.[126]

The seeming reluctance of the old regime to recognize William and Mary and to take the requisite steps to ally themselves formally to the new government in London provided further evidence to the Leislerians that the old Council and their supporters were Jacobites. Council members had, after all, received their commissions from James II and were part of the "arbitrary" Dominion government that the New York militia had overthrown.[127] The old regime had also shown tolerance to Roman

Catholics, even promoting them to positions of trust in the civil government and colonial military, and, with the exception of the unfortunate Mr. Plowman, most Catholics were still in those positions. Leislerians gave credence to the rumors that the old regime had conspired, hand in glove, with Catholics in the province to bring about its ruin and could thus never be trusted with authority and never be true friends of William and Mary.[128]

Supporters of Leisler contended that they had undertaken the Revolution in New York with popular support and in allegiance with the Prince of Orange in order to defend the colony from James' arbitrary government.[129] Jacob Leisler wrote that the "inhabitants by the encouragement of the Prince of Orange (now our gracious King), . . . for their security have secured the fort for their Ma[jesties] King William and Queen Mary."[130] Leislerians alleged that New York had long been governed by "commission," its rulers having "quite forgot the English Constitution of calling the representatives of the People."[131] They further claimed that the old regime had been prepared to join with the French and local Catholics to destroy the colony rather than to allow it to fall into the hands of William and Mary's supporters and loyal subjects, the people of New York. To that end, the colonial militia had taken the fort, secured the city, sought out and neutralized Catholics and their allies who lived among them, and strengthened the city fortifications the better to preserve the colony from their Majesties' foreign enemies.[132]

New Yorkers after 1692 were still a factious people, but the discourse of New York politics had changed. No prominent leader in the colony would ever again promote the oligarchical constitution that had been the chief political feature of the colony since its occupation in 1664. In fact, the old Dominion Council members like Bayard and Robert Livingston adopted the language of the glorious Revolution in their rhetorical struggle against Leisler's regime. They and their adherents accused their political adversaries of much the same misconduct that James Stuart and his minions had been criticized for by New Yorkers in the past. Indeed, the old party members conveniently glossed over their own past sins against the people of New York. Anti-Leislerians like the author of *A Modest and Impartial Narrative* grew adept at celebrating the "good providence of Almighty God, in their Majesties happy accession" and the "Late Happy Revolution in England," without expending much ink on the causes of that Revolution and accession.[133] Neither did they mention their own complicity in the government of the colony under the "Late King James," beyond claiming that the legitimacy of the Dominion government was founded in James' authority. Anti-Leislerians protested that the Dominion leaders in New York were no Jacobites, however, and did everything they could to comply with the desires of William and Mary once they were made known.[134] Leislerians, in turn, claimed that the legacy of the Glorious Revolution was theirs and accused their opponents of rank Toryism, even Jacobitism. Both factions were in agreement that they supported the set of political values that reflected the English Whig principles of the Glorious Revolution—liberty, the protection of personal property, and the Protestant religion, and both factions accused the other of violating them, and of unfaithfulness to their new rulers.

As was the case in Massachusetts, perceived interests encouraged Revolutionary principles and promoted loyalty to William and Mary's government in England. The new Monarchs' devotion to Parliament and fervent anti-Romanism provided validation to Long Island Puritans who had long pleaded for a representative assembly and worried about increasing Papist influence in their colonial government. Ethnic political and economic differences between English and Dutch residents were no longer relevant by the 1690s.[135] The merchants of New York, both Dutch and English, saw the alliance of England and Holland through the agency of their new rulers as an opportunity to profit concomitantly from Dutch trade and benevolent English rule. All of the political factions competed with each other for the support of the English government in London and the English Governor in New York, and they all viewed the adoption of the Whig principles of the English Revolution and the enthusiastic support of the English monarch as good politics. Regardless of their political affiliations in local affairs, New Yorkers agreed that the new rulers and their successors were guarantors of the lives, liberty, property and Protestant religion of their subjects wherever they might reside. New Yorkers grew to acknowledge English monarchs as allies—protectors of their rights—rather than as potential tyrants. In short, New York colonists accepted the Whig premises of government and kingship that became the standard line of thought of eighteenth century English political culture. In fact, in New York, there was no competing political paradigm for a politician to embrace. In 1698 Governor Bellomont noted that there were "parties here as in England, Whigs and Tories, or rather Jacobites," but the New York politician who might accept the latter title was rare and had little future in the politics of the province or the Empire.[136] Even during Queen Anne's reign, Toryism did not take in New York. So while political factionalism became the rule in New York, all parties gave unflagging support to their king, and to the principles of the Glorious Revolution: to liberty, property and the Protestant religion.

Notes

1. [Anon.], *Loyalty Vindicated from the Reflections of a Virulent Pamphlet. . .* (London, 1698), in *Narratives of the Insurrections, 1675-1690*, Charles M. Andrews, ed. (New York: Charles Scribner's Sons, 1915), 376.

2. Andrews, *Narratives*, 375. For the history of New York under James, both as Proprietor and King, see Patricia Bonomi, *A Factious People: Politics and Society in Colonial New York* (New York: Columbia University Press, 1971), 19-75; Michael Kammen, *Colonial New York: A History* (New York: Charles Scribner's Sons, 1975), 73-127; John Webb Pratt, *Religion, Politics and Diversity: The Church-State Theme in New York History* (Ithaca, New York: Cornell University Press), 27-46; Jerome R. Reich, *Leisler's Rebellion: A Study in Democracy in New York, 1664-1720* (Chicago: University of Chicago Press, 1953); Robert Ritchie, *The Duke's Province: A Study of New York Colonial Politics and Society, 1664-1691* (Chapel Hill: University of North Carolina Press, 1977); Voorhees, "'In Behalf of the True Protestants Religion': The Glorious Revolution in New York" (Ph.D. diss., New York University, 1988), 98-121, 251-265. Jerome Reich and, to a lesser extent, Lovejoy give a balanced coverage to the wide range of constitutional, economic and religious grievances that New Yorkers had against their government under James Stuart, and note that there was no single overriding cause that stimulated the Revolution in the province. Ritchie concentrates on the interaction between the people of the colony and their government through the social, political and economic developments over the period of Stuart domination there. The religious tensions in the province are the focus of Pratt's and Voorhees' studies, and Voorhees attributes the Revolution and its aftermath under Jacob Leisler primarily to religious tensions, both anti-Romanist and internecine among the Calvinists of the province. Kammen and Bonomi focus on the social and economic diversity of New York and the tensions and conflicts caused by the diverse ethnicity and economy in the province. The demographics of the colony and city of New York are the focus of several helpful works by Thomas J. Archdeacon, among them *New York City, 1664-1710: Conquest and Change* (Ithaca, New York: Cornell University Press, 1972), 32-96, and "The Age of Leisler—New York City, 1689-1710: A Social and Demographic Interpretation," in *Aspects of Early New York Society and Politics*, Jacob Judd and Irwin H. Polishook, eds. (Tarrytown, New York: Sleepy Hollow Restorations, 1974), 63-82.

3. *D.H.N.Y.*, 4:21. Of course, a number of Native American tribes also lived within the territory of the New York Charter as self-governing groups who interacted with the colonial government. On the ethnic diversity of the early New

York (and New Netherlands) population, see Milton M. Klein, "New York in the American Colonies: A New Look," in Judd and Irwin, *Aspects of Early New York Society and Politics*, 16-17; Bonomi, *A Factious People*, 18-27; Pratt, *Religion, Politics and Diversity*, 4-5; Michael Kammen, *Colonial New York*, 23-72. For a detailed examination of the population of colonial New York, see Archdeacon, *New York City*, 32-77.

4. *N.Y.H.S.C.*, 2:118.

5. Governor Stuyvesant to the Duke of York, *N.Y.C.D.*, 3:164; "Answers of Governor Andros to Enquiries about New York," *N.Y.C.D.*, 3:261.

6. For the treaty itself, see "Articles of Capitulation on the Reduction of New Netherland . . ., August 27, Old Style, 1664," *N.Y.C.D.*, 2:250-253. For a discussion of expectations of the Dutch, and their understanding of the treaty, see Reich, *Leisler's Rebellion*, 8-10, *passim.*, and Ritchie, *The Duke's Province*, 22-23, *passim.* Governor Nicholls had good reason to forge articles that were lenient to the Dutch residents of the province. Since the Dutch made up two-thirds of the population, Nicholls and future governors often sought their cooperation and looked to Dutch leaders for support. See Steve Stern, "Knickerbockers who Insisted and Asserted: The Dutch Interest in New York Politics, 1664-1691," *New York Historical Society Quarterly* 58:2 (1974), 117-119, 129-131.

7. For more on religious guarantees and the Dutch Reformed Church, see Milton Klein, "New York in the American Colonies: A New Look," in Judd and Polishook, *Aspects of Early New York Society and Politics*, 19-20.

8. "Articles of Capitulation," *N.Y.C.D.*, 2:251-252.

9. See Reich, *Leisler's Rebellion*, 9-10. For a petition from Peter Stuyvesant, see *N.Y.C.D.*, 3:163-164.

10. Reich, *Leisler's Rebellion*, 9.

11. Reich, *Leisler's Rebellion*, 9. Trade with Holland continued after 1665 with some regularity, but never reached the magnitude necessary to sustain the demand for Dutch goods. See Jan Kupp, "Aspects of New York-Dutch Trade, 1670-1674," *New York Historical Quarterly* 58:2 (1974), 141. See also A.J.F. Van Laer, ed. and translator, *Correspondence of Jeremias Van Renselaer, 1651-1674* (Albany: The University of the State of New York, 1932), 376, 390-391, 408, 431, 446, passim; and A.J.F. Van Laer, ed. and translator, *Correspondence of Maria Van Renselaer, 1669-1689* (Albany: The University of the State of New York, 1935), 9, 83, 40, 82.

12. "Order of the King's Council on the Petition of Peter Stuyvesant," *N.Y.C.D.*, 3:166-167.

13. The Board of Trade to the King, *N.Y.C.D.*, 3:176.

14. "Petition of Olive Stuyvesant Van Cortlandt, and others . . .," *N.Y.C.D.*, 3:179.

15. "Order in Council, 11 December, 1668," *N.Y.C.D.*, 3:179.

16. Governor Stuyvesant to the Duke of York, 1667, *N.Y.C.D.*, 3:162.

17. "Petition of the Common Council of New York, December, 1669," *N.Y.C.D.*, 3:187. See also Reich, *Leisler's Rebellion*, 10, and Lovejoy, 103.

According to Patricia Bonomi, the Fur traders found a substitute for duffel in the form of English Stroudwaters, "a course woolen cloth produced in superior quality, at less cost in England." See Patricia Bonomi, *A Factious People*, 42.

18. Governor Stuyvesant to the Duke of York, 1667, *N.Y.C.D.*, 3:162.

19. *N.Y.C.D.*, 2:739-740; 3:236. See also Reich, *Leisler's Rebellion*, 31.

20. Reich, *Leisler's Rebellion*, 31. See John Werden to Governor Andros, *N.Y.C.D.*, 3:239. Werden was James' personal secretary.

21. "Answers of Governor Andros to Enquiries about New York," *N.Y.C.D.*, 3:261.

22. See John Werden to Governor Andros, January 28, 167^5/$_6$, *N.Y.C.D.*, 3:236.

23. "Governor Dongan's Annual Report on the State of the Province, including his Answers to certain Charges against him," *N.Y.C.D.*, 3:398.

24. Reich, *Leisler's Rebellion*, 4.

25. Reich, *Leisler's Rebellion*, 4.

26. "Grant of New Netherland to the Duke of York," *N.Y.C.D.*, 3:660.

27. Lovejoy, *Glorious Revolution*, 106.

28. *N.Y.C.D.*, 14:501, cited in Reich, *Leisler's Rebellion*, 11.

29. "Declaration of the Deputies of Long Island, 1 March, 1665," *N.Y.C.D.*, 3:91; *Cal. St. P.*, 6:286.

30. Nicholls to the Duke of York, November, 1665, in *N.Y.C.D.*, 3:104.

31. Reich, *Leisler's Rebellion*, 12.

32. See Reich, *Leisler's Rebellion*, 14-17, and Lovejoy, *Glorious Revolution*, 107-108.

33. Lovejoy, *Glorious Revolution*, 108. See also Reich, *Leisler's Rebellion*, 14-15.

34. *Records of the Town of Jamaica*, 1:41, cited in Reich, *Leisler's Rebellion*, 15.

35. Reich, *Leisler's Rebellion*, 15; Lovejoy, *Glorious Revolution*, 108; *Cal. St. P.*, 7:381.

36. For James Stuart's finances with relation to the New York colony, see Robert Ritchie, "The Duke of York's Commission of Revenue," *New York Historical Society Quarterly* 58:3 (1974), 177-187.

37. Reich, *Leisler's Rebellion*, 13.

38. Lovejoy, *Glorious Revolution*, 109.

39. Duke of York to Governor Andros, *N.Y.C.D.*, 3:230.

40. Duke of York to Governor Andros, *N.Y.C.D.*, 3:235.

41. Duke of York to Governor Andros, *N.Y.C.D.*, 3.235.

42. Duke of York to Governor Andros, *N.Y.C.D.*, 3:230.

43. Duke of York to Governor Andros, *N.Y.C.D.*, 3:230.

44. Duke of York to Governor Andros, *N.Y.C.D.*, 3:235.

45. *N.Y.C.D.*, 14:681.

46. *N.Y.C.D.*, 14:683, cited in Reich, *Leisler's Rebellion*, 22.

47. See *N.Y.C.D.*, 14:723, 744.

48. *N.Y.C.D.*, 3:412.

49. *N.Y.C.D.*, 3:370.

50. *N.Y.C.D.*, 389. For a longer summary of the events, see Lovejoy, *Glorious Revolution*, 110-111.

51. Lovejoy, *Glorious Revolution*, 110. The charges against him were dismissed in England because no one from New York appeared to bring charges. Dyer was promoted to another post.

52. *N.Y.C.D.*, 3:292.

53. *N.Y.H.S.C.*, 45:14, Cited in Lovejoy, *Glorious Revolution*, 111.

54. *N.Y.H.S.C.*, 45:14.

55. *N.Y.H.S.C.*, 45:16.

56. Lovejoy, *Glorious Revolution*, 112. See also Reich, *Leisler's Rebellion*, 42-43.

57. On the liberalization of religious tolerance under Dutch rule, see Kammen, *History*, 61-63, and Pratt, *Religion, Politics and Diversity*, 15, 20-21.

58. "Answers of Governor Andros to Enquiries About New York," *N.Y.C.D.*, 3:262.

59. "Governor Dongan's Report," *N.Y.C.D.*, 3:415.

60. Charles Wolley, *A Two Years Journal in New York and Part of Its Territories in America* (1701), cited in Voorhees, "Glorious Revolution in New York," 71.

61. See Voorhees, "Glorious Revolution in New York," 72-73. For religious tensions in New York from the English occupation to the Glorious Revolution, see Voohres, "Glorious Revolution in New York," 70-80; Langdon G. Wright, "In Search of Peace and Harmony: New York Communities in the Seventeenth Century," *New York History*, 64 (January, 1980), 5-21; Donna Merwick, "Becoming English: Anglo-Dutch Conflict in the 1670s in Albany, New York," *New York History* (October, 1981), 389-414; and Patricia Bonomi, *Under the Cope of Heaven: Religion, Society and Politics in Colonial America* (New York: Oxford University Press, 1986), 74-75. Religious tensions and competition were not new to the colony, for evidence of religious controversies under Dutch rule, see Kammen, *History*, 60-62, and Bonomi, *Cope of Heaven*, 25-26.

62. Voorhees, "Glorious Revolution in New York," 72-73.

63. See Voorhees, "Glorious Revolution in New York," 170. See also Captain Leisler to King William and Queen Mary, *N.Y.C.D.*, 3:615-616; and *Loyalty Vindicated*, Andrews, *Narratives*, 398.

64. "Commission of Governor Dongan, June 1686," *N.Y.C.D.*, 3:379. See also Ritchie, *The Duke's Province*, 144-146.

65. See Kammen, *History*, 85; Reich, *Leisler's Rebellion*, 33-34; and Voorhees, "Glorious Revolution in New York," 75-76. For more on the Van Renselaer controversy, see Lawrence Leder, "The Unorthodox Domine: Nicholas Van Renselaer," *New York History* 35:2 (1954), 166-176.

66. Leder, "Unorthodox Domine," 169, and Ritchie, *The Duke's Province*, 144-147. Leder notes that Van Renselear's theology was quite unusual—at least two individuals had remarked on some of his rather odd ideas. Charles II apparently assumed, on conversing with Van Renselaer, that he was a Quaker (Leder, "Unorthodox Domine," 167-168). Ritchie claims that the controversy went beyond theology. The Van Renselaer family was unpopular in Albany because of a long-standing altercation over Albany real estate, so a member of that family was a poor choice for an Albany pulpit regardless of Nicholas' religious affiliation. In addition, Van Renselaer was foisted on the Dutch Reformed Congregation by a Catholic Duke and Catholic Governor and was thus viewed as at least a Catholic "sympathizer." Ritchie notes that "being English subjects was one thing, but suffering crypto-Catholics in their Churches was another" (Ritchie, *The Duke's Province*, 147).

67. "Governor Andros to Officials at Albany Concerning Charges Brought by Jacob Leisler and Jacob Milbourn Against Domine Nicholas Van Renselaer, September 16, 1676," in *The Andros Papers: Files of the Provincial Secretary of New York During the Administration of Governor Sir Edmund Andros, 1674-1680*, 2 Vols., Peter R. Christoph and Florence A. Christoph, eds. (Syracuse, New York: Syracuse University Press, 1989), 1:435. Henceforth cited as *Andros Papers*.

68. Voorhees, "Glorious Revolution in New York," 76. Tesschenmaker's ordination was confirmed by the Amsterdam Classis the following year.

69. Voorhees, "Glorious Revolution in New York," 76-77.

70. "Randolph to Sir Nicholas Butler Proposing a Romanist Mission," *Randolph Papers, 6:243*.

71. "Deposition of Andries and Jan Meyer," *D.H.N.Y.*, 2:17.

72. See "Letter from the Members of the Dutch Church in New York to the Classis in Amsterdam, October 21, 1698," *N.Y.H.S.C.*, 1868, 398-399; and Leisler to the Governor at Boston, August 13, 1689, *D.H.N.Y.*, 2:14.

73. Voorhees, "Glorious Revolution in New York," 76. See also "Early Catholic Clergymen in New York," *D.H.N.Y.*, 3:110-111.

74. Voorhees, "Glorious Revolution in New York," 68.

75. Voorhees, "Glorious Revolution in New York," 9-11.

76. *A Catalogue of all the Discourses Printed Against Popery* (London, 1689), cited in Voorhees, "Glorious Revolution in New York," 31.

77. Voorhees, "Glorious Revolution in New York," 29-32.

78. "Affidavit of Andries Greveraet and George Brewerton, 22 March, 1689," *N.Y.C.D.*, 3:660.

79. "Affidavit of Andries Greveraet and George Brewerton, 22 March, 1689," *N.Y.C.D.*, 3:660.

80. Voorhees, "Glorious Revolution in New York," 120.

81. Robert Livingston to Edward Randolph, Albany, 22 March, $168^{8}/_{9}$, *Randolph Papers*, 4:262.

82. "Minutes of the Council of New York," *N.Y.H.S.C.* (1868), 242, 244.

83. "Minutes of the Council of New York," *N.Y.H.S.C.* (1868), 245-246.

84. "Declaration of the Freeholders of Suffolk County, Long Island in the Territory of New England, 3 May, 1689," *N.Y.C.D.*, 3:577.

85. *N.Y.H.S.C.* (1868), 254-255.

86. "Account of Ensign Joost Stol's Proceedings," *N.Y.C.D.*, 3:632-633.

87. "Henry Cuyler's Disposition Concerning Governor Nicholson, 10 June, 1689," *N.Y.H.S.C.* (1868), 292-293. Reich notes that Cuyler's "uncorroborated evidence would be highly suspect, except for the fact that it was never frankly denied." (Reich, *Leisler's Rebellion*, fn.16, 58). Whether it was true or fabricated by Cuyler, the anecdote quickly became the foundation for rumors that Nicholson was part of a conspiracy to fire the town.

88. "A Declaration of the Inhabitants Soudjers Belonging Under the Severall Companies of the Train Band of New York, 31 May, 1689," *D.H.N.Y.*, 2:7.

89. "Affidavit Against Col. Bayard & Certain Papists on Staten Island," *D.H.N.Y.*, 2:17-18.

90. *N.Y.H.S.C.* (1868), 400.

91. "Declaration of the Inhabitants Soudjers," *D.H.N.Y.*, 2:7.

92. "Commission from the Committee of Safety [of New York]," *D.H.N.Y.*, 2:7; Stephen Van Cortlandt to Governor Andros, July 9, 1689, *Cal. St. P.*, 13:81, and *N.Y.C.D.*, 3:595-596.

93. Voorhees, "Glorious Revolution in New York," 130.

94. John Tudor to Francis Nicholson, October 23, 1689, *Cal. St. P.*, 13:131.

95. See "Colonel Bayard's Narrative of Occurrences in New York from April to December, 1689," *N.Y.C.D.*, 3:636-644. See also Lovejoy, *Glorious Revolution*, 255-256; Kammen, *History*, 122; Reich, *Leisler's Rebellion*, 76-78. Reich notes that if Bayard, a detractor, was correct in his assertion that about one-third of the people of the province participated in the selection of the Committee of Safety, this turnout was "amazingly large" and signifies wide popular support for the Revolutionary government in New York (Reich, *Leisler's Rebellion*, 77).

96. Voorhees, "Glorious Revolution in New York," 165-166. Leisler, the son of a German Calvinist minister, had married into an old Dutch family in 1663 and become prosperous. He had connections to the leading Dutch merchant families, the Bayards, Van Cortlandts, and Lookermans, among them. For a biographical sketch of Leisler, see David William Voorhees, "The Fervent Zeale of Jacob Leisler," *William and Mary Quarterly*, 3rd ser. 51:3 (1994), 447-472.

Kammen argues that the Leislerian Revolution represented an attempt by the older Dutch elite, among them Leisler, to regain their primacy over the new "Anglo-Dutch establishment." He quotes Colonel Bayard's statement that Leisler's supporters were mostly Dutch in support of his thesis. Bayard's accusations appear inconsistent with the outcome of the election. If the "ignorant and innocent" Dutch populace had dominated the elections, why were no old Dutch trading families represented in the outcome? Why was only one Dutch member selected by the freeholders? Why did the predominately Dutch community of Albany consistently oppose Leisler and his government throughout his regime? All of these facts seem inconsistent with Kammen's thesis. (Kammen, *History*, 120-124). Voorhees' argument that Committee of Safety members' religion was more significant than their ethnic ties or class seems to hold more substance. See also Stern, "Knickerbockers," 133-136.

97. Leisler to William Jones in New Haven, July 10, 1689, *D.H.N.Y.*, 2:6.

98. *D.H.N.Y.*, 2:17-18; *N.Y.C.D.*, 3:610.

99. See Voorhees, "Glorious Revolution in New York," 170-171. For the Committee and Quakers, see Lieutenant Governor Leisler and Council to the Bishop of Salisbury, January 1, 1689[/90], *N.Y.C.D.*, 3:656. For Anglicans, see Captain Leisler to King William and Queen Mary, *N.Y.C.D.*, 3:615-616. Several Dutch Reformed Ministers who did not feel the zeal of their Voetian and Congregationalist brethren were harassed by Committee representatives. See *A Letter from a Gentleman of the City of New York*, Andrews, *Narratives*, 367, and Leisler's comments, Lieutenant Governor Leisler and Council to the Earl of Shrewsbury, October 20, 1690, *N.Y.C.D.*, 3:753.

100. William Smith, Jr., *The History of the Province of New York*, 2 vols., Michael Kammen, ed. (London, 1757; reprint, Cambridge, Massachusetts: Belknap Press of Harvard University, 1972), 1:70.

101. "Declaration of the Freeholders of Suffolk County, Long Island," *N.Y.C.D.*, 3:577. See also "Address of the Militia of New-York to William and Mary," *N.Y.C.D.*, 3:583; and *Loyalty Vindicated*, Andrews, *Narratives*, 375.

102. "Letter from Members of the Dutch Church in New York to the Classis of Amsterdam," *N.Y.H.S.C.* (1868), 399. See also *Letter from a Gentleman in New York . . .*, Andrews, *Narratives*, 361.

103. Voorhees, "Glorious Revolution in New York," 179-180.

104. Kammen, *History*, 169.

105. "Address of the Merchants of New York to the King and Queen, May 19, 1690," *N.Y.C.D.*, 3:748. Dutch, French and English names appear upon the address.

106. See Bonomi, *A Factious People*, 46.

107. *D.H.N.Y.*, 2:5.

108. See Mr. Livingston to Mr. Ferguson, March 27, 1690, *N.Y.C.D.*, 3:699. Reich notes that while the Albany elite who led the Convention refused to negotiate with Leisler's government, the "common people" of the town were more sympathetic to the New York Committee of Safety, as some one hundred Albany residents "menaced the members of the convention" in support of the Leislerians (Reich, *Leisler's Rebellion*, 81-82). Both Bonomi and Reich cite delicate relations between Albany and the Iroquois and a distrust of Leisler's diplomatic abilities as the chief reasons why Albany leaders, influenced by Peter Schuyler and Robert Livingston, refused to support Leisler (Reich, *Leisler's Rebellion*, 81; Bonomi, *A Factious People*, 46). Voorhees cites religious differences between Leisler and the

Voetians who supported his regime and the Cocceian clergy of Albany, especially Godfrey Dellius, the most influential of the Albany Reformed clergymen (Voorhees, "Glorious Revolution in New York," 306-307). Lawrence Leder also refers to religious differences between Leisler and Albany leaders going back as far as the Van Renselaer controversy as a reason why Albany refused to support the New York City regime (Lawrence Leder, *Robert Livingston (1654-1728) and the Politics of Colonial New York* (Chapel Hill: University of North Carolina Press, 1961), 59). Voorhees notes that the major centers of resistence to Leisler came from areas where either non-Pietist Cocceian Dutch Reformers were in the majority, like Albany, or where Anglican or Quaker leaders were predominate in local society (Voorhees, "Glorious Revolution in New York,", 310-312). Long-standing economic differences between New York and Albany over fur trade and export, and Albany commercial leaders' fear of domination by the New York City merchant community also contributed to the split. See Kammen, *History,* 107-108; Leder, *Robert Livingston,* 61-62; Voorhees, "Glorious Revolution in New York," 309-310.

109. "Address of the Militia of New York to William and Mary," *N.Y.C.D.,* 3:583; See also *D.H.N.Y.,* 2:64-65; Stephen Van Cortland to Captain Nicholson, August 5, 1689, *N.Y.C.D.,* 3:609; *A Modest and Impartial Narrative . . .,* Andrews, *Narratives,* 321; *D.H.N.Y.,* 2:64-65; and "Leisler's Declaration or Protest against Ingoldsby, March 10, 1691," *N.Y.H.S.C.* (1868), 306.

110. *D.H.N.Y.,* 2:61.

111. *Cal. St. P.,* 13:192. See also *A Modest Narrative,* Andrews, *Narratives,* 340-341.

112. See Lovejoy, *Glorious Revolution,* 276.

113. "By the Leiut. Governor & Council, December 28, 1689," *D.H.N.Y.,* 2:30. See Reich, *Leisler's Rebellion,* 91-92. The author of *A Modest Narrative,* possibly Dominion Councillor (and Leisler's bitter rival) Nicholas Bayard, ignored the fact that the taxes were raised by a representative assembly and claimed that the taxes were levied by the Catholic Governor Dongan and were thus void. Ironically, the author of the *Narrative,* a supporter of the Dominion government, accused Leisler of taxing the people of the colony "without and contrary to their own consent, notwithstanding the many wholsome laws" of England (*A Modest Narrative,* Andrews, *Narratives,* 341).

114. See Lovejoy, *Glorious Revolution,* 277. See also Mr. Van Cortland to Sir Edmund Andros, May 1690, *N.Y.C.D.,* 3:717.

115. In 1691 Jacob Leisler refused to surrender the New York City fort, now Fort William, to Captain Ingoldsby, an officer who preceded the new Governor to the colony. Ingoldsby had no written orders, but, encouraged and supported by his new friends, members of the old Dominion Council, he demanded control of the fort. Leisler refused to surrender under those circumstances. When Governor Sloughter arrived, he too allied with the old regime. Leisler quickly surrendered the fort to him, only to find himself and a number of his followers arrested for high

treason. For a more detailed narrative of these events, see Reich, *Leisler's Rebellion*, 108-126.

116. See Reich, *Leisler's Rebellion*, 131-134. For relevant primary documents, see *N.Y.H.S.C.* (1868), 314-396.

117. Lovejoy, *Glorious Revolution*, 301-302. For a few examples of accusations against Anti-Leislerians, see *N.Y.H.S.C.* (1868), 341, 366-368, 383, 387, 391, 393, 414-415; *Loyalty Vindicated*, Andrews, *Narratives*, 383, 385, 393; "Depositions of Sundry Persons," *D.H.N.Y.*, 2:226-233; "Humble Petition of Johannes Provoost," *D.H.N.Y.*, 3:239. For accusations against Leislerians, see *Letter from a Gentleman of the City of New York*, Andrews, *Narratives*, 364, 369; *A Modest Narrative*, Andrews, *Narratives*, 321, 329, 331-333; "House of Representatives of the Province of New York, April 17, 1691," *D.H.N.Y.*, 2:207; "A Narrative in Answer to their May[ties] Letter," *D.H.N.Y.*, 2:222; John Lyon Gardiner, "Notes and Observations on the Town of East Hampton," *N.Y.H.S.C.* (1869), 246; and Cadwallader Colden, "Letter on Smith's History, July 5, 1759," *N.Y.H.S.C.* (1869), 203.

118. *Letter from a Gentleman*, Andrews, *Narratives*, 364. See also Messrs. Philips and Van Cortland to Secretary Blaithwayt, August 5, 1689, *N.Y.C.D.*, 3:608; "Col. Bayard's Narrative," *N.Y.C.D.*, 3:637; and Governor Slougher to the Committee, May 7, 1691, *N.Y.C.D.*, 3:762.

119. See Mr. Tudor to Captain Nicholson, *N.Y.C.D.*, 3:617; "Col. Bayard's Narrative," *N.Y.C.D.*, 3:637-645; Col. Bayard to Mr. John West, *N.Y.C.D.*, 3:661; "Memorial of the Agents from Albany to the Government in Massachusetts, March 20, 16[89]/[90]," *N.Y.C.D.*, 3:696-697; Mr. Newton to Captain Nicholson, May 26, 1690, *N.Y.C.D.*, 3:721; and John Clapp to the Secretary of State, *N.Y.C.D.*, 3:754-755.

120. *A Modest Narrative*, Andrews, *Narratives*, 329.

121. *A Modest Narrative*, Andrews, *Narratives*, 341, 333, 332. See also "Dispositions," *D.H.N.Y.*, 2:208-209; and "A Narrative in Answer to their Maj[ties] Letter," *D.H.N.Y.*, 2:222.

122. Mr. William Nicholls to Mr. George Farewell, January 14, 1689, *N.Y.C.D.*, 3:662. "Col. Bayard's Narrative," *N.Y.C.D.*, 3:638-639. See also Col. Bayard to Mr. John West, *N.Y.C.D.*, 3:661; Mr. Livingston to Mr. Ferguson, March 27, 1690, *N.Y.C.D.*, 3:699; Mr. Livingston to the Government of Connecticut, May 13, 1690, *N.Y.C.D.*, 3:730; "Address of the New-York Merchants to the King and Queen," *N.Y.C.D.*, 3:748; John Clapp to the Secretary of State, *N.Y.C.D.*, 3:754-755; and Chidley Brooke to Sir Robert Southwell, April 5, 1691, *N.Y.C.D.*, 3:757.

123. "Col. Bayard's Narrative," *N.Y.C.D.*, 3:645. See also "Memorial of the Agents from Albany to the Government of Massachusetts, March 20, 16[89]/[90]," *N.Y.C.D.*, 3:696; Mr. Livingston to Mr. Ferguson, March 27, 1690; *N.Y.C.D.*, 3:699; "Address of the New-York Merchants to the King and Queen," *N.Y.C.D.*, 3:748; and "Answer to the Memorial Presented by Captain Blagge to the King," *N.Y.C.D.*, 3:764-765.

124. Stephen Van Cortland to Governor Andros, July 9, 1689, *N.Y.C.D.*, 3:596; "Abstract of Colonel Bayard's Journal," *N.Y.C.D.*, 3:682; and Messrs. Philips and Van Cortland to Secretary Blathwayt, August 5, 1689, *N.Y.C.D.*, 3:608.

125. See "The Case of Mr. Jacob Leisler," *N.Y.H.S.C.* (1868), 262-263; *Loyalty Vindicated*, Andrews, *Narratives*, 378, 380, 382; "Letter from Members of the Dutch Church in New York to the Classis of Amsterdam," *N.Y.H.S.C.* (1868), 399-400. Bayard claimed that the council and aldermen of New York City were prepared to announce the accession of the new rulers publicly as soon as they received the official announcement from London, but that the militia intercepted the royal proclamation en route to the Council and thus deprived them of the opportunity to act before Leisler did. See "Col. Bayard's Journal," *N.Y.C.D.*, 3:600-601.

126. "Col. Bayard's Journal," *N.Y.C.D.*, 3:602-603.

127. See *Loyalty Vindicated*, Andrews, *Narratives*, 376-377; "Petition of Captain Benjamin Blagg to the King," *N.Y.C.D.*, 3:737; Leisler to William Jones, *D.H.N.Y.*, 2:5-6; and "At a Convention &c., Albany, November 9, 1689," *D.H.N.Y.*, 2:64.

128. See *Loyalty Vindicated*, Andrews, *Narratives*, 377-379; "Deposition of Robert Sinclair, February 23, 1691," *D.H.N.Y.*, 2:229; "Deposition of Jacob Williams, February 24, 1691," *D.H.N.Y.*, 232; and "Deposition of Citizens of New York, August 22, 1691," *N.Y.H.S.C.* (1868), 345-346.

129. See "Commission of Capt. Leisler to be Commander in Chief, August 16, 1689," *D.H.N.Y.*, 2:14-15; "By the Governor & Council &c., December 30, 1689," *D.H.N.Y.*, 2:32; "A Memoriall of What Has Occurred in their Mat^{ies} Province of New York," *D.H.N.Y.*, 2:23; "Representation of Joost Stol for the Committee of Safety in New York," *N.Y.C.D.*, 3:630; Lieutenant Governor Leisler to the King, January 7, 16^{89}/$_{90}$, *N.Y.C.D.*, 3:654; "Leisler's Declaration and Protest Against Ingoldsby," *N.Y.H.S.C.* (1868), 306-307; "Affidavit of George Dolstone, February 19, 1691[/2]," *N.Y.H.S.C.* (1868), 314; "Affidavit of Thomas Jeffers, February 19, 1691[/2]," *N.Y.H.S.C.* (1868), 319-320; "Affidavit of Isaac De Riemer, February 24, 1691[/2]," *N.Y.H.S.C.* (1868), 324-325; "A Letter from Members of the Dutch Church in New York to the Classis of Amsterdam," *N.Y.H.S.C.* (1868), 399; and *Loyalty Vindicated*, Andrews, *Narratives*, 381-383.

130. Leisler to the Governor of Barbadoes, November 23, 1689, *D.H.N.Y.*, 2:24.

131. *Loyalty Vindicated*, Andrews, *Narratives*, 379.

132. See Leisler to the Governor of Barbadoes, November 23, 1689, *D.H.N.Y.*, 2:24-25; "A Memoriall of What Has Occurred in their Mat^{ies} Province of New York," *D.H.N.Y.*, 2:33; "Humble Petitions to Governor Sloughter . . .," *D.H.N.Y.*, 2:209; "Dying Speeches of Leisler and Milbourne," *D.H.N.Y.*, 2:213-215; "Depositions of Sundry Persons," *D.H.N.Y.*, 2:226-228, 230-231; "Petition of Captain Jacob Mauritz, May 10, 1699," *D.H.N.Y.*, 2:238; "Representation of Joost Stol," *N.Y.C.D.*, 3:630; "Affidavit of George Dolstone," *N.Y.H.S.C.* (1868), 314;

Chapter 3

"Affidavit of Isaac De Reimer," *N.Y.H.S.C.* (1868), 325; "Affidavit of Kiliaan Van Renselaer, March 7, 168$^1/_2$," *N.Y.H.S.C.* (1868), 328, 330, 331; "Deposition of Citizens of New York," *N.Y.H.S.C.* (1868), 345-346; "Petition and Remonstrance of the New York House of Representatives to Governor Bellomont . . ., May 15, 1699," *N.Y.H.S.C.* (1868), 413-414; and *Loyalty Vindicated*, Andrews, *Narratives*, 377, 379-380, 384-385.

133. *A Modest and Impartial Narrative*, Andrews, *Narratives*, 320-321. *A Letter from a Gentleman of the City of New York*, Andrews, *Narratives*, 360.

134. *A Modest and Impartial Narrative*, Andrews, *Narratives*, 332, 344; *A Letter from a Gentleman of the City of New York*, Andrews, *Narratives*, 363-364, 369, 370.

135. At least one scholar, Steve Stern, argues that these differences had all but vanished by the Revolution in New York, replaced by differences of class and geography (i.e. competition between Albany and New York) (see Stern, "Knickerbockers," *passim.*).

136. Alison Gilbert Olson, *Anglo-American Politics, 1660-1775: The Relationship between Parties in England and Colonial America* (New York: Oxford University Press, 1973), 101.

4

A Nursing Father:
The Whig Image of Kingship

How great a Mercy ought a People to account it, when God gives such to rule over them who are concerned to promote their best Interests, and desirous to shew them all the Affection and Tenderness of kind Fathers. And such a Mercy our Nation and Land enjoy in his present MAJESTY, our *Rightful and most Gracious Sovereign King* GEORGE II, who, we trust, esteems it a greater Honour to be the Common Father of his Loyal Subjects, than to wear the Imperial Crown of *Great-Britain*. — Daniel Lewes.[1]

Men are bound to honour in their Hearts, and with their Lips, those whom God hath vested with his Authority, and advanced, by his Providence to rule over them . . . *Fear God; Honour the King*: If we obey the first, we shall not despise the second of these divine Precepts. Magistrates are God's Representatives upon Earth, they bear his Character, and shine with some Rays of his Majesty; and ought therefore to be highly respected according to the dignity of their Station. — Ebenezer Gay.[2]

The rhetoric of the Glorious Revolution in America, as in England, was shaped by those precepts that Englishmen understood to be the cornerstones of their constitution. American participants in the Revolution against James II and his colonial regimes equated Stuart government with tyranny, slavery and Popery, and saw in William and Mary and the post-Revolutionary settlements in England and America a return to the traditional English constitutional values and institutions that protected the liberty, property and religion of English subjects wherever they might reside. The Glorious Revolution was thus regarded not as a radical movement toward some new innovation in government but as a return to first principles, as Samuel Johnson would have it, "a course . . . which returns to the point at which it began to move."[3] Colonists explained that they had joined in the Revolution to restore representative government, to protect their property, and to defend their lives and Protestant consciences against the unacceptable innovations in government and religion fostered by James Stuart and the men to whom he gave precedence over his American possessions. The colonists had not been alone in their struggles. They credited William and Mary for assisting in their salvation and for the restoration of their constitutional rights and privileges. Thus the inhabitants of Kent in Maryland gave thanks to God for their Majesties' "endevours for the restitution of our ancient Laws, religion, and properties to their primitive lustre and splendor."[4] Cotton Mather noted that under William's rule, the "Charters and Ancient Privileges should be restored to the English Nation" and intimated to his colleagues in Boston that the King would surely do no less for them.[5] This new alliance of king and people became an integral part of the Revolutionary settlement and a political idea that would endure in the colonies until the summer of 1776. The power and prerogatives of the monarch and the liberty of the subject were viewed, not as competing interests, but as complimentary aspects of the English constitution.[6] Increasingly, American colonists viewed the reigning English monarch as the defender of their laws, liberties, properties and religion.

Colonists who had overturned Stuart governments, or who, in the case of Maryland, toppled the government of a proprietor to whom they attributed Stuart principles, claimed to have done so in allegiance with William and Mary and in keeping with the Whig ideals of the English Revolution. Revolutionaries in Massachusetts, Connecticut, New York, and Maryland announced that they had rebelled against corrupt colonial administrators who abused the laws, deprived the people of their say in government, taxed unconstitutionally, and conspired with Papists, both domestic and foreign, toward the ruination of the English colonies and the residents thereof.[7] As has been seen, Jacob Leisler and his government based their legitimacy on an alliance with William and Mary, and Leisler's adherents continued to claim that the Revolution in New York had been undertaken in support of the Revolution in England.[8] Like Jacob Leisler, John Coode, the leader of the Maryland Revolution, justified his actions and those of his supporters by linking the Revolution in Maryland with that of England. He wrote, "wee know our duty which is obliged our lives and fortunes for the service of King William and Queen Mary."[9] Coode claimed that the "most eminent Protestants" of Maryland supported the new monarchs and had resolved that "as God Almighty had given their Majesties a just call to the Crown . . . ., so accordingly . . . they would give their lives and fortunes to mainteyne their Majesties Right and Title to the Faith and Allegiance Obedience and Subjection of their subjects in the said Province."[10]

Even those who had resisted the colonial revolutions were quick to give their obedience to the new rulers once they were firmly ensconced on the throne and to congratulate them, albeit somewhat belatedly, on their accession. The "Jacobite" colonists tried to gain the high moral ground as quickly as possible. Connecticut "Loyalists," for instance, protested that the revolutionary government that ousted them had no legitimacy—"it is not derived from the Crown, for the Crown gives no liberty to erect a government . . . This Government [was] erected in opposition to and contempt of the Crown . . .; the benefit of their Majesties laws are denied us."[11] A Dominion sympathizer in Boston wrote that the Boston Committee of Safety had "subverted their Majesties Government and . . . such was their design, to rend themselves from the Crown of England."[12] Nicholas Taney of Maryland characterized the conflict there as a "rebellion for persons here without order from theire Majestys to take up armes against the lawful authority" of the Lord Proprietor and the King and Queen.[13] Richard Hill echoed Taney's sentiments in a letter to Lord Baltimore. He wrote that under the Proprietor's protection he and his fellow colonists had "always enjoyed our free libertie in the exercise of our religion together with the benefit of the laws of our native Countrey England," and that these privileges were lost to them since the Maryland Revolution. He described the revolutionary government's "practices and proceedings" as "not only contrary but in defiance of all laws both humane and divine."[14] In an address to the new rulers, Anglican supporters of the Proprietary government of Maryland congratulated William and Mary upon "dispersing all malitious and threatening Clouds of Popery" and nourishing the Church of England. Then they asked for the new rulers' aid against the "several persons who call themselves Protestants" who had "overturned the Lawfull and peaceable Government" for no other reason "then to gratifie their own ambitions and mallitious designes."[15] Although some colonists were opposed to the revolutionary governments that were the result of the Glorious Revolution in their home provinces, none appear to have been particularly enthusiastic about restoring Stuart rule. Support for James II seems to have evaporated with the accession of the Orange Prince, and James' progeny in France, James the Old Pretender and Bonnie Prince Charlie, found very few adherents in America. There was no significant Jacobite movement in the colonies; according to John Adams, they were as rare "as a comet or an earthquake."[16] Americans' "king over the water" resided at the Court of St. James, not St. Germain. Even those colonists who had been the most vocal in their protests against the revolutionary regimes in New England, New York and Maryland gave their loyalty and allegiance to William and Mary and celebrated (though perhaps with less enthusiasm) the abdication of James II.

The generation of the Glorious Revolution and succeeding generations of American colonists viewed the provincial conflicts of 1689 as a continuation of the Glorious Revolution fought in America—in essence, campaigns of the same war fought on distant shores. Cotton Mather noted that the Revolution in Boston was "a great service . . . done for their Majesties: King William and Queen Mary, whom God grant long to Reign."[17] Mather was seconded by Edward Rawson and Samuel Sewell, who wrote that "no man does really approve of the *Revolution* in *England*, but must justifie that in New England also; for the latter was affected in compliance with the former."[18] As time passed, the Glorious Revolution became a part of Americans' political legacy, at once illustrating the patriotism, love of liberty, and Protestant fervor of the forefathers and linking successive good English Protestant kings with their American subjects. Charles Chauncy preached nearly fifty years later that when "our fathers in NEW-ENGLAND groaned under an oppressive burden of . . . *popish* and tyrannical power," Bay Colonists threw off their oppressors in imitation of their English brethren and in allegiance with "the glorious King WILLIAM, under God, the great Deliverer of the Nation from Popery and Slavery."[19]

Regardless of the form that the Revolution had taken in individual provinces, Americans everywhere considered the Glorious Revolution and the subsequent accession of William and Mary to be crucial events in the political and constitutional history of the English world. It was celebrated in all of the American colonies for years to come. On St. George Day in 1732, residents of Charlestown, South Carolina, "under a Discharge of Cannon round the Battery . . . drank to the pious Memory of King *William* the 3rd."[20] In 1755, the trustees of the College of New Jersey named a new building on their campus Nassau Hall to "express the Honour we retain, in this remote part of the Globe, to the immortal Memory of the glorious King *William* the Third . . ., who was the great Deliverer of the *British* Nation from those two monstrous Furies—*Popery* and *Slavery*."[21] In 1774, John Adams wrote that the Glorious Revolution in New England was affected when the people there "made an original express contract with King William."[22] Three years later the New York Presbyterian Patriot minister, Abraham Keteltas, cited William's Revolution and accession "by the votes of a free Parliament" among the precedents that lent justification to the then current revolution against the tyrannical rule of George III and his ministers.[23]

When the Hanoverian Dynasty was ushered in with the accession of King George I in 1714, there was a broad consensus among American colonists in favor of the German ruler. Although the dynastic change and ensuing politics in England caused stress and social disorder there, Americans appear to have accepted their new rulers with equanimity. George I's reputation proceeded him in the colonies as well as in England. In 1714, Cotton Mather extolled the virtues of the new king in his funerary sermon for Queen Anne. "We see ascending the *British Throne*," intoned Mather, "A KING whose Way to it is Prepared in the Hearts of his Joyful Subjects, by the Accounts which they have long had of his Princely Endowments, and of His Excellent Conduct in His German Dominions."[24] Mather praised the new King for his tolerance of Protestant dissent in his German realm, for his solicitous conduct toward his subjects and for his justice. In 1716, Benjamin Colman praised George for his piety, wisdom and justice. Coleman declared, "O what a GIFT of God, not only to us, but to Europe and to the Reformed Churches, [that] a Wise and Just King [sits] upon the Throne of Britain."[25]

In the age of the Hanovers, American political writers devoted a great deal of their attention in political sermons and tracts relating to the good governance of the colonies and the Empire to the king. He was viewed as the chief executive of Great Britain as well as each colony. He was the linchpin that connected each American province to the British Empire. He existed as the head of state, the protector of a Protestant religious polity, the dispenser of justice, the promoter of prosperity, the chief arbiter of morality and order, and the apex of the British social hierarchy.

Colonists viewed themselves as both subjects of the British Empire and citizens of their own colony. As the latter they were protected by additional contractual relationships (their charters) which gave them certain rights or liberties peculiar to themselves because of their colonial status. Since the colonial charters were presumed to be contractual agreements between each colony and the Crown, colonists viewed their relationship with the British Empire as a connection between the reigning monarch and themselves. Although the Crown might not have interpreted the charter relationships in the same light as colonists did, the means by which the Empire administered her colonies tended to support the colonists' views. The king either chose or gave his imprimatur to his royal governors; colonial laws were conditional upon their acceptance by the governors and the king in council (both, in effect, extensions of the British Crown).

The colonial charter relationship was personal as well as political. Colonial newspapers, serials and sermons conveyed an interest in the monarch that was considerably more intimate than a merely constitutional relationship with a political entity. Newspapers frequently carried stories about the day to day lives of the ruler and the royal family, the parties and events that they attended, their dress, and their public demeanor. Royal family weddings were celebrated and royal deaths were mourned in print and from the pulpit even when these distant events had no effect on the succession or on colonial relations with the mother country.[26] In addition to the public lives of the royal family, colonial subjects were also interested in the political lives and personalities of their rulers. This interest was conveyed in newspaper articles and tracts, in addresses to royal officials and the king, and in sermons in which colonial ministers declaimed upon the ideal attributes of rulers and compared the behavior of the reigning monarch and his antecedents with the ideal.[27] Americans' preoccupation with the monarch and royal family even permeated the landscape itself as colonists named towns and counties, streets and even the physical features of the land after kings and princes, queens and royal consorts, from Lake George on the Vermont frontier to Fort King George in Georgia, from the James River to the Cumberland Gap.

A number of historians, among them Gordon Wood and Richard Bushman, have explored the position and importance of the monarch in colonial society. He sat at the top of a vertical social hierarchy.[28] Differences of rank from majesty to noble, to husbandman, to yeoman, to tenant, to itinerant—from the one to the few to the many—"was part of a natural order of things, part of that great chain of existence that ordered the entire universe."[29] Admittedly, this hierarchical chain was less distinct in the British colonies in North America than it was in the mother country. In the American colonies there were very few hereditary lords, and the relative availability of land, and the scarcity of labor made for a larger freeholder class than in England, a more affluent and respected mechanic class, and a much smaller itinerant class. Although by the middle of the eighteenth century, distinctions between the highest and lowest economic classes in the colonies had become starker, and the distribution of wealth more skewed than it had been in the past, class stratification "remained remarkably shallow and stunted by contemporary English standards."[30] Although scholars might disagree as to the significance of the economic and social structural developments within colonial society in the eighteenth century, they generally agree that the American colonial social ladder was shorter than that of Great Britain. Edwin Perkins notes that poverty increased, especially in the northern towns after the middle of the century, but still concludes that the standard of living for the "typical white family was almost certainly the highest in the world by the 1770s."[31] Perhaps class differences and the potential for class conflict were the most apparent in the growing northern urban centers and in those areas of the colonies where, by the mid-eighteenth century, new land was becoming scarce. There, conflicts of interest between manufacturers, workers, consumers, farmers and speculators caused friction.[32] In spite of these differences, however, American colonists still viewed society in the same terms as their English cousins and agreed that the king held a paramount place in it as both the apex of British society and the political father of those below him on the chain.

Colonists frequently portrayed their king in patriarchal terms. Although redefined from the Filmerian construction by Whig ideas of constraint on the executive and the elective nature of kingship, the concept of the king as father held on with tenacity both in Britain and in the colonies and was revitalized during the first half of the eighteenth century. Robert Filmer had justified Stuart absolute kingship by equating it with the power a patriarch exercised over his family under the divine ordinance of the Commandment to "honor thy father." For Filmer, a tyrannical father was a father nevertheless, answerable only to God, and not to his children, for his actions.[33] British Whig writers of the first half of the eighteenth century stressed that only good rulers deserved the title of father. Political fatherhood was not the divine right of the ruler but an accolade from the people. Writers stressed the paternal love, benevolence and protection that a good father bestowed upon his family rather than the authoritative power that a patriarch wielded over his progeny.[34] "In order to answer the ends of civil Government," Daniel Lewes stated, "Rulers should behave towards their People, with the tenderness and affection of FATHERS . . . by protecting them to the utmost of their Power."[35] Lewes continued:

The Parent who governs his Children with Lenity and Gentleness and appears to be deeply concerned for their welfare on all Accounts, takes the surest Course to entitle himself to their sincere Respect, and to be truly honoured by them. Where as he that is rigorous and always treats them in a churlish imperious Manner, is only slavishly feared, but not cordially loved.[36]

Lewes attributed to George II, "all the Affection and Tenderness" of a loving father.[37] According to Ebenezer Pemberton, a Presbyterian minister in New York, George II "may truly be stiled the indulgent FATHER of his people, under whose administration we may worship God according to the dictates of our conscience, and have none to terrify and disturb us,—may dwell under our vines and Figtrees, and have none to make us afraid."[38]

With increasing frequency during the period from the rise of the Hanovers through the 1760s, colonial ministers and other writers compared good kings (monarchs since the Revolution of 1688) with bad kings (usually the Stuarts), and employed biblical citations that stressed the paternal nature of monarchy to illustrate the qualities of good rulers. "Such Kings," Samuel Checkley noted, "as they expect love, honour and loyalty from their Subjects, so they endevour to be themselves *nursing fathers* unto them, which was the great blessing God promised his People of old."[39] Ebenezer Gay stressed that "Rulers are political *Fathers* of their People." When they encourage virtue and suppress vice, "such rulers are called . . . the *Breath of a People's Nostrils*." Gay continued, "our *KING* is a nursing Father, and our *QUEEN* a nursing Mother, who have expressed their tender care of, and Concern for us, their poor but dutiful Children in these distant parts of their Dominion."[40] Nathaniel Eells preached at the Hartford election sermon in 1748 that "in order to answer the Ends of civil Government. . . Rulers should behave towards their People, with the Tenderness and Affection of Fathers."[41] Daniel Lewes took a more Classical turn when he compared George II to Augustus Caesar, "one of the best and wisest" Roman Emperors, "that when the People offered him the title of *Lord*, . . . thought the title of *Pater Patria* more honourable."[42]

Since good kings were "civil Fathers" to their subjects, colonial writers argued that good subjects ought to exercise a filial duty "to honour them as such."[43] As good rulers protected and guaranteed their subjects' liberties, property and religion, so subjects were obliged to pray for and obey their king and to do all that they could to protect and preserve the power and prerogatives of their ruler. To do so was not a matter of blind or slavish obedience, but of reciprocal self-interest and obligation, and was thus good practice. After all, if the king employed his powers to the benefit of his subjects, then self-interest dictated that the subject, in turn, should strive to preserve those royal powers that the king exercised to his people's benefit. Good rulers worked "with Heart, and Head, and Hand, to promote the great Ends of Rule, and Government, the Good and Welfare of their People, and are willing to Spend and be Spent, for the common weal."[44] Should not good subjects then support their rulers, for "what an inexcusable and shameful Ingratitude to God, as well as Blindness to their own Interests, is it for a People to bite the Hand that thus kindly feeds them?"[45] Indeed, the Scripture enjoined good Christian citizens that "whosoever therefore resisteth the power," of rulers, "resisteth the ordinance of God."[46] Divine writ, however, did not extend the requirement "to all who bear the title of rulers in common," but only to those who "actually perform the duty of rulers by exercising a reasonable and just authority for the good of human society . . ., such as are in the exercise of their office and power, benefactors."[47] Good rulers were ever vigilant and solicitous of the temporal and spiritual interests of their subjects. They encouraged virtue and punished vice.[48] "Under their shadow" the people "possess[ed] the comforts and conveniences of Life, with security from Rapine, from solicitude, from continual fears of Wrong and Outrage."[49] Philadelphia minister Archibald Cummings stated that "where *Princes* Protect and Defend their Subjects, and injure them not in their *legal Rights* and *Liberties*, the Subjects are bound to Reverence and Obey their Princes."[50] Such *"reciprocal Duties"* were "founded on the eternal respects of things; for natural Equity, plain Reason, and the unavoidable necessities of our state and condition, exact and require them."[51] Because kings were the "Instruments in the Hand of Providence," it was incumbent upon their subjects to pray for them. In doing so, "we are at the same time in the most Effectual and Successful manner promoting our own Interest."[52] In short, so long as the king evinced a paternal care for the needs of his subjects, they were obliged by God, by society and by their own self-interest, to offer him the allegiance, obedience and protection that good children afforded their parents.

Colonists saw the hand of Providence at work in the events that they associated with their kings. Just as a divine hand and a Protestant wind had brought William, Prince of Orange, to England to deliver the English world from Popery and slavery in 1688, Providence continued to bless Englishmen into the eighteenth century. Colonial writers viewed the Hanoverian succession as a providential stroke that guaranteed a new dynasty of good Protestant rulers to Englishmen wherever they might reside.[53] In 1746, "the GOD of BATTLES" intervened on the field at Culloden in Scotland, insuring victory to George II's son William, the Duke of Cumberland, and his army over Charles Edward Stuart, the Young Pretender, thus preserving the continuation of Hanover rule.[54] Royal events were prodigious, sometimes even causing effects far away in the provinces at the fringe of the Empire. The editor of the *New England Weekly Journal* noted that, after the celebration of the accession of George II in Boston "a welcome *rain*, after a time of much heat and drought put an end to the Ceremony." He observed that "a like merciful rain" had auspiciously fallen, ending a prolonged drought "on the evening of the Day when George *the First* was proclaim'd here." This Bostonian concluded with the hope that "the royal smiles" and "happy influences of" the new monarch's "wise and just Government" might fall on all of his dominions, Massachusetts in particular, "like the rain upon the mown grass & as showers that water the earth; that in his days the righteous may flourish."[55]

As Whig notions of royal patriarchy developed, so also the idea grew that, although British kings were not specifically chosen by God, but governed by the consent of the British people through their representative legislatures, good kings were, nevertheless, "raised up by divine Appointment and Providence to Rule and Judge the People."[56] The phrase "his sacred majesty" was employed as a title for British kings. The notion of assigning divine approval and even status to rulers who were also assumed to hold their office and prerogatives by the election and consent of those whom they ruled may seem paradoxical to the modern reader; however, ministers found a precedent for this new model of divine kingship in the Old Testament story of the establishment of a monarchy over the Children of Israel.[57] "When they had become a settled Nation," John Barnard said, "in the Land which God had promised to their Fathers," the Israelites chose "to come under a *Monarchical* Form of Government."[58] In 1754, Jonathan Mayhew cited biblical precedent to illustrate the legitimacy of the Hanoverian succession when he noted that after the establishment of monarchy in Israel:

> the crown, instead of descending uniformly to the elder branch of the male line, was often bestowed on a younger; sometimes transferred to another family; and sometimes even into another tribe—and this not without divine approbation.[59]

Colonial ministers and writers adopted a curious mixture of scriptural authority and English Whig political principles to forge a synthesis that, while hostile to the Stuart notion of divine right, nevertheless insisted that a good monarch, though chosen by the consent of those ruled and constrained by Parliament, was the anointed of God and held both secular prerogatives and divine authority. Barnard argued that, since the king was placed at the head of government by the people, a bad king might be removed by the people; however, a good king, howsoever chosen, was both anointed and ordained by God.[60] An "Independent" puts the point rather succinctly:

Men are made *kings* by the Grace of God,—but not *tyrants*, because they have not the grace of God in them. And that *grace of God* which makes kings comes by means of the *good will of the people*. Those that hold their power by this right, as the *present royal family do*, have the best, the justest, and the most natural right in the world. Properly speaking, men are made kings by *the grace of the people*, and they behave as worthy of such an office, by *the grace of God*.[61]

In short, for Englishmen, only *good* kings could hold the position of God's anointed before their subjects, and good kings were those rulers who were solicitous of the religion, liberties and property of those over whom they ruled.

Good rulers were assigned a status even greater than divine ordination. Good rulers were "God's Vicegerents [sic], and therefore called Gods."[62] For Samuel Mather, "with respect to the Power, Rule and Authority, which they have over others," kings resembled "*the Almighty* who is the Original of all Dominion, Might and Majesty."[63] While some writers described the divine, or divinely inspired, attributes of kings, others stressed the kingly attributes of God. Jonathan Edwards, admitting that "all things upon earth are insufficient to represent to us" the glory of God and of Heaven, employed the language of monarchy to describe them "because we are most apt to [be] affected by those things which we have seen with our own eyes, and heard with our own ears, and had experience of."[64] Edwards noted that the capital cities of kingdoms "are commonly, above all others, stately and beautiful" and Heaven, being the seat of the King of Kings, was the most beautiful of capitals as it displayed the glory of God.[65] Like a good English king, Edwards stated, Christ governs by laws that are "exceedingly tending in their own nature to the peace, comfort, joy and happiness of his people."[66] Christ's government provides his subjects with the "greatest liberty," and the Holy Ghost "rules over his subjects as a father amongst his dear children, . . . his commands are but fatherly counsels."[67] Benjamin Colman also invoked the qualities of a good king in describing God. As the King of Kings, He held his sovereignty by inalienable right.[68] He is a benevolent monarch, providing "Protection, Defense or Maintenance" to his subjects.[69] God is the law made manifest, who like earthly kings, distributes dignity and rewards to the righteous and punishes the wicked, "thus the Lord is our King, the Lord is our Judge."[70] Significantly, both

Edwards and Colman characterized God primarily as a benefactor, solicitous of the cares of His subjects—a far cry from the vengeful God who might visit "nothing but horrible disorders, agonies, and vexations" upon his strayed children.[71] He is an English Whig God, portrayed with the stern but benevolent and paternal attributes of a good English king, not the unrestrained and often arbitrary and wrathful ruler of the Old Testament and the Jeremiad. God's benevolence was all the more remarkable because, unlike good English kings, His powers and prerogatives were unrestrained. He had no Parliament to protect His subjects from arbitrary rule. There could be no revolution, and no abdication in His Kingdom. God truly ruled by "inalienable right," and, as the creator and preserver of all things in Heaven and on Earth, He exercised "Government and Rule over all."[72] God's Throne rested upon the pinnacle of the metaphysical pyramid that was the "Great Chain of Being," and, given that there was no possible appeal to temper His wrath, His benevolence was all the more wonderful and worthy of emulation by his ministers, the kings of the Earth.

Colonial political writers rarely considered the likelihood that any future British ruler might become a tyrant so long as the Settlement of 1688 and the Hanoverian succession held; however, should a Stuart somehow return to the throne—a very real threat in the minds of American colonists throughout the period—there was general consensus that tyranny must surely follow. Indeed, fears of the restoration of a Roman Catholic ruler were a fundamental part of the political ideology of most Englishmen, and especially of His Majesty's colonists in North America. Colonists, like the majority of their English cousins, equated tyrannical government with Catholic monarchs in general and with the Stuarts in particular. Colonial ministers and editorialists asked what could be more terrifying than a Catholic Stuart prince who was educated on absolutist principles by his father at the court of a French monarch? American divines used the reign of James II and the administration of his servants in the Dominion of New England to illustrate the cataclysmic consequences of a Stuart restoration. Charles Chauncy wrote, "Our Fathers groaned under the oppressive Burden of a *popish* and tyrannical Power . . . [when] the then Governor of Massachusetts, Sir Edmond Andros, unhappily copied after the Measures of his Royal Master."[73] So might new governors reduce a new generation of Anglo-Americans to oppression and slavery under a Stuart Restoration. William Dawson of William and Mary College agreed that, "should it prevail (which Heaven avert) Life, Liberty, and Fortune would be Precarious."[74] A New Yorker expanded on the theme, stating that under a restored Stuart king "our Lives, Laws, Liberties, Properties, Wives,

Children, and Religion must be sacrificed."[75] Should the Pretender succeed, said Maryland Anglican minister and poet Thomas Cradock, "how miserable had we been! better by far not to have lived . . . , we should have been governed with a Rod of Iron;" forced to submit to a Catholic Tyrant, "had we been so obstinately honest as to have stood to this, then what remains for us but the *Smithfield* fire?"[76] For American colonists the success of the Jacobite cause augured nothing more than a return to the misery and oppression that their forefathers had experienced under the Pretender's father, James II, and a renewed threat to their Protestant faith.

Most English Protestants viewed the Glorious Revolution as a triumph over Roman Catholicism. English Protestants in North America believed that William had saved the nation from Popery and that his successors were the defenders and protectors of English Protestantism. The king of England was, after all, the "Defender of the Faith," and colonists evidently took this royal title seriously. Americans celebrated the Hanoverian succession because the German line had impeccable Protestant credentials. The Hanovers were "a powerful Bulwark of the Protestant interest in Europe."[77] British subjects considered the Hanoverian succession a guarantee against the encroachment of Popery. American colonists feared Catholicism as much as Englishmen did at home. Memories of the persecutions of English Protestants under Mary Tudor and the "popish plots" of James II colored American colonists' perceptions of Catholicism as much as those of Englishmen across the Atlantic. These fears were brought into starker contrast by the fact that the English colonies in North America were surrounded on all sides by foreign Catholic powers that periodically challenged Britain for control of Anglo-America and thus threatened their very existence. Colonists' fears of Catholic incursion from France and Spain increased between 1715 and 1746, because those two nations were seen as allies to the Stuart pretenders who threatened the security and religion of England. Colonists, like many Englishmen, dreaded the possibility of a Stuart restoration that would inevitably be accompanied by the curse of Popery and the undoing of William's Revolution.[78] George Whitefield summed up the sense of foreboding that Englishmen had about their religious future under a restored Roman Catholic Stuart Pretender. While Stuart tyranny chiefly threatened bodily harm and thus "must necessarily terminate in the grave," English Protestants must also suffer "Spiritual mischiefs." England and the colonies would be overrun by "whole swarms of monks, Dominicans and friars, like so many locusts" and "foreign titular bishops," would fill England's sees. English universities would teach "all the superstitions of the church at Rome." Protestant Bibles would be taken away, "and ignorance every where set up as the mother of devotion." How long, Whitefield asked Philadelphians, would English Protestants be able to keep their faith? How soon would it be before their new Catholic masters instituted the inquisition, replete with all "the tortures which a bigotted zeal, guided by cruel principles, could possibly invent? How soon would that mother of harlots have made herself once more drunk with the blood of saints?"[79] Whitefield announced to his Philadelphia listeners that these horrors were put off because George II's son, William, the Duke of Cumberland, "like his glorious predecessor the Prince of Orange, has once more delivered three kingdoms from the dread of popish cruelty and arbitrary power."[80]

If William III was seen as a defender of Protestantism in general, Dissenting Protestants viewed the Hanovers as special friends. Through much of her reign, Queen Anne's government, while reasonably tolerant of dissenting sects until 1714, had been generally staunchly Tory and Anglican. In that year, while the Queen was on her death bed, Bolingbroke used the old Tory slogan, "The Church in Danger," to promote his own primacy in government with the passage of the Occasional Conformity and Schism Acts.[81] Dissenters expected better treatment from George I, who had promised to help them.[82] Dissenting leaders praised the new German house for their Protestant tolerance as much as for their wisdom as rulers, and their sentiment on the subject appears to have speedily crossed the Atlantic. "We see ascending the throne a KING" Cotton Mather wrote of George I, "in whose Dominions *Lutherans* and *Calvinists* live Easily with One Another . . . [who] will discern and Pursue the TRUE *Interest of the Nations*; and give the Best Friends of His House and the Nations, cause to Rejoice."[83]

George I, himself a Lutheran, had a reputation for religious tolerance toward his German subjects, and his new Whig government wished to reward Dissenters for their support of their party and king. Thus, Whig leaders like James Stanhope and Robert Walpole saw both justice and political gain in maintaining a more liberal policy toward Calvinist Dissenters and Quakers in Britain. Parliament repealed the Occasional Conformity Act and the hated Schism Act in 1718 and two years later attempted to reform the established Church in order to bring at least some Dissenters back into the fold. The government closed the 1719 Convocation when Whig clergy under the leadership of Bishop Hoadly failed to execute its church reform measures because of High Church opposition in the Lower House. After that embarrassment, the Whig government generally ignored laws meant to force conformity and

Anglican church attendance among Dissenters.[84] In 1732, Robert Walpole was able to get an annual grant of £500, the *Regium Domum*, to be dispersed among the widows of Dissenting ministers, and from 1728 on he promoted annual Indemnity Acts that gave some protection to Dissenters who were in office but could not take the sacrament of the Church of England.[85] Toleration of dissent and Church reform was one of the political footballs of the first half of the eighteenth century. Ministerial leaders continually tried to maintain a wider coalition to preserve their governments by trying to balance the interests and needs of Dissenters and Old Whigs against those of Church Whigs and staunchly Anglican country backbenchers. Often, as in the case of Walpole's pre-election policies of 1735, these flirtations were brief and disappointing for the Dissenters and Old Whigs. Nevertheless, they were frequent enough to preserve the impression, sometimes undeserved, that the Hanovers and their ministries supported the dissenting religious interests.[86] American Dissenters were gratified at the government's policies of toleration and credited their king with the efforts. Massachusetts Governor Jonathan Belcher even went so far as to remind the colonial assembly that, if King George II could exercise his "Royal Indulgence" and tolerate English Dissenters at home, the Massachusetts assembly should surely do no less in a colony founded as a haven for dissenting Protestants.[87]

As the protectors of Protestant religion, the Hanovers simultaneously became the protectors of English liberty. Just as Popery and slavery were inextricably bound, so also Protestantism and liberty went together. Hanover rulers quickly acquired a better reputation in the colonies as rulers who were solicitous of the rights and liberties of their subjects than they had at home, where there was still an active Jacobite movement hostile to the Whig political ascendancy and fearful for the preservation of the High Church, as well as a constant "highly vocal and rancorous" Whig opposition movement.[88] From the beginning of the reign of George I, colonial political sermons reflected support for the Hanover ascendency. In his eulogy for Queen Anne, Cotton Mather dwelt in detail on the attributes of the new Hanover king.[89] In proceeding sermons New England divines characterized George I and George II as ideal English monarchs, benefactors to their subjects, solicitous, paternal rulers, who zealously guarded and protected the rights and religion of Englishmen. Colonial religious leaders of all flavors praised the German monarchs and frequently tied their religious and political liberty to the continuation of the Hanover line. Samuel Sewell, as moderator for the 1747 convention of Massachusetts ministers, remarked that, "[w]e chearfully rely on your

Majesty's Royal Goodness, under God . . . to protect us and our Churches in the Possession of our invaluable Rights." Sewell went on to link the continuing security of their liberties with the "longer Posperity [sic] of your Majesty's Reign, and the Continuance of your Crown in your Royal Family, through the Generations."[90] Ministers and newspapers frequently characterized the Hanover rulers as being especially solicitous of the rights of their colonial subjects, especially in those times when the Hanover succession appeared to colonists to be in danger.[91]

The Rebellions of 1715 and 1745 lent an urgency to fears of a Stuart return, and fears of slavery and Popery reverberated through the texts of colonial writers throughout the mid-eighteenth century. This threat, combined with the tendency among some Anglican clergy in the 1750s to elevate the execution of Charles I to martyrdom and revive Filmerian notions of kingship, gave American clergy of all denominations food for both thought and declamation. The source of ideas of absolute monarchy associated with Stuart rule—"the hereditary, inalienable right of succession; of the despotic unlimited powers of kings by the immediate grant of heaven," according to Jonathan Mayhew, were not "drawn from holy Scriptures but from a far less pure and sacred fountain . . . from him who was a politician from the beginning."[92] Mayhew was not the only minister in America (or Britain) during the mid-eighteenth century to revive visions of the fires of Smithfield, the admonitions of Pym and Prynne in the 1630s and 40s, and the rhetoric of the Popish Plot and the Revolution of 1688.[93] "Would one that brings his Religion from ROME," asked Charles Chauncy of the Pretender, "turn enemy to the POPE, and encourage and promote the Cause that is opposite to his and subversive to it? Had not the *Nation* full experience of this in the Reign of Queen Mary, not withstanding her Promises to the contrary?"[94] In general, however, so long as a Hanover was on the throne, fears of arbitrary rule were dismissed. As John Gordon of Annapolis stated of George II:

> Blessed be God, we are favoured with a KING, who may truly be stiled the indulgent FATHER of his people, under whose administration we may worship God according to the dictates of our conscience, and have none to terrify and disturb us, . . . [we] *may dwell under our own vines and figtrees, and have none to make us afraid.*[95]

As a result of the development of Whig notions of kingship, the English ruler became an active participant along with his subjects in the preservation of the liberty, property and religion of those under his care.

The pre-Glorious Revolution stereotype of the king as "dread sovereign," distant, aloof, and independent, an estate unto himself, and hence always a potential danger to the well-being of his subjects, gave way to the Whig characterization of the king as an active participant in the pursuance of the first great aim and goal of government, the preservation of "the true rights, liberties, and privileges of the subject."[96] Although the ideal Whig ruler was kind and benevolent, solicitous of the liberties of his subjects–in short a "nursing father"–colonists still characterized their Hanoverian rulers in terms that the staunchest enthusiast of the divine right of kings would not find inappropriate. Good English kings ruled with a divine authority. They were ministers of God among their people.

Yet the divinity of Whig kings was conditional. It was contingent upon their good behavior and adhered to the ruler only so long as he continued to govern by law and for the good of those whom God had placed under his care. The king and the people were principals in a contract, what Richard Bushman calls a "protection-and-allegiance covenant," in which the king was obligated to rule by the laws of the nation and to protect and defend the lives, liberties, property and Protestant faith of his subjects. Britons, in turn, were obliged to obey and serve the king, to pray for him, and to help, where necessary and proper, to preserve his powers and prerogatives.[97] From the Hanoverian Accession up to the summer of 1776, American colonists imagined their king to be a benevolent protector, a powerful ally, who, godlike by definition, never slept, never died, and could do no wrong. The protection-allegiance covenant gave colonists an ally against those who would deprive them of their rights, even when, as was often the case, the people's adversaries were the agents of the king himself. The covenant allied the king with his assembly in each colony, creating a sort of "king in parliament" in miniature in each of his Majesty's provinces and uniting king and people in the defense of the liberties, property, and religion of the English subjects in the King's possessions far away in North America.

Notes

1. Daniel Lewes, *Good Rulers the Fathers of their People, and the Marks of Honour Due Them* . . . [Massachusetts election sermon] (Boston: John Draper, 1748), 23.

2. Ebenezer Gay, *The Duty of a People to Pray for and Praise their Rulers . . .* (Boston: Thomas Fleet, 1730), 25.

3. *Samuel Johnson's Dictionary of the English Language*, Alexander Chalmers, ed. (Rep. London: Studio Editions, 1994), 617.

4. "Address of the Justices of the County of Kent to the King . . ., February 7, 1689[/90],", "Proceedings of the Council of Maryland," *Archives of Maryland*, William Hand Browne, ed. (Baltimore: Isaac Friedenwald for the Maryland Historical Society, 1890), 8:143.

5. Increase Mather, *A Brief Account of the Agents of New-England*, in *Narratives of the Insurrections, 1675-1690*, Charles M. Andrews, ed. (New York: Charles Scribner's Sons, 1915), 292-293.

6. See Richard L. Bushman, *King and People in Provincial Massachusetts* (Chapel Hill: University of North Carolina Press, 1985), 22; Gordon Wood, *The Creation of the American Republic, 1776-1787* (New York: W.W. Norton & Co., 1969), 269-270. For the English equivalents of the idea, see J.R. Western, *Monarchy and Revolution: The English State in the 1680s* (Totowa, New Jersey: Rowman & Littlefield, 1972), 30, and H.T. Dickinson, *Liberty and Property*, 75-78.

7. For a compilation of Marylanders' complaints against the proprietary government of Lord Baltimore, see "Mariland's Grevances Wiy The Have Taken Op Arms," Beverly McAnear, ed., *The Journal of Southern History*, 8:3 (1942), 392-409. For studies of proprietary government in Maryland, see James Hugh, "A Facet of Sovereignty: The Proprietary Governor and the Maryland Charter," *Maryland Colonial Historical Magazine*, 55 (June, 1960), 67-81; and Francis Edgar Sparks, "Causes of the Maryland Revolution of 1689," *Johns Hopkins University Studies in Historical and Political Science*, Herbert Adams, ed. 14th Series, 11-12, (November-December, 1896), 7-108. Studies of the causes of the Maryland Revolution include Michael Kammen, "The Causes of the Maryland Revolution of 1689," *Maryland Historical Magazine*, 55 (December, 1960), 293-333; Lovejoy, *Glorious Revolution*, 70-97, 257-274; and Michael D. De Michele, "The Glorious Revolution in Maryland: A Study in the Provincial Revolution of 1689" (PhD. diss., Pennsylvania State University, 1967).

8. See *D.H.N.Y.*, 2:9, 14, 20, 30, 34-35; and *Loyalty Vindicated*, Andrews, *Narratives*, 386, 388, 392.

9. Mr. Coode to Mr. Bacon, February 8, $16^{89}/_{90}$, *Maryland Archives*, 8:169.

10. "The Answer of John Coode and Kenelm Cheseldine Agents and Commissioners from the Late Convention of Their Majesties Province of Maryland . . .," *Maryland Archives*, 8:227.

11. "Some Objections Against the Pretended Government in Connecticut," *Cal. St. P.*, 13:705-706.

12. C.D., *New England's Faction Discovered*, Andrews, *Narratives*, 265, 257.

13. Nicholas Taney to Madam Barbara Smith, September 14, 1689, *Maryland Archives*, 8:119.

14. Richard Hill to Lord Baltimore, September 20, 1689, *Maryland Archives*, 8:122.

15. "Address of the Protestants of Calvert County to His Maj^tie," *Maryland Archives*, 8:130-131.

16. John Adams, "On the Canon and the Feudal Law," *Works of John Adams*, Charles Francis Adams, ed. (Boston: Little & Brown, 1850), 3:456.

17. Cotton Mather, *The Present State of New England* . . . (Boston: Samuel Green, 1690), 33-34.

18. E.R. & S.S., *The Revolution in New England Justified, and the People there Vindicated from the Aspersions Cast upon them by Mr. Joseph Palmer, in his Pretended Answer to the Declaration, Published by the Inhabitants of Boston, and the Country Adjacent* . . . (Boston, 1691), 1.

19. Charles Chauncy, *A Counsel of Two Confederate Kings to Set the Son of Tabeal on the Throne of Israel . . . A Sermon Occasion'd by the Present Rebellion in Favour of the Pretender . . .*, (Boston: D. Gookin, 1746), 28. See also John Gordon, *A Sermon on the Suppression of the late Unnatural Rebellion* (Annapolis: Jonas Green, 1746), 18; John Swift, *Election Sermon* (Boston: B. Green, 1732), 13; and Charles Chauncy, *Civil Magistrates Must Be Just, Ruling in the Fear of God . . .* [Massachusetts election sermon] (Boston, 1748), 34.

20. *South Carolina Gazette*, April 29, 1732.

21. *Maryland Gazette*, October 30, 1755. For similar sentiments, see also "Killigrew's Political Maxims," *South Carolina Gazette*, July 13, 1747; Thomas Prince, *The People of New-England Put in Mind of the Righteous Acts of the Lord . . .*, (Boston, 1730), in A.W. Plumstead, *The Wall and the Garden: Selected Massachusetts Sermons, 1670-1775* (Minneapolis: University of Minnesota Press, 1968), 201; John Barnard, *The Throne Established by Righteousness . . .* (Boston, 1734), Plumstead, *The Wall and the Garden*, 276; [Peter Annet?], *A Discourse on Government and Religion. Signed by an Independent* (Boston: D. Fowler, 1750), 18, 42; and Samuel Cook, *An Election Sermon* (Boston, 1770), Plumstead, *The Wall and the Garden*, 340-341.

22. John Adams, "Novanglus," *Works of John Adams*, 4:114.

23. Abraham Keteltas, *God Arising and Pleading the People's Cause . . .*, (Newburyport, Massachusetts, 1777), in Ellis Sandoz, *Political Sermons of the Founding Era, 1730-1805* (Indianapolis: Liberty Press, 1990), 596. See also Moses Mather, *America's Appeal to an Impartial World* (Hartford, 1775), Sandoz, *Political Sermons*, 453, 476; Samuel Cooper, *A Sermon on the Day of the Commencement of the Constitution . . .* (Boston[?], 1780), Sandoz, *Political Sermons*, 639; and Elhanan Winchester, *A Century Sermon on the Glorious Revolution* (London, 1788), Sandoz, *Political Sermons*, 995-996.

24. Cotton Mather, *The Glorious Throne . . .* (Boston: B. Green 1714), 33.

25. Benjamin Colman, *A Sermon Preach'd at Boston in New England, on Thursday the 23rd of August, 1716. Being the Day of Public Thanksgiving, for the Suppression of the Late Vile and Traitorous Rebellion in Great Britain* (Boston: Fleet & Crump, 1716), 6.

26. For Weddings, see *Boston Weekly Rehearsal*, June 9, 1733, August 13, 1733; *Virginia Gazette*, October 1, 1736; *Pennsylvania Journal*, February 21, 1744. For Deaths, see *Virginia Gazette*, March 1, 1737, March 24, 1737, April 7, 1737; *Pennsylvania Gazette*, January 15, 1761, January 26, 1761; Cotton Mather, *The Glorious Throne;* Samuel Checkley, *The Duty of a People to Lay to Heart and Lament the Death of a Great KING . . .* (Boston: Benjamin Gray, 1727); Thomas Prince, *A Sermon on the Sorrowful Occasion of the Death of His Late Majesty King George of Blessed Memory . . .* (Boston, 1727); Jonathan Mayhew, *A Sermon Preached at Boston in New England, May 26, 1751. Occasioned by the Much Lamented Death of his Royal Highness, Frederick, Prince of Wales . . .* (Boston: Richard Draper, 1751).

27. See "From the Portland Gazette, October 21, 1745," *Maryland Gazette*, February 25, 1746; *New York Weekly Journal*, January 17, $17^{37}/_{38}$; "Twelve Good Reasons for Rejecting the Pretender, Which Ought to Be Kept in the Study of Every Protestant," *New York Weekly Journal*, February 17, 1746; "Answer to the Pretender's Declaration," *Pennsylvania Gazette*, February 11, 1746.

28. Gordon Wood, *The Radicalism of the American Revolution* (New York: Alfred A. Knopf, Inc., 1992), 12, *passim*. See also Jerrilyn Greene Marston, *King and Congress: The Transfer of Political Legitimacy, 1774-1776* (Princeton, University Press, 1987), 23, *passim*; and Bushman, *King and People*, 19-22, 46-48.

29. Wood, *Radicalism*, 19. See also Bushman, *King and People*, 18-20.

30. Wood, *Radicalism*, 112.

31. Edwin J. Perkins, *The Economy of Colonial America*, 2nd ed. (New York: Columbia University Press, 1988), 212. See also Theodore Draper, *A Struggle for Power: The American Revolution* (New York: Times Books, A Division of Random House, 1996), 123-127; Alice Hanson Jones, *Wealth of a Nation to Be* (New York: Columbia University Press, 1980), 67-68, 72. David Hackett Fischer remarks on the "truncated system of social orders in New England" and adds that Virginia's more stratified social order was based less on economic determinants than on "worthy descent, virtue and valor, reputation and fame" (David Hackett Fischer, *Albion's Seed: Four British Folkways in America* (New York: Oxford University Press, 1989), 383-384). See also Rhys Isaac, *Transformation of Virginia, 1740-1790* (New York: W.W. Norton & Co., 1988), 118. Richard Hofstadter argued that the significant feature of American colonial society was that the preponderance of the population fell somewhere into a wide middle class. See Richard Hofstadter, *America at 1750: A Social Portrait* (New York: Vintage Books, 1973), 132-135. Robert Brown and other historians note the fairly broad based and essentially democratic features of the American colonial class structure. See Robert Brown, *Middle-Class Democracy and the Revolution in Massachusetts, 1691-1780* (Ithaca, New York: Cornell University Press, for the American Historical Association, 1955); Robert E. and Katherine T. Brown, *Virginia, 1705-1780: Democracy or Aristocracy?* (East Lansing: Michigan State University Press, 1964); Daniel Boorstin, *The Genius of American Politics* (Chicago: University of

Chicago Press, 1953) and *The Americans: The Colonial Experience* (New York: Random House, 1958).

32. These tensions have been the focus of works by Progressive and neo-Progressive historians. For a few examples, see Carl L. Becker, *The History of Political Parties in the Province of New York* (Madison, Wisconsin: University of Wisconsin Press, 1909); J. Franklin Jameson, *The American Revolution Considered as a Social Movement* (Princeton: Princeton University Press, 1926); Arthur M. Schlesinger, *The Colonial Merchants and the American Revolution, 1762-1776* (New York, 1918); Allan Kulikoff, "The Progress of Inequality in Revolutionary Boston," *William and Mary Quarterly*, 3rd series, 28 (July, 1971), 375-412; Marc Egnal and Joseph Ernst, "An Economic Interpretation of the American Revolution," *William and Mary Quarterly*, 3rd series, 29 (January, 1972), 3-33; Gary B. Nash, *The Urban Crucible: The Northern Seaports and the Origins of the American Revolution* (Cambridge, Massachusetts: Harvard University Press, 1979); Kenneth Lockridge, *A New England Town: The First Hundred Years* (New York: W.W. Norton, 1985),150-159, *passim.;* and the recently published 1962 dissertation of Jesse Lemisch, *Jack Tar vs. John Bull: The Role of New York's Seamen in Precipitating the Revolution* (New York: Garland Publishing, 1997).

33. See Robert Filmer, *Patriarchia*, in *Two Treatises of Government, by John Locke. With a Supplement Patriarchia by Robert Filmer*, Thomas I. Cook, ed. (New York: Hafner Press, 1947), 281.

34. In *The Radicalism of the American Revolution*, Gordon Wood focuses on the more negative aspects of Early Modern familial relations and the analogous patriarchal political relationship between king and people. He stresses the inequality and dependency of paternalism, the "stark forms of unfreedom," and "other kinds of inferiority and dependence" of Early Modern family and monarchical society rather than the more protective and benign aspects of paternity within the family relationship (see Wood, *Radicalism*, 46-56). Wood notes that the American Revolution was, in part, the continuation of a "revolution against patriarchal society," that transformed parents from "arbitrary" to "limited monarchs" (149-156). Although Wood's assumptions about the liberalization and increasingly indulgent nature of parenthood through the late eighteenth and nineteenth centuries are valid and well supported by writers like Lawrence Stone and Daniel Blake Smith, Wood largely ignores that even in the earlier works by Americans of the Hanoverian Age, writers stressed the protective, benign and indulgent nature of the British monarch as patriarch. See Lawrence Stone, *The Family, Sex and Marriage in England, 1500-1800* (London: Weidenfeld & Nicholson, 1977); Daniel Blake Smith "Study of the Family in Early America," *William and Mary Quarterly*, 3rd Series, 39 (1982), 2-28; Karen Calvert, "Children in American Portraiture, 1670-1810," *William and Mary Quarterly*, 3rd Series, 39 (1982), 87-113.

35. Daniel Lewes, *Good Rulers*, 14,15.

36. Daniel Lewes, *Good Rulers*, 21.

37. Daniel Lewes, *Good Rulers*, 23.

38. Ebenezer Pemberton, *A Sermon Delivered at the Presbyterian Church in New York . . .* (New York: James Parker, 1746), 20. For a few other examples, see Ebenezer Gay, *The Character and Work of a Good Ruler, and Duty of an Obliged People . . .* [Massachusetts election sermon] (Boston: D. Gookin, 1745), 11; Daniel Lewes, *Good Rulers*, 25, *passim*; Samuel Mather, *A Funeral Discourse Preached on the Occasion of the Death of the High, Puissant, and Most Illustrious Prince Frederick Lewis, Prince of Great Britain . . .* (Boston: J. Draper, 1751), 27; Jonathan Mayhew, *A Sermon Preached at Boston*, 23; "To the Author," *New England Courant*, May 28, 1722; "Humble Address of the Maryland House of Delegates," *Maryland Gazette*, January 26, 1755.

39. Samuel Checkley, *The Duty of a People*, 14. See also Nathaniel Appleton, *The Cry of Oppression Where Judgement is Looked for . . .* (Boston: J. Draper, 1748), 13-15, 25; and "To the Honourable Cadwallader Colden . . . The Humble Address of the Council of His Majesty's Province of New York," *Pennsylvania Journal*, March 18, 1762.

40. Ebenezer Gay, *The Duty of a People to Pray for and Praise their Rulers . . .* (Boston: Thomas Fleet, 1730), 16, 19, 33.

41. Nathaniel Eells, *The Wise Ruler, a Loyal Subject . . .* [Connecticut election sermon, 1748] (Boston: Timothy Green),14.

42. Lewes, *Good Rulers*, 13. See also Samuel Mather, *A Funeral Discourse*, 27.

43. Lewes, *Good Rulers*, 24.

44. Nathaniel Hunn, *The Welfare of a Government Considered . . .* [Connecticut election sermon] (New London: Timothy Green, 1747), 9.

45. Nathaniel Hunn, *The Welfare of a Government Considered*, 9. See also Samuel Davies, *Religion and Patriotism the Constituents of a Good Soldier . . . Hanover County, Virginia, August 17, 1755 . . .* (Philadelphia: James Chattin, 1755), 3-4.

46. Rom. xiii, 2. Cited in Jonathan Mayhew, *Discourse Concerning Unlimited Submission . . .* (Boston: D. Fowle, 1750), in *Pamphlets of the American Revolution*, Bernard Bailyn, ed. (Cambridge, Massachusetts: Belknap Press, 1965), 215.

47. Jonathan Mayhew, *Discourse Concerning Unlimited Submission*, Bailyn, *Pamphlets*, 226.

48. See Benjamin Colman, *A Sermon Preach'd at Boston in New England, on Thursday the 23rd of August, 1716. Being the Day of Public Thanksgiving, for the Suppression of the Late Vile and Traitorous Rebellion in Great Britain* (Boston: Fleet & Crump, 1716), 2-4; Ebenezer Gay, *The Duty of a People*, 18-19; John Swift, *Election Sermon*, 13; Benjamin Colman, *God is a Great King* (Boston: S. Kneeland & T. Green, 1733), 4; Nathaniel Hunn, *The Welfare of the Government Considered*, 6-7; Nathaniel Eells, *The Wise Ruler*, 17-18; William Balch, *A Public*

Spirit, as Express'd in Praying for the Peace and Seeking the Good of Jerusalem, Recommended to Rulers and People ... [Massachusetts election sermon] (Boston, 1749), 13-14.

49. Ebenezer Gay, *The Duty of a People*, 18-19.

50. Archibald Cummings, *The Character of a Righteous Ruler. A Sermon Upon the Death of the Honourable Patrick Gordon* ... *Christ's Church, Philadelphia, August 8, 1736* ... (Philadelphia: Andrew Bradford, 1736), 10. See also Ebenezer Gay, *The Character and Work of Good Rulers*, 14; Nathaniel Hunn, *The Welfare of the Government Considered*, 7-8.

51. Jared Eliot, *Give Cesar His Due: or, the Obligation that Subjects Are Under to Their Civil Rulers* ... *A Sermon Preached before the General Assembly of the Colony of Connecticut* ..., *May 11th, 1736* (New London: Timothy Green, 1738), 18. See also Ebenezer Gay, *The Character and Work of Good Rulers*, 13; Charles Chauncy, *The Counsel of Two Confederate Kings*, 43; John Gordon, *A Sermon*, 30.

52. Eliot, *Give Cesar His Due*, 16.

53. See Benjamin Colman, *A Sermon Preach'd at Boston*, 7; Ebenezer Gay, *The Duty of the People*, 33; Archibald Cummings, *The Character of a Righteous Ruler*, 13; Thomas Prince, *The People of New England*, Plumstead, *The Wall and the Garden*, 209; John Gordon, *A Sermon*, 18; Charles Chauncy, *The Counsel of Two Confederate Kings*, 32; Mr. Thornton [sic], "To His Highness the Prince of Wales. An Ode," *South Carolina Gazette*, December 15, 1737; "A Short Eulogium on His Present Majesty King George II," *Maryland Gazette*, December 31, 1746; "The Humble Address of the Pastors of the Churches in His Majesty's Province of the Massachusetts Bay in New England, Assembled in Boston, at their Annual Convention, May 25, 1743," *New York Weekly Journal*, February 2, 1747; "Humble Address of the Synod of *Philadelphia*, Conven'd May 25, 1743," *Pennsylvania Gazette*, June 9, 1743.

54. Ebenezer Pemberton, *A Sermon*, 7. See also Charles Chauncy, *The Counsel of Two Confederate Kings*, 28; "Victory Celebration at Annapolis, July 22, 1746," *Pennsylvania Gazette*, July 31, 1746; "Address of the House of Representatives of the Colony of Nova Caesaria, or New Jersey, in America ...," *Pennsylvania Gazette*, June 4, 1747. George Whitefield, though English, conveyed similar sentiments in a sermon he preached in Philadelphia shortly after hearing news of the victory at Culloden. See George Whitefield, *Britain's Mercies, and Britain's Duty; Represented in a Sermon Preach'd at the New-Building in Philadelphia* ... (Boston: Kneeland & Green, 1746), in Sandoz, *Political Sermons*, 125.

55. *The New England Weekly Journal*, August 21, 1727.

56. Nathaniel Eells, *The Wise Ruler*, 1. See also Benjamin Colman, *A Sermon Preach'd at Boston*, 6; John Hancock, *Rulers Should be Benefactors* ... (Boston, 1722), 3; Edward Holyoke, *Integrity and Religion to be Principally Regarded by Such as Design Others to Stations of Public Trust* [Massachusetts election sermon, 1736] (Boston: J. Draper, 1736), 13; Daniel Lewes, *Good Rulers*, 8; and "The

Humble Address of the Synod of *Philadelphia*, Conven'd May 25, 1743," *Pennsylvania Gazette*, June 9, 1743.

57. I Samuel 8.

58. John Barnard, *The Throne Established by Righteousness . . .* (Boston, 1734), Plumstead, *The Wall and the Garden*, 238. See also Charles Chauncy, *The Counsel of Two Confederate Kings*, 32. For comparisons of Hanover kings to David, see Benjamin Colman, *Fidelity to Christ . . .* (Boston: T. Fleet, 1727), 2-3; John Barnard, *The Throne Established*, Plumstead, *The Wall and the Garden*, 247; Ebenezer Gay, *The Character and Work of a Good Ruler*, 28; and "Observations," *Virginia Gazette*, July 3, 1746.

59. Jonathan Mayhew, *An Election Sermon*. May 29th, 1754, Plumstead, *The Wall and the Garden*, 292.

60. John Barnard, *The Throne Established*, Plumstead, *The Wall and the Garden*, 243-244. See also "The Chronicle of the *Queen* of *Hungary* with the mighty Acts of GEORGE King of *England* at the Battle of Dettingen," *Pennsylvania Journal*, December 15, 1743.

61. [Peter Annet?], *A Discourse on Government*, 16.

62. Jared Eliot, *Give Cesar his Due*, 16. See also John Hancock, *Rulers Should be Benefactors*, 3; Ebenezer Gay, *The Duty of a People*, 25; and Jonathan Mayhew, *A Discourse Occasioned by the Death of King George II. And the Happy Accession of His Majesty King George III* (Boston, 1761), 30-34; "To the Author," *New England Courant*, May 28, 1722.

63. Samuel Mather, *The Fall of the Mighty Lamented. A Funeral Discourse Upon the Death of Her most Excellent Majesty Wilhelmina Dorothea Carolina* (Boston, 1738), 11.

64. Jonathan Edwards, *Nothing on Earth Can Represent the Glories of Heaven*, in *The Works of Jonathan Edwards*, Kenneth P. Minkema, ed. (New Haven: Yale University Press, 1997), 14:139-140.

65. Edwards, *Nothing on Earth*, 14:141.

66. Jonathan Edwards, *The Threefold Work of the Holy Ghost, Edwards' Works*, 14: 427.

67. Edwards, *The Threefold Work*, 14:432.

68. Benjamin Colman, *God is a Great King . . .* (Boston: S. Kneeland & T. Green, 1733), 2-3.

69. Colman, *God is a Great King*, 3. See also Thomas Prince, *The People of New England*, Plumstead, *The Wall and the Garden*, 208; Samuel Cook, *An Election Sermon* (Boston: Edes & Gill, 1770), Plumstead, *The Wall and the Garden*, 335; Samuel Wigglesworth, *God's Promise to an Obedient People, of Victory Over Their Enemies* (Boston: S. Kneeland, 1755), 2, and *The Blessedness of Such as Trust in* CHRIST *the King Whom* GOD *Hath Exalted* (Boston: S. Kneeland, 1755), 9, 24-25.

70. Colman, *God is a Great King*, 4

71. Cotton Mather, *The Way to Prosperity*... [Massachusetts election sermon, 1689] (Boston: Richard Pierce, 1690), Plumstead, *The Wall and the Garden*, 129. See also Edward Holyoke, *Integrity and Religion*, 13.

72. Coleman, *God is a Great King*, 2-3.

73. Charles Chauncy, *The Counsel of Two Confederate Kings*, 28. See also John Barnard (Harvard 1709), *The Presence of the Great God in the Assembly of Political Rulers*... [Massachusetts election sermon, 1746] (Boston: J. Draper), 12-13.

74. "Open Letter to the Clergy of Virginia from William Dawson of William and Mary College," *Virginia Gazette*, Jan. 16, 1746.

75. "Twelve Good Reasons for Rejecting the Pretender, Which ought to be Kept in the Study of Every Protestant," *New York Weekly Journal*, Feb. 17, 1746.

76. Thomas Cradock, *Two Sermons. . . Preached on the Occasion of the Suppression of the Scotch Rebellion*... (Annapolis, 1747), 9. Under Mary Tudor, Protestants were burned at the stake at Smithfield which became an English symbol for Protestant martyrdom. See also John Barnard (Harvard 1709), *The Presence of the Great God*, 11-12; Charles Chauncy, *The Counsel of Two Confederate Kings*, 24; and George Whitefield, *Britain's Mercies*, Sandoz, *Political Sermons*, 126-127.

77. Edward Holyoke, *Integrity and Religion*, 13. See also Charles Chauncy, *The Counsel of Two Confederate Kings*, 43; John Gordon, *A Sermon*, 30; Ebenezer Pemberton, *A Sermon*, 22; George Whitefield, *Britain's Mercies*, Sandoz, *Political Sermons*, 125; "Governor Belcher's Speech to the Massachusetts Assembly, February 10, 1731," *Pennsylvania Gazette*, February 10, 1731; "Governor of New-York's Speech to the General Assembly, April 15,1741," *General Magazine*, April, 1741; "The Humble Address of the Synod of Philadelphia, conven'd May 25, 1743," *Pennsylvania Gazette*, June 9, 1743; "Address of the Rev. Presbyteries of New-Brunswick and New-Castle," *Pennsylvania Journal*, May 31, 1744; "From the *Portsmouth Gazette*, October 21, 1745," *Maryland Gazette*, February 25, 1746; "Celebration of the Duke of Cumberland's Victory, Annapolis," *Pennsylvania Gazette*, July 31, 1746.

78. See Charles Chauncy, *A Sermon Occasioned by the Present Rebellion*, 24; John Gordon, *A Sermon*, 12-17; Thomas Cradock, *Two Sermons*, 10; "Copy of a treaty between the Pretender and the King of France, (from a South Carolina Gazette Reader)," *South Carolina Gazette*, February 9, 1747; "Address of the House of Representatives or Nova-Caesaria, or New Jersey . . ., St. James, February 17, 1747," *Pennsylvania Gazette*, June 4, 1747; "Twelve Good Reasons," *New York Weekly Journal*, February 17, 1747; "From the *Portsmouth Gazette*, October 21, 1745," *Maryland Gazette*, February 25, 1746; "Open Letter to the Clergy of Virginia from William Dawson of William and Mary College," *Virginia Gazette*, January 11, 1746; "A Genuine Intercepted Letter, From Father Patrick Graham, Almoner and Confessor to the Pretender's Son, in Scotland, to Father Benedict Yorke, Titular Bishop of St. David's at Bath," *Virginia Gazette*, January 23, 1746.

79. George Whitefield, *Britain's Mercies,* Sandoz, *Political Sermons,* 127.

80. Whitefield, *Britain's Mercies,* 130. For a similar view of England under a restored Pretender, see "Cato's Vision," *New England Courant,* May 3, May 10, 1725; and Davies, *Religion and Patriotism,* 13.

81. The Occasional Conformity Act allowed dissenters to qualify for office if they took the Anglican communion intermittently. The act had been promoted by the Tories in order to draw country Whig Dissenters away from the Whigs. The Schism Act was primarily created for the purpose of excluding Dissenters from the universities. See Sir David Lindsay Keir, *The Constitutional History of Modern Britain Since 1485,* 9th ed. (New York: W.W. Norton, 1967), 284.

82. Owen, *The Eighteenth Century,* 10-11.

83. Cotton Mather, *The Glorious Throne,* 35. See also Benjamin Colman, *A Sermon Preached at Boston,* 13; Daniel Lewes, *Good Rulers,* 18, 25; Samuel Mather, *Funeral Sermon,* 28; and Jonathan Mayhew, *A Sermon Preached at Boston,* 29-30.

84. Mark Goldie, "The Nonjurors, Episcopacy, and the Origins of the Convocation Controversy," in *Ideology and Conspiracy: Aspects of Jacobitism, 1689-1759,* Eveline Cruickshanks, ed. (Edinburgh: John Donald Publishers Ltd., 1982), 17-18.

85. Owen, 39.

86. T.F. Kendrick, "Sir Robert Walpole, the Old Whigs and the Bishops, 1733-1736: A Study in Eighteenth-Century Parliamentary Politics," *The Historical Journal* 11: 3 (1968), 429-445.

87. Governor Belcher to the Massachusetts Assembly, *Pennsylvania Gazette,* September 24, 1730.

88. Jack P. Green, "The Gifts of Peace: Social and Economic Expansion and Development in the Periodization of the Early American Past, 1713-1763," in Jack P. Green, *Negotiated Authorities: Essays in Colonial Political and Constitutional History* (Charlottesville: University Press of Virginia, 1994), 98. Green states that "A number of international and metropolitan conditions," notably peace, political stability, and government promotion of the expansion of trade, especially under Walpole, positively impacted the American colonial economy and eased tensions between the colonies and London (99-100).

89. Cotton Mather, *The Glorious Throne,* 33, 35.

90. "The Humble Address of the Pastors of the Churches . . . of the Massachusetts Bay . . . at Their Annual Convention, May 28, 1746," *New York Weekly Journal,* February 2, 1747. A few more examples with similar content in addresses to the King or governors include "Address from the Reverend Presbyterians of New Brunswick and New-Castle . . .," *Pennsylvania Journal,* May, 31, 1744; "Humble Address of the Presbyterian Synod of Philadelphia, May 27, 1747." *Pennsylvania Gazette,* June 4, 1747; "Address of the Clergy of South Carolina to Governor James Glen, Esq.," *South Carolina Gazette,* April 16, 1744; and addresses of the South Carolina Royal Council, and Commons House, *South*

Carolina Gazette, November 26, 1750. See also John Gordon, *A Sermon*, 30; Ebenezer Pemberton, *A Sermon*, 33; Charles Chauncy, *Civil Magistrates Must be Just*, 34; Cotton Mather, *A Funeral Discourse*, 28.

91. For a few examples, see "Address of the Representatives of New Jersey," *Pennsylvania Gazette*, May 21, 1730; "Letter to the Editor," *South Carolina Gazette*, April 29, 1732; *New York Weekly Journal*, January 14, 1733; "Ode for His Majesty's Birthday, by Colly Cobber," *Virginia Gazette*, February 11, 173⁶/₇; "Address of the Clergy to Governor James Glen," *South Carolina Gazette*, April 16, 1744; "Address of the Rev. Presbyteries of New-Brunswick and New-Castle," *Pennsylvania Journal*, May 31, 1744; "Twelve Good Reasons," *New York Weekly Journal*, February 17, 1746; "Humble Address of the House of Delegates to His Excellency Thomas Blader, esq., Governor of Maryland," *Virginia Gazette*, April 3, 1746; "A Short *Eulogium* on His Present Majesty King George II," *Maryland Gazette*, December 31, 1746; "Humble Address of the Pastors of the Churches in His Majesty's Province of Massachusetts, May 28, 1746," *New York Weekly Journal*, February 2, 1747; "Speech of William Ball, Representative of the South Carolina Assembly, to the Lft. Governor, Council and Assembly," *South Carolina Gazette*, March 28, 1761.

92. Jonathan Mayhew, *Election Sermon*, Plumstead, *The Wall and the Garden*, 291.

93. Jonathan Mayhew, *A Discourse Concerning Unlimited Submission*, Bailyn, *Pamphlets*, 213-247, and *An Election*, Plumstead, *The Wall and the Garden*, 283-319. See also as examples, John Barnard (Harvard 1709), *The Presence of the Great God*; [Peter Annet?], *A Discourse on Government*. Fears of the return of a Stuart Pretender were long lived in the Colonies, stretching even into the Revolutionary Era. John Adams as "Humphrey Ploughjogger" parodied anxiety about the return of a "pritandur" and "popiree" in his first letter in 1763. See *Papers of John Adams*, Robert J. Taylor et al., eds. (Cambridge, Mass.: Belknap Press, 1977), 1:62.

94. Charles Chauncy, *The Counsel of two Confederate Kings*, 24.

95. John Gordon, *A Sermon* , 20.

96. John Barnard, *The Throne Established*, Plumstead, *The Wall and the Garden*, 250. See also Ebenezer Gay, *The Character and Work of a Good Ruler*, 12; Elnathan Whitman, *The Character and Qualifications of Good Rulers, and the Happiness of Their Administrations* . . . (New London: T. Green, 1745), 24; Charles Chauncy, *The Counsel of Two Confederate Kings*, 31; John Gordon, *A Sermon*, 30; Nathaniel Hunn, *The Welfare of the Government Considered*, 10; Gilbert Tennant, *A Sermon Preach'd at Philadelphia, January 7, 174⁷/₈* (Philadelphia: W. Bradford, 1748), 13; Jonathan Mayhew, *A Sermon*, Plumstead, *The Wall and the Garden*, 298-299; Jonathan Mayhew, *A Discourse Concerning Unlimited Submission*, Bailyn, *Pamphlets*, 231, 247.

97. See Bushman, *King and People*, 51-52.

5

King and Colony:
Colonial Politics and Whig Kingship

As the Religion, Liberty, Property, and a due Execution of the Laws, are the most valuable Blessings of a free People & the peculiar Privileges of this Nation, it shall be My constant Care to preserve the Constitution of this Kingdom, as it is now happily established in Church and State inviolable in all its parts; and to secure to All My Subjects, the full Enjoyment of their religious and civil Rights. — His Majesty's Most Gracious Speech to Both Houses of Parliament, on Tuesday the 27th day of June, 1727.[1]

These Sir, we beg Leave to assure you, are the only Sentiments of our Hearts; and, thus animated, we will unite in every Means our Power can reach, to promote the Interest of our Country, and to give the amplest Proof of our Duty and Affection to His Majesty King *GEORGE*, and our Zeal to maintain the Succession of the Crown, in His Royal House; the surest Bulwark of our Religion, the best Guardian of our Liberties, and the strongest Support of our happy Constitution: Thus, endeavouring to deserve that favourite and amiable Character, so justly, from these Motives, acquired by our Ancestors, of Loyal Subjects, and True Patriots. — Address of the Virginia House of Burgesses to the Governor, February 21, 1745.[2]

The protection-allegiance covenant was an integral part of colonists' understanding of the workings of their government. According to the covenant interpretation, among the king's principal constitutional duties was his obligation to protect his subjects from any who would threaten their lives, liberty, property or religion. The English king ruled over a free people, and both reveled in and protected their freedom. New York Governor William Burnet described this aspect of the covenant when he met with the leaders of several local Indian tribes at Albany in 1721:

The Great King of Great Britain . . . will always be a kind father to you as
he is to your Brethren on the other side of the Great Lake . . . His greatest
pleasure is the happiness of his people their liberty is dear to him he loves
and values you because you are a free People and will lose your lives rather
than be slaves.[3]

In return for the king's solicitude and protection, his subjects, and most
especially those who had been placed in positions of authority in his
realms, were obligated to show their sovereign loyalty and obedience, and
to support his prerogatives. Virginia Governor William Gooch reminded
the Burgesses that the first among their chief duties was to support their
king, because "by Him and His Family, next under God, is our happiness
secured."[4] Gooch observed that even in the American wilderness, the
liberties of Englishmen were secure "while we live under a Prince who
esteems it his greatest Glory to rule over a free People" and who protected
his subjects' rights and properties.[5] In 1754, Charles Knowles, the
Governor of Jamaica, told his Assembly that it was their duty to promote
both "the Prerogative of the Crown and the Liberties of the People" and to
do other than both would ultimately be destructive to the "Rights and
Property of the Inhabitants" of the colony.[6] The Maryland House of
Delegates responded similarly in 1755, noting that they held "a just sense
of [the king's] paternal Care of all his Subjects, however remote from the
happy Influence of his more immediate Protection." In the same sentence
the House pledged both their loyalty to the king and their "steady
Adherence, and immoveable Attachment to the true Interests, Rights and
Privileges, of those from whom our Power of forming Resolutions is
delegated."[7]

A central tenet of the contract between the king and his subjects in the
Hanoverian Age was that the king ruled by the laws settled upon by custom
and tradition and legislated by the people through their representatives. It
was thus the duty of legislatures to make laws that were both in the best
interests of the people and conformable to the prerogatives of the ruler.
Hence colonists understood that their representative assemblies had the
right to legislate for them, and that the king was obliged, so long as
legislation did not overstep the bounds of the prerogatives or threaten the
people's liberty, property or religion, to assent to, honor, and enforce the
colonial legislation. As an English country judge would have it:

Allegiance from the People to their Sovereign, and the Prince's Protection
to his Subjects are reticprocally [sic] stipulated by laws: For as by Laws the

Prerogative of the Prince, and the People's Liberty, are a support and Security to each others, when moving in their proper Spheres.[8]

The protection-allegiance covenant was a central feature in relations between the colonial government and royal authority. Since the covenant idea made it possible for colonists to conclude that the first goal of both the king and his provincial governments was the preservation of the liberties of his subjects, the king became a potent symbol that provincial political leaders could employ in support of their arguments in the various political controversies that arose in the American colonies after 1715. Most of these controversies centered around the question of power in the colonial constitution. They were essentially domestic in nature, challenging the authority, powers, and independence of the royal governor within the structure of colonial government, rather than the power or prerogatives of the king over his provinces in North America. Over the course of the eighteenth century, the powers of royal governors tended to diminish while those of the colonial assemblies increased. Colonists reasoned that their assemblies, as popular representative bodies, were best qualified to legislate in the interests of the freeholders whom they represented. This development of democratic institutions in America did not, of necessity, imply any diminution in loyalty or dependence toward the king among his colonial subjects.

Colonists considered their assemblies to be the fundamental guardians of their liberties. This role was shared throughout the branches of government, but the assembly, as the people's representatives, was understood to be the most able to judge the needs and rights of those whom they represented. Assembly members argued an intimate alliance of purpose with the king "whose interest, and that of his posterity are inseparable from his People's."[9] The colonial assemblymen understood it to be their role to provide a balance between royal power and the good of the people of the colony. This was not a competition in which one side was seen to lose when the other won, because the goals of both the king and his colonial assembly were viewed as identical—the protection of the lives, liberties, property and religion of colonists. Thus the Lieutenant Governor of South Carolina could tell the assembly to "dispatch all of the affairs that come before you, in such a manner as shall demonstrate, that . . . [the] Royal Prerogative, and the Welfare of this Province is what we have nearest to Heart."[10] The South Carolina Assembly replied similarly that "we are met with Hearts full of Zeal to Dispatch the Affairs that come before us, with a full regard to the Duty we owe his most sacred Majesty and the Welfare of this Province."[11] As defenders of both the Royal prerogative in the colony and the people's rights, colonial assemblies could, and often did, claim a tacit royal consent to their legislation and to their resistence to the demands of royal governors, even when the policies that they resisted were demanded by the Crown itself.

Assemblies, as the representatives of the people, claimed their obedience and loyalty to the king and assumed his support in their endeavors, even when they were actively engaged in thwarting his purposes. The perennial conflicts between assemblies and governors were thus not viewed by the former as disloyalty to the Crown, even though the latter was the royal representative in the colony. The purpose of the assembly in the colonial constitution was to preserve the interests of the people. Since this was also the primary object of the king, then no conflict of interest between the king and the representatives of his subjects was conceivable. Royal governors were sometimes mystified when they attempted to get the colonial assembly to enact legislation requested by the king, only to find that the assemblies opposed the legislation and claimed the king as an ally in opposition to it. Governors often accused the colonial assemblies of disobedience to the king, or of duplicity when the legislature claimed loyalty and obedience to the monarch while actively thwarting his royal will.[12] Assemblies, in turn, often accused royal governors of serving the interests of neither the king nor the people—of "making the general good and welfare of the Province subservient to [their] own private particular interest."[13]

Between 1700 and 1750 several issues prompted conflicts between royal governors and the colonial assemblies. Among these were appointments of speakers, adjournment of the assemblies, auditing of expenditures, payment of quitrents, and the question of a permanent salary for the governor. The popular parties within the assemblies demanded that they have the powers to appoint their own speaker, to adjourn themselves, to monitor government spending to prevent the governor from using public revenues to benefit himself, and to control the governor's salary, hence keeping him dependent upon the will of the people. In most instances, when one of these conflicts arose, the Crown, through the Privy Council or Board of Trade, sided with the governor and sent instructions requiring the assembly to conform to the wishes of the Crown. The assembly ignored royal instructions while sending loyal remonstrances to Whitehall in which they often explained that they were taking contrary action out of loyalty to the king and in the interests of his obedient subjects.[14]

During these and other controversies between the colonial legislatures and Crown officials, both sides represented themselves as acting out of loyalty to the king. Both sides felt their actions and loyalty justified because their understanding of their own functions under the constitution confirmed their rightness. The assemblies perceived it their duty to protect the king's subjects from the avarice of officials who, according to prevailing political wisdom, would, if unrestrained, fill their pockets at the expense of both the Crown and the people. The governors assumed their duty to lie in following royal instructions and protecting colonial subjects by maintaining the balance of government against an unrestrained, and hence dangerously democratic, popular legislature.

The controversy over fixed salaries for colonial governors exemplified this formula. In most of the royal colonies in North America, governors were dependent on acts of the colonial legislature for their support.[15] By 1700, the authorities in London had come to the conclusion that this practice was open to abuse by both governors and provincial assemblies. On the one hand, a sufficiently avaricious governor might use his authority to coerce funds from the colony over which he ruled. On the other, colonial assemblies could grant or withhold funds from the governor as they saw fit, rewarding those who acquiesced to legislation, and essentially starving those who would not submit to their will.[16] On rare occasions lower houses simply ignored their fiduciary obligation to support their governors. This was the case with unpopular executives like New Jersey's first royal Governor, Lewis Morris. The New Jersey legislature refused to pass any legislation for support of the colonial government until the Council and Morris assented to their paper emission bill.[17] Morris complained that "there is nothing more common in the mouths of the populace than, Saying . . . that if the Governor doth not Assent to such Laws as are Offr'ed for his Assent, the Assembly are Justifyable in not raising a support for his Majesty's Government."[18] Sometimes colonial legislatures deprived even popular governors of support. This appears to have been almost the rule with several royal governors of North Carolina. In 1746, for instance, the respected Gabriel Johnston complained that he had not received any pay during the previous eight years of his tenure.[19] By withholding the governor's salary, the provincial legislature might force the king's most important colonial representative to become a mere cipher.

In response to the first problem, that of corrupt governors, the Lords of Trade under Queen Anne required that no money be granted directly to the governor by the assembly, but that grants be voted to the Crown with the request that the monies be put to the governor's use should the queen see fit to do so. In response to both problems, from 1703 on governors received instructions from Whitehall requesting that they urge their legislatures to settle a permanent, fixed salary on them during their tenure in the province and forbidding them to accept any gifts from the colony under pain of the royal displeasure.[20] These instructions, and various governors' attempts to implement them, gave rise to the "salary question" that plagued several royal colonies into the middle of the century. The arguments that royal governors and colonial assemblies put to each other over the question yield significant evidence of the understanding of each *vis à vis* their respective relationships, real or imagined, with the king. Massachusetts provides the best illustration of the controversy, because there the debate that lasted over thirty years was played out, at least in part, in the local newspapers.

A series of governors from 1704 to 1728 confronted the Massachusetts General Court with requests for a fixed salary, and all of them eventually surrendered to the assembly.[21] The request became a sort of annual ceremony in which the governor dutifully asked the legislature for a permanent salary as per his Majesty's instructions, and the Assembly responded with the enactment of either an annual or temporary grant to defray the governor's expenses. The grant was often the last piece of legislation considered, and, on rare occasions, the General Court refused to give any grant of support until the governor had assented to the bills enacted during the session.[22] Perhaps the most blatant and extortionate example occurred in 1721, when a committee of the General Court made Governor Shute's salary contingent upon his approval of the bills and appointments made by the Massachusetts Assembly during the current session.[23] By 1721, the state of affairs in Massachusetts was such that Whitehall despaired of exercising any real control over that province at all. The Lords Commissioners wrote to the king that:

> the unequal Balance of their constitution having lodged too great a power in the Assembly, this province is & is always likely to continue in great disorder. They do not pay a due regard to your Majesty's Instructions; they do not make a suitable provision for the maintenance of their Governor, & on all occasions they affect too great an independence on their Mother Kingdom.[24]

In 1728, this by now traditional state of affairs was challenged when William Burnet became governor of the Bay Colony. Burnet was determined to force the colonial assembly to comply with the king's will and enact a permanent, fixed salary for his tenure in the province.

Massachusetts gave Burnet a warm welcome with the usual pomp—cannon, flags, parades, and so forth—and the House of Representatives produced a glowing congratulatory address dwelling on his excellent lineage (his father, the Bishop of Salisbury, had been among those who invited William of Orange to England) and the new Governor's past accomplishments.[25] Perhaps the assemblymen should have paid closer attention to Burnet's first address that preceded their welcoming speech. In it, the new Governor noted that the "excellency of the *British* Constitution" depended on each branch being "able to support its own Dignity and Freedom."[26] Significantly, Burnet caused his Majesty's 23rd Instruction, which required the Massachusetts Assembly to grant a fixed salary for the governor's upkeep, to be printed in the same issue of the *New England Weekly Journal* that carried his first address to the Assembly.[27] In his next address, Burnet informed the Assembly that, in granting him a permanent salary, it did no more than the Parliament did when it granted each new king a civil list for his reign. The Assembly replied that "we do not put as much Confidence in the Governour as the Parliament do in our most Gracious Sovereign." It asked, "is it reasonable or possible that we should confide in any Governour whatsoever so much as in our most Gracious KING the Common Father of all his Subjects?" The king was "known to delight in nothing so much as the Happiness" of his subjects, and his "Interest and Glory," and that of his progeny, were "inseparable from the Prosperity and Welfare of his People." On the other hand, a governor had a real interest "neither [in] the Prosperity nor Adversity of a People" and his tenure was ephemeral; he had no stake in the long term happiness, prosperity or freedom of those over whom he governed.[28] Burnet responded by accusing the House of "ill grace" toward the king and reminded the Assembly that the salary was not to go directly to him but to the king, for the use of his Majesty's servant. Should Burnet betray the king's trust and abuse the people of Massachusetts, the Governor assured the General Court that "upon just complaint" the king would remove him. Burnet concluded that, should the House disregard the king's request, his Majesty would certainly look "upon it as a manifest Mark of your Undutiful Behavior to himself."[29] The Assembly responded that giving the governor a fixed salary defied precedent. It was "an untrodden Path which neither we nor our predecessors have gone in & we cannot certainly foresee the many Dangers there may be in it." The Assembly also noted that the Governor, by attempting to coerce a settlement, violated the right of the people's representatives to raise monies "of their own free accord, without compulsion . . . the undoubted right of all Englishmen by *Magna Charta*."

Finally, it reported that the power to grant fixed salaries went beyond the scope of the colonial charter which empowered the Assembly to make laws for the "good & welfare of the Inhabitants;" to enact salary legislation that was not specifically allowed by the charter "might justly be deem'd a betraying of the Rights and Priviledges" of the people, and might thus "justly incur the King's Displeasure."[30] The House protested their unfailing loyalty to the king and voted Burnet a gift of £1,700 to enable him to "manage the Affairs of Government."[31] The Governor rejected the grant, explaining that his Majesty's instructions forbade him to receive gifts from the colony.[32]

At the same time that the Massachusetts government was wrangling over the salary issue, the General Court promoted a money emission scheme to raise £60,000. Burnet advised the House that the king would most certainly veto the bill but might assent to it if part of the interest were to go toward the governor's salary.[33] The House responded that, if it did as Burnet suggested, it would, in effect, fix a permanent salary upon the governor, "which is concluded by this House to tend very much to the hurt of the People of this Province."[34] Burnet replied that the House displayed a spirit "better adapted to the Republic of Holland than the British Constitution" and, to avoid exposing the representatives to the highly charged anti-salary political atmosphere of Boston, moved the General Court to Salem until they should comply with the king's instructions.[35] The House vowed to do no business until the governor allowed it to return to Boston. To do so, it argued, was prejudicial to the rights and liberties of the people, and certainly "detrimental to the peace of the King and his Subjects in the Province."[36]

Until early September of 1729, Burnet and the General Court wrangled over the salary question. The House continued to maintain that a fixed salary violated the liberties of the people, and that, since the king's interests and the people's were the same, such a step would amount to disloyalty to the king.[37] Burnet continued to accuse the Assembly of disloyalty and ungratefulness toward their sovereign. The General Court had the last word in the argument with Burnet. In a reply published after his death, the House reproved the Governor for implying that it displayed a want of duty to the king. The House and the people, it responded, "will ever remain and appear to be sincerely and heartily Loyal to our most gracious and rightful Sovereign King George; and they have and always will seek the true Interest and Welfare of this People."[38]

The Board of Trade chose Jonathan Belcher to replace Burnet. Belcher was a native of Massachusetts, a Congregationalist, a member in good standing of the Boston merchant community, and a well established local politician whose career was associated with the popular party. In 1728, he was chosen by the Assembly to represent their interests in London and to assist the official agent, Francis Wilks. Belcher's chief purpose there had been to promote the Assembly's side in the debate over permanent executive salaries. The Council refused to appropriate funds for Belcher because he was not a legitimate agent but only a lobbyist for the popular majority in the Assembly. So, the Assembly raised the needed funds by popular subscription.

Belcher's tenure as governor of Massachusetts provides another good example of the relationship between viceregents and the Massachusetts Assembly. Once appointed governor, Belcher changed his position on the salary question and convinced the ministry that he wielded sufficient influence and prestige in the colony to achieve a permanent salary for the royal governor and to exercise control over the popular elements in Massachusetts who wanted a more inflationary monetary policy.[39] Belcher was appointed to the position in November of 1729. He received royal instructions that stipulated that he prevent inflationary money policies in Massachusetts and settle the question of a permanent salary for the royal governor once and for all. The Board of Trade stipulated that if Belcher should fail in obtaining a permanent salary, he was to return to London and a new governor would be appointed who, presumably, might be expected to use means other than prestige and influence to achieve the king's purpose.[40]

In February of 1730, the province learned that the king had appointed Jonathan Belcher to replace Burnet as Governor of Massachusetts. The newspapers in Boston celebrated the royal choice, noting that Belcher had always "manifested a hearty concern for the Civil and Religious Interest [sic] of this People."[41] The colony celebrated Belcher's arrival with parades, cannonades, entertainments and sermons of thanksgiving. Bay Colony leaders observed that his Majesty's choice of a well respected native of their colony to lead them provided further proof of "the Paternal care of our good and gracious KING for the Welfare and Happiness of his Subjects."[42] One local poet even compared the new Governor with William III:

> Immortal Nassau! How Angelick Great!
> That Could Retrieve Three Sinking Kingdoms' Fate.
> How Justly too, shall Belcher's Deathless Name,
> Shine Bright for ever in the Rolls of Fame.

Three destin'd Provinces, that erst deplor'd
Their Bleeding Liberties, has He restor'd.[43]

After the usual ceremonies of installation were concluded, the celebration of the new Governor moved to the streets where a "vast multitude of Spectators without, express'd in their united shouts, an unusual Joy and Elevation of the Soul."[44] Next Belcher received the blessings of the Boston clergy, who evinced pleasure that a Congregationalist of known piety had been selected to be the new governor. Benjamin Colman, pastor of the prestigious Brattle Street Church, announced, "the KING could not have chosen any One" of the colony's "*Sons*, more worthy to represent His Royal Person," and stressed the new governor's piety and traditionalist faith.[45] Belcher, in turn, assured the clergy that he had agreed to the position, not from self interest, "but from a hope of advancing His Majesty's Service, and the Interest and Prosperity of this Country."[46]

The honeymoon ended rather abruptly, however, when the new governor announced to the Assembly on September 9 that he, like his predecessors, in keeping with the desires of his Majesty, required a fixed and permanent salary, and threatened to quit the province and return to England if it were not forthcoming.[47] Belcher's arguments in favor of a permanent salary were both more complimentary to the Assembly and more sophisticated than those of his predecessors. At first, he refrained from accusing the House of disloyalty to the king. He made his appeal not only as the king's servant, but as a native of the province who was thus sympathetic to the interests and needs of the people. "Ye are my Brethren: Ye are my Bones and my Flesh," announced Belcher, "& I have no Interest separate from your true and real Interest." The new Governor could reasonably argue that unlike his predecessors who were strangers, he shared a long-term interest in the prosperity of the colony and the liberties and privileges of its people.[48] Belcher stated that he would say little more upon the subject of a permanent salary because he had already made the king's will on the matter known to the province, and he himself was not a party in the dispute which was really between the king and his subjects in Massachusetts. He could only convey his hope that the Assembly would comply out of loyalty and obedience to the king and end the contention that had "turned out to the great Loss and Disadvantage of the good People of the Province." In a statement that would have warmed the heart of any "True Whig," Belcher informed the General Court:

How happy should we be, if there might be no Parties or Contentions among us for the future, but who shall approve themselves the best of Patriots, by their steady Loyalty and Obedience to the King, as well as by their just and prudent care of the Liberties and Properties of this People.[49]

Faced with Belcher's veiled accusation that the General Court had become a factious body that acted in the best interests of neither the people nor the king, the Assembly tried to frame its own reasons for non-compliance with royal instructions so as to deny the Governor's charges, yet contrive to show a friendly face toward the popular and respected Belcher. The General Court voted the new Governor a grant of £1,000 for his support and stated that this act complied with the spirit of his Majesty's Instruction, but pleaded that more than that it could not do. Loyalty to the king and a "high respect for the great Confidence in" the Governor made the Assembly "willing to do everything consistent with the Safety, Rights, and Priviledges of His Majesty's free-born Subjects." In voting a temporary grant, it had done everything possible "in faithfulness to His Majesty's good People here, whose real Good, conformable to His Majesty's glorious Example, we hope your Excellency will ever seek and desire."[50]

It was ultimately the controversy over inflationist policies rather than constitutional issues that brought Belcher's tenure to a close. When the governor refused to give ground on the subject, popular leaders combined with Belcher's enemies in other colonies to wage a war of petitions both in the colony and in London, in which he was accused of oppression and corruption. The war was not very successful because Belcher's reputation for honest dealings and his personal fortune of some £60,000 made charges of avarice and corruption less credible both in Boston and Whitehall. Finally, according to Thomas Hutchinson, political machinations over Parliamentary elections in Britain led to Belcher's dismissal and replacement in 1741 by William Shirley.[51] The governor, who had achieved something of a favorite son status early in his tenure, thus left office considerably less popular for having attempted to follow his royal directives. "It is the duty of governors and rulers," he stated in his defense "to stand upon the watch towers and warn their people of their danger and to hide them from evil. A tender parent wont let a foolish, mad child run into a fire."[52]

The debate over a permanent salary between Governors Burnet and Belcher and the Massachusetts Assembly provides an excellent illustration of the different understandings of the constitution that were held by both sides. The Assembly argued in an address to the king that distance and misinformation made it impossible for him to assess the performance of his representatives in all of his colonies. Thus, it was in the king's best interest "and very necessary to the tranquility and flourishing of this your Province, that the Governor should be induced by his own interest, as well as duty to your Majesty, to consult the interest and welfare of the people."[53] This, they argued, might best be effected by voting the governor an annual, rather than permanent salary. An annual salary would link the chief executive of Massachusetts to the people of that colony, and since the chief object of British government was the good of the people, the Crown would also be well served.

Burnet replied that the key to good government under the British constitution was the separation of powers. The British government was made up of "three distinct Branches of the Legislature, preserved in a due Ballance, . . . [and if] any one of these Branches should become less able to support its own Dignity and Freedom, the Whole must inevitably suffer by the Alteration."[54] The independence of the royal branch of colonial government could only be preserved if the governor received a permanent salary that rendered him independent of the other branches of government and responsible only to the Crown. The Assembly replied that, on the contrary, the "mutual Dependence of our King and Parliament is the only support, and great Happiness of our Constitution," and if either might subsist without the other, "our Constitution is at an end."[55]

Ironically, Burnet's argument that government best protected the governed when the branches of government were independent of each other echoed Bolingbroke and other country party thinkers, while the Assembly argued for that very interdependency of the branches of government that Country Whig writers condemned as the root of constitutional corruption. No matter what the source of their constitutional thought, however, both argued that their actions were motivated by loyalty to the Crown. The Assembly thought they could best serve the king's interests if the governor were restrained; the governor reasoned that he best served his royal master's interest, as well as those of the people of the province, if he remained independent of democratic influences. Similarly, Jonathan Belcher's arguments had a decidedly "Real Whig" flavor when he accused the assembly of factional interests and politics, and reminded the Massachusetts representatives that true "patriots" eschewed party causes and contention for service to the king and the people.

Well versed in colonial politics, Jonathan Belcher understood the precarious nature of a colonial governorship. While he might be treated with deference by Bay citizens, feted, praised and complimented, he had little real authority beyond personal suasion to dictate the legislative agenda of the colony, regardless of his instructions from his royal master. Other colonial governors who had less experience with the nature of the office were often mystified by the apparent contradictions between their theoretical and actual authority.

In February of 1731, George Burrington arrived in North Carolina to assume his duties as that province's first royal governor. He was quite pleased with his reception and must have assumed that the enthusiastic welcome boded well for his future relations with the colonial government. He wrote the Board of Trade that he had been received "with the Greatest Demonstrations of Joy by the People of the Province" at his installation, but evinced shock that, in spite of his good reception, the assembly refused to pass any of the acts required by the king's instructions, "which were only designed for the Ease of the People, and their own Good."[56] The king had instructed Burrington, among other things, to enact legislation to regulate quitrents and paper emissions within the colony and to settle adequate salaries on royal officials.[57] At first, the North Carolina Assembly's response to the Governor's recommendations was cordial. It complimented Burrington on his zealous care for the welfare of the province, pledged loyalty and obedience to the king, promised to consider Burrington's and the king's proposals with all due weight and gravity, and to do all that it could to demonstrate its "Duty and Loyalty to his Majesty, Zeal and Affection for your Excellency, and the Welfare of the Province."[58] In ensuing meetings, however, the Assembly refused to pass any of the recommended legislation. It declared them "contrary to Law," "an Oppression of the Subjects, . . . disagreeable to the known Justice of his Sacred Majesty" and "hurtfull to the just Freedom of the subjects" of North Carolina.[59] Burrington's personality was such that he took the conflicts with colonial representatives and magistrates personally. Ultimately his relations with North Carolina and its government became so acrimonious that, in response to the complaints of the colonists, he was recalled by London authorities.[60]

By 1730, the colonial assemblies had taken their cues from the British Parliament and its Whig masters. They had learned to employ the protection-allegiance covenant idea to promote their own interests and those of the colonists that they represented, often at the political expense of the Crown. The employment of the Whig idea that the king's interests and those of his subjects were inseparable gave the assemblies leverage in provincial affairs and made it possible for colonial representative bodies to effect the gradual erosion of Crown authority in the colonies in the king's name. Colonial laws, justice, and power were all derived from the sovereign authority of the king; yet increasingly, because of the link assumed to be inherent between the British Sovereign and his people, it was the popular assemblies, rather than the king's direct representative, the royal governor, that exercised those powers. Royal governors' powers within their colony were greater, at least in theory, than those of the king over England, where statute, politics and custom had all eroded royal authority. Governors took great risks, however, should they actually try to exercise their authority in order to restrain the colonial assemblies. They were impotent to do more than refuse their assent to legislation and did even that at some risk. A governor who consistently failed to go along with his colonial assembly quickly became the object of complaints from the colony to London. Colonial agents and memorials would accuse him of corruption and avarice, and of disloyalty to the Crown. Where the governor's support fell to the whim of the colonial legislature, the price of serving the interests of the king was often penury. A governor, like Burrington, who consistently impeded the colonial legislature faced recall from London and the possible loss of future promotion in government service. Even governors like George Burrington and Jonathan Belcher, who had ample support in London and who were directly appointed by Lord Newcastle himself, could not weather a storm of well organized protests from influential colonists and their supporters in London and entreaties of suitable replacement candidates who also claimed political favors from Whitehall.[61]

Colonial governors' authority was increasingly undermined not only from within the colony, but also from without, as influential members of the government in London jockeyed to get places for their own favorites, often at the expense of sitting governors. In this way, Jonathan Belcher's tenure was threatened by the influential Board of Trade member, Martin Bladen, who disliked Belcher and perhaps, more importantly, was the friend of Belcher's political adversaries in New Hampshire.[62] Similarly, New York Governor William Cosby found himself the target of an alliance of Board of Trade officials and the "Morris faction" in his colony in the late 1720s. His career was saved when Newcastle himself persuaded Robert Walpole to support the Governor against his political adversaries.[63] A royal governor who consistently opposed the colonial assembly faced recall at the behest of colonists and their London political allies, and a governor who was too conciliatory toward his assembly might be recalled for dereliction of duty. Only an individual with reputation and connections might sail, as it were, between both obstacles, and survive long as a royal governor. One such was William Gooch, perhaps the most well-liked Governor that ever served in American colonial administration. During his long tenure as chief executive of Virginia (1727-1749), Gooch consistently gave his assent to laws that did not meet with the immediate approval of the Board of Trade or the English merchants. He was a consummate diplomat and had enough influence at London to gain the support of London merchants, courtiers and politicians.[64] Gooch was also able to survive numerous disputes with influential London officials like William Keppel, the Duke of Albemarle (the absentee Governor of Virginia), and Anglican Commissary James Blair, representative to the Bishop of London.[65] Gooch "acquiesced gracefully," indeed, even tacitly encouraged, the steady constitutional growth of the Virginia House of Burgesses and thus remained popular among his subjects in Virginia. At the same time Gooch was reasonably safe from political fallout in London because his family and Robert Walpole were neighbors and old friends in Norfolk, his brother was the Bishop of Norwich, and he was well liked by such minor luminaries in colonial affairs as Martin Bladen.[66] Gooch was certainly the exception and not the rule in colonial politics.

It was not only the governor who might become embroiled in domestic controversies with colonial assemblies over the welfare of the people and the prerogatives of the Crown.[67] In 1744 the Royal Council of New Jersey appointed Robert Hunter Morris, a councilman and son of the Governor, to be chief justice of the province.[68] The Lower House responded, "that our Governour's own Son should be Chief Justice and at the same time one of his Majesty's Council . . . may be very prejudicial to the Interest of the People."[69] The Assembly resolved that it was inconsistent with the constitution of the colony that an individual should be both a legislator and a chief justice at the same time. Interestingly, the Assembly appeared to attribute little significance to the fact that Morris *pére* was the governor. The chief thrust of its complaint was over separation of the powers of the Council and judiciary and the possible growth of conflicts of interest between branches of government that made laws and those that enforced them.[70]

The Morris appointment touched off a long and bitter debate between all of the branches of New Jersey colonial government. The Council responded to the Assembly's allegations that it was "his Majesty's undoubted right and prerogative" to appoint anyone he desired to the highest bench, even a Councilor, that the two positions were in no way incompatible with the rights and welfare of the people of the province, and that the Council, as the king's representatives might make the appointment in the king's name. The Council further alleged that the Assembly's challenge ought to be looked upon "as an attack on the prerogative of the Crown . . . [and] a publick attempt to alter the Constitution."[71] The Assembly countered the Council's arguments by voting down a supply bill and other legislation that the governor and Council wanted. At that point Governor Morris rather tactlessly joined in the fray in support of the Council. In his address to the first sitting of the Assembly of 1745, Morris noted, with some justice, that it was not uncommon for colonial council members to sit on the judicial bench, even in New Jersey, and that no conflict of interest existed between the two positions. The Governor stated that no such restraints lay upon English Peers, who might also be judges, "and would it not be strange," Morris queried, "that this incompatibility, or inconsistency should never be discovered either in England or in America, till hit upon by our late Sagacious Assembly, tho' founded in Nature?"[72] Morris accused the Assembly of exposing the Council, "which is the Great Guardian of the Liberties and properties of the People" and the prerogatives of the king, to popular contempt.[73]

The judicial controversy was, in fact, only a minor issue, even something of a red herring, as the New Jersey Assembly's response to Morris's address indicated. The new Assembly stated that it had wanted to put the acrimony of the past behind it and move on to legislation that the province needed for the welfare of the people. "We cannot think ourselves accountable for the Transactions of former Assemblies," observed the new Speaker, "neither can we believe that Our King intended, or that our Country ever expected that we should be called together, to enter into unnecessary Disputes with any other Branch of the Legislature." Then the Speaker got to the crux of their complaints. Past Legislatures had promoted numerous bills for the good of the colony, only to have them quashed by either the governor or the Council before "his Majesty's Pleasure should be known."[74] The Assembly alleged that the other branches of the colonial government had interfered with the legislative relations between the representatives of the people of New Jersey and the king. The Speaker stated that the New Jersey Assemblies had always zealously supported the king and that they had never forgotten the duty that they owed to the Crown.[75]

The controversy between the Assembly and the other branches of the New Jersey government, at least in part, centered on the question of assent to bills from the popular legislature. In November of 1744, a committee of the Lower House complained to Governor Morris that, in the past sessions of the New Jersey government, the Assembly's legislation created "out of tender regard for the welfare" of the colonists, had been repeatedly rejected by the Royal Council.[76] While the Assembly admitted that the Council had the right to disallow legislation, it argued that it did so far too often and to the detriment of the public welfare. The Council also denied the king his right to review and give his assent to the laws of his colony. The Assembly stated that if its bills had not been disallowed before they could be seen in London and properly represented there, "from his Majesty's known Candour and Goodness," the Assembly had "the utmost reason to think" that the king would have assented to their legislation and redressed their grievances.[77]

The principals in these provincial controversies—assemblies, councils and governors—employed general arguments about the nature of their colonial constitutions and governmental authority that were prevalent in political discourse in England at the same time. The representative assemblies generally argued that the government that governed best was comprised of branches that were interdependent and that the English system of government protected the people because the various branches of government were bound, within the constraints of their constitutional functions, to cooperate with each other in the creation and enforcement of law. "The glory of the *British* Constitution," the Massachusetts General Court observed, was "that every Part of it had a mutual Relation to and Dependence on each other according to the different Powers and Privileges respectively belonging to each."[78] According to this interpretation of the English constitution, the various branches of government made up a "Natural Body," each part functioning in concert with the others and none capable of exercising sole authority without imperiling the whole. This organic notion of government was virtually identical to that of the English Whig oligarchs like Robert Walpole, whose *London Journal* noted similarly that "'tis necessary" that the legislative and executive branches "in order to the due exercise of government, that the powers which are distinct, and have a negative on each other, should also have a mutual dependency and mutual expectations."[79] Increasingly into the Augustan Age, establishment Whigs explicitly denied that complete independence and separation of the branches of the government were a requirement for good governance.[80] As one historian of Parliament observed during the period:

Ours is a mixed government, and the perfection of our Constitution consists in this, that the monarchical, aristocratic, and democratical forms of

government are mixt and interwoven in ours, so as to give all the advantages
of each without subjecting us to the danger and inconvenience of either.[81]

Ironically, colonial governors, appointees of such institutional Whig
luminaries as Walpole and Newcastle, found themselves framing
arguments that might have been cribbed from Viscount Bolingbroke or
other "True Whigs" in order to defend their master's instructions from
colonial assemblies. Both institutional and Country Whigs understood that,
in the normal workings of government, some independence existed
between the branches of government. As *The Craftsman* would have it, "an
Independent House of Commons, or an Independent House of Lords is as
inconsistent with our Constitution as an Independent, that is absolute
King."[82]

The independence of the colonial executive was not the whole issue
when the governor's authority and autonomy from the assembly came into
question. The actual chief executive of each royal colony was the king,
whose distance from his province, sovereignty, wealth and prestige made
him theoretically incorruptable. But the king's first minister in the province
was another matter altogether. William Burnet stated that "His Majesty is
the Head of the Legislature here," just as he was in England, and "the
Governor is but an officer to act by his Instructions, and to have no
Inclinations, no Temptations, no Byass, that may divert him from obeying
his Royal Master's Commands."[83] A governor who could be reduced to
beggary by the provincial assembly or who was beholden to another branch
of the government for his daily bread was perforce the creature of that
branch and could not be expected to fulfill his duties to his king. He was
corrupted and dependent, a slave to those who sustained him. According to
this "Country" interpretation of the colonial constitution, if the Assembly
rendered the governor, the king's most intimate representative, ineffectual,
then it also divorced the king from his sovereignty in the colony. The king
was excluded from government when his eyes, ears, and hands, as
manifested in the form of his governor, were reduced to serving the
assembly. Here was the "True Whig's" complaint. It was not the
constitutional separation and balance of powers, or the normal
interdependency of the branches of government that led to tyranny, but the
subversion of any one branch of government to another by means of
importune influence or corruption. In essence, colonial governors argued
that any undue influence that the colonial legislature might assume over the
executive subverted the colonial constitution.[84]

Assemblies were not always Walpolian in their arguments, nor governors consistently "True Whig." These were the rhetorical conventions available to them in English political culture of the eighteenth century, and so they essentially chose the language, the rhetorical construction, that best lent themselves to their particular argument. Occasionally, as in the case of the New Jersey Assembly and its controversy with Lewis Morris and the Royal Council, the legislature made a "True Whig" argument about the possible corruption of the judiciary by sitting a Council member on the bench, then argued in Walpolean fashion that frequent vetoes of bills by the Council had a tendency to exclude the king from his just place in provincial legislation, thus separating the king from his assembly.

Perhaps as significant as the actual debates within the colonies was the extent to which all sides reflected the protection-allegiance idea in their rhetoric. Both governors and assemblies assumed that the preservation of the people's welfare was the chief object of the king and his colonial governments and that the provincial assembly should do nothing that might overstep the bounds of the protection-allegiance covenant and weaken the king's authority or prerogatives. Time and again, governors addressed their assemblies with statements that stressed their shared duty to the king "in support of His Just Honour and Authority, in seeking the Welfare and happiness of His good People."[85] Gabriel Johnson observed in his speech to the North Carolina Assembly that the king's "grand and constant design of his whole auspicious Reign" was "the happiness and prosperity of all his Subjects," and that no one should ever "presume to make a distinction between the Interest of the Crown and the Interest of the Country."[86]

Assemblies, whatever their disagreement with the other branches of colonial government, struck the same note as their governors when it came to their understanding of the relationship between the king and his people, and their duties to both. Assemblies increasingly claimed precedence in the legislative matters of their respective colonies and employed the "king in parliament" analogy to their own situation in provincial government. If the king ruled Britain through his Parliament there, it was not such a stretch to infer that the same system must apply in each royal colony in America. After all, as the Council of South Carolina put it, "it is the opinion of this House that His Majesty does allow the Commons House of Assembly, the same Privileges as the House of Commons doth enjoy in England."[87] As one newspaper editor stated, the British king was "pleased to invest his Subjects with [the] Power necessary to make Laws for their Welfare and good Government" in a manner comparable to the role of the House of Commons. "But at the same time," this editor observed, in the interests of preserving the constitution, colonial subjects, like their English counterparts, were "Duty bound to support and maintain the just Prerogatives of the Crown."[88]

From the accession of George I until the 1760s, these assumptions about kingship and colonial government met no serious resistence from the British government. Colonial legislation, it was true, frequently received royal disallowances, usually through the agency of the Board of Trade or the Privy Council, but these acts only confirmed the constitutional link between king and colony in the minds of American colonists. The king had an undisputed right to disallow any laws in any of his realms that he saw fit. This was one of the constitutional prerogatives of the king, and, if anything, the manner of the exercise of the royal veto only made the analogy between the English House of Commons and the provincial legislatures stronger.[89] The good relations between the king and his people in his provinces of North America endured, and, in the perception of the colonists, the Empire prospered under the paternal protection of the best of kings through the first two Hanoverian rulers. Colonists' assumptions about the nature of English kingship and their own place within the British Empire were rarely challenged until the reign of George III.

Notes

1. *New England Weekly Journal*, September 18, 1727.

2. *Journals of the House of Burgesses of Virginia, 1742-1747, 1748-1749*, H.R. McIlwaine, ed. (Richmond: Virginia State Library, 1909), 156.

3. "Conference Between Governor Burnet and the Indians, September 7, 1721," *N.Y.C.D.*, 5:635.

4. *Journals of the House of Burgesses, 1727-1740*, 4. For similar, see "Governor Belcher to the Massachusetts Assembly," *New England Weekly Journal*, June 3, 1734.

5. *Journals of the House of Burgesses, 1727-1740*, 58.

6. "Speech of His Excellency Charles Knowles, Captain General and Governor, &c. to the Hon. Assembly . . . November 8, 1754," *Maryland Gazette*, January 16, 1755.

7. "Humble Address of the Maryland House of Delegates, June 25, 1755," *Maryland Gazette*, June 26, 1755. See also "To the Author," *New England Courant*, May 28, 1722.

8. "Some Paragraphs from the Charge of James Montague, esq., to the Grand Jury of Wilts, 1720," *New York Weekly Journal*, January 20, 1734. See also "A Short *Eulogium* on his Present Majesty King George II," *Maryland Gazette*,

December 31, 1746; "Americo-Britaneus," *Maryland Gazette*, June 4, 1748; "On the Happy Nuptuals of His Royal Highness the Prince of Wales," *Virginia Gazette*, October 1, 1736.

9. "Massachusetts House of Representatives Reply to Governor Burnet, August 30, 1729," *Pennsylvania Gazette*, September 29, 1729.

10. "Speech of Thomas Broughten to the Commons House of Assembly," *South Carolina Gazette*, November 29, 1735.

11. "Address of the Commons House of Assembly," *South Carolina Gazette*, November 29, 1735. For similar exchanges between governor and assembly, see "William Burnet to the General Assembly," and "The Congratulatory Address of the House of Representatives," *New England Weekly Journal*, July 29, 1728; "Governor John Montgomerie to the New York Assembly, June 21, 1728," and "Reply," *New England Weekly Journal*, August 19, 1728; "Speech of James Glen," *Pennsylvania Gazette*, April 5, 1744, and "Address of the Assembly of South Carolina to His Excellency James Glen," *Pennsylvania Gazette*, April 12, 1744.

12. For a few examples, see, "His Excellency's Reply," *New England Weekly Journal*, September 9, 1728; Speech of Governor John Montgomerie to the New York Assembly, June 23, 1728," *New England Weekly Journal*, August 19, 1728; "Governor Belcher to the Assembly of Massachusetts, September 9, 1730," *New England Weekly Journal*, September 14, 1730; "Governor Burnet's Last Message to the General Court, September 7, 1729," *Pennsylvania Gazette*, October 2, 1729; "Lieutenant Governor Dummer to the General Court, September 20, 1729," *Pennsylvania Gazette*, October 9, 1729.

13. Francis Wilks and Jonathan Belcher to the King, 1729, *Cal. St. P.*, 36:489. See also "Answer of the House to Governor Burnet, September 3, 1728," *New England Weekly Journal*, September 9, 1728; "Extract of a Letter from Mr. Dummer, London, March 25, 1729," *Pennsylvania Gazette*, July 10, 1729; "North Carolina Council and Assembly's Address to Gabriel Johnson," *South Carolina Gazette*, February 22, 1733.

14. See Bushman, *King and People*, 111-120.

15. Some exceptions existed. Virginia governors received a fixed salary from tobacco taxes after 1682. See Labaree, *Royal Government*, 315. In 1720 the governor of South Carolina was guaranteed an annual income as commander of an independent company of infantry in the province. See Labaree, *Royal Government*, 330. In 1730, an annual salary of £700 was authorized by the Board of Trade for the governor of North Carolina to come from provincial quitrents, but as these rents were inefficiently collected, they rarely yielded more than a fraction of the revenues necessary to actually pay the salary. See Labaree, *Royal Government*, 332-333. For specific coverage of colonial governors' incomes, see Beverly McAnear, *the Income of the Colonial Governors of British North America* (New York: Pageant Press, 1967), *passim*.

16. See Labaree, *Royal Government*, 312; Evarts Boutell Greene, *The Provincial Governor in the English Colonies of North America, Harvard*

Historical Studies, Vol. VII (New York: Longman, Green and Co., 1907), 167; Draper, *A Struggle for Power*, 38-41.

17. See *N.J.C.D.*, 15:81-83, 15:200-201.

18. *N.J.C.D.*, 15:272.

19. See Charles Raper, *North Carolina: A Royal Province, 1729-1775* (Chapel Hill: The University Press, 1901), 19.

20. Greene, *The Provincial Governor*, 168-169; Larabee, *Royal Government*, 318. In reference to New York, see McAnear, *Income*, 17.

21. For Massachusetts governors from Joseph Dudley (1703) to William Shirley (1768), and their attempts to promote a fixed salary, see Labaree, *Royal Government*, 346-348, 355-370. Labaree covers the salary controversies in several colonies, both in North America and the West Indies (312-372).

22. See Governor Burnet to the House of Representatives, *New England Weekly Journal*, November 18, 1728; Governor Burnet to the House of Representatives, *New England Weekly Journal*, September 8, 1729.

23. See Larabee, *Royal Government*, 357; Draper, *A Struggle for Power*, 58.

24. "State of the British Plantations in America, in 1721," cited in Draper, *A Struggle for Power*, 58.

25. "Congratulatory Address of the House of Representatives to William Burnet," *New England Weekly Journal*, July 29, 1728.

26. "Speech of William Burnet to the General Assembly," *New England Weekly Journal*, July 29, 1728.

27. *New England Weekly Journal*, July 29, 1728.

28. "Answer of the House to Governor Burnet Respecting a Fixed Salary," *New England Weekly Journal*, September 3, 1728.

29. "Governor Burnet's Reply to the House, September 3, 1728," *New England Weekly Journal*, September 9, 1728.

30. *New England Weekly Journal*, September 16, 1728.

31. *New England Weekly Journal*, September 23, 1728.

32. See Larabee, *Royal Government*, 361.

33. "Burnet to the House of Representatives," *New England Weekly Journal*, October 7, 1728.

34. "House of Representatives Reply to Governor Burnet," *New England Weekly Journal*, October 28, 1728.

35. "Governor Burnet to the House of Representatives," *New England Weekly Journal*, November 4, 1728; "Governor Burnet to the House of Representatives," *New England Weekly Journal*, November 18, 1728.

36. "House of Representatives to the Governor," *New England Weekly Journal*, December 9, 1728.

37. See "House of Representatives to the Governor," *New England Weekly Journal*, December 9, 1728; "Belcher's Message to the House, 3rd Instant," *New England Weekly Journal*, September 15, 1729.

38. *New England Weekly Journal,* September 22, 1729. For Burnet's obituary, see *New England Weekly Journal,* September 15, 1729.

39. Belcher convinced the Board of Trade that the salary conflict in Massachusetts was primarily the result of colonial officials' and representatives' acrimony toward Burnet rather than any specific constitutional differences between the Crown and Bay Colonists. See Labaree, *Royal Government,* 364; Bushman, *King and People,* 68.

40. In addition, the Board stated that, should Belcher fail to gain the requisite salary, on his return the matter would be brought before Parliament and settled there. Labaree notes that both Belcher and the Massachusetts Assembly rightly assumed that "the threat of parliament's intervention was nothing but a colossal bluff" (Labaree, *Royal Government,* 364).

41. *New England Weekly Journal,* February 9, 1730.

42. *New England Weekly Journal,* February 9, 1730. See also the "Speech of Lieutenant Governor William Taylor, June 30, 1730," *New England Weekly Journal,* July 17, 1730.

43. "A Congratulatory POEM to his Excellency Governour Belcher; At His Arrival," *New England Weekly Journal,* August 17, 1730. See also "A Letter to ***," *New England Weekly Journal,* August 11, 1730.

44. *Boston News-Letter,* August 6-13, 1730.

45. Benjamin Coleman, *Government the Pillar of the Earth,* ii. See also "Address of the Reverend Dr. CUTLER, Minister of CHRIST CHURCH . . . to His Excellency Governour Belcher, August 11, 1730," *New England Weekly Journal,* August 17, 1730; "Address of the Select Men of the Town of Boston," *New England Weekly Journal,* August 17, 1730; and "Address of the Merchants of Boston, August 19, 1730," *New England Weekly Journal,* August 24, 1730.

46. *Boston News-Letter,* August 6-13, 1730. Cited in John Langdon Sibley, *Biographical Sketches of Graduates of Harvard University, in Cambridge, Massachusetts . . .,* 4 vols. (Cambridge, Massachusetts: C.W. Sever, 1873-1919), 4:441.

47. "Speech of Governor Belcher," *New England Weekly Journal,* November 9, 1730.

48. "Governor Belcher's Speech to the Assembly of Massachusetts, September 9, 1730," *New England Weekly Journal,* September 14, 1730.

49. "Governor Belcher's Speech to the General Assembly, October 2, 1730," *New England Weekly Journal,* October 2, 1730.

50. "Extract from the Journal of the House of Representatives, December 31, 1730" *New England Weekly Journal,* January 11, 1731.

51. Hutchinson, *History of Massachusetts Bay,* 2:398-9. For details of Belcher's recall and London politics, see Henretta, *"Salutory Neglect": Colonial Administration Under the Duke of Newcastle* (Princeton: Princeton University Press, 1972), 208-215.

52. Cited in Sibley, *Harvard Graduates*, 4:441.

53. "Address of the House to the King, Nov. 22, 1728," *Cal. St. P.*, 36:311.

54. *Journals of the House*, VIII, 246. Cited in Bushman, *King and People*, 125.

55. *Extract from the Political State of Great Britain, for the Month of December, 1730* (Boston, 1730), 14-15.

56. *C.R.N.C.*, 3:331.

57. For Burrington's account of some of his instructions and his comments on the Assembly's treatment of them, see Burrington to the Duke of Newcastle, July 2, 1731, *C.R.N.C.*, 3:142-156.

58. *C.R.N.C.*, 3:296-297.

59. *C.R.N.C.*, 3:297, 3:304-305.

60. See Raper, 11-15. For a summary of Burrington's complaints against the Chief Justice of North Carolina and other "nefarious" political opponents, see "Memorial of Govr. Burrington, 15 Nov. 1732," *C.R.N.C.*, 3:373-375.

61. For the case of Burrington's recall and the subsequent promotion of Gabriel Johnson to the governorship of North Carolina, see Henretta, *Salutory Neglect*, 151-154.

62. See Olson, *Anglo-American Politics*, 129-131.

63. Olson, *Anglo-American Politics*, 133-134.

64. See Richard L. Morton, *Colonial Virginia*, 2 vols. (Chapel Hill: University of North Carolina Press, for the Virginia Historical Society, 1960), 2:507-510, 2:512-513, 2:519-520.

65. For Gooch and Albemarle, see Olson, *Anglo-American Politics*, 132, Blair, see Olson, *Anglo-American Politics*, 138. Olson notes that James Blair's political activities in the Southern colonies were infamous, even prompting complaint from his master, the Bishop of London: "Commisary Blair managed to unseat three, possibly four, Virginia Governors, and at one time was even acting governor of the colony himself" (94). For more on Blair, see Morton, *Colonial Virginia*, 2:467-469, 2:481, 2:532, passim; Daniel Esten Motley, *The Life of Commissary Blair, Johns Hopkins University Studies in History and Political Science*, Ser. 19, No. 10 (October, 1901).

66. Olson, *Anglo-American Politics*, 132.

67. For an overview of the various controversies within New Jersey colonial government under Morris, see John E. Pomfret, *Colonial New Jersey: A History* (New York: Charles Scribner's Sons, 1973), 147-152.

68. See Labaree, *Royal Government*, 390.

69. *N.J.C.D.*, 15:371.

70. *N.J.C.D.*, 15:371-372.

71. *N.J.C.D.*, 15:375.

72. *N.J.C.D.*, 15:406.

73. *N.J.C.D.*, 15:405.

74. *N.J.C.D.*, 15:411.

75. *N.J.C.D.*, 15:414.

76. *N.J.C.D.*, 15:369-371, 15:379.

77. "Extracts from the Votes of the House of Assembly of the Province of New Jersey, Thurs., Nov. 22nd, 1744," *Pennsylvania Journal*, December 20, 1744.

78. *Journals of the Massachusetts House of Assembly*, cited in Bushman, *King and People*, 126.

79. *Journals of the Massachusetts House of Assembly*, cited in Bushman, *King and People*, 127.

80. See Dickinson, *Liberty and Property*, 144-148; and Isaac Kramnick, *Bolingbroke and His Circle: The Politics of Nostalgia in the Age of Walpole* (Cambridge, Massachusetts: Harvard University Press, 1968), 123-127, *passim*.

81. *IX Parliamentary History*, cited in Kramnick, *Bolingbroke*, 124.

82. *The Craftsman No. 258*, June 12, 1731.

83. "Speech of William Burnet to the General Assembly," *New England Weekly Journal*, July 29, 1728.

84. Bushman claims that the arguments of Massachusetts governors were primarily concerned with the separation of powers within the colonial constitution, but fear of corruption by colonial assemblies was also a tenet of governors' arguments. Short term payments and legislated salaries dependent upon executive assent certainly had the look of attempts to subordinate the colonial executive to the assembly. See Bushman, *King and People*, 125.

85. "Governour Belcher's Speech to the New Jersey House of Assembly, March, 16, 1746," *N.J.C.D.*, 16:134. For similar examples, see "Governor Gooch to the Virginia House of Burgesses, February 1, 1727," *Journals of the House of Burgesses, 1727-1734, 1736-1740*, 4-5; "Governour Belcher's Speech to the Massachusetts House of Representatives, February 10, 1731," *Pennsylvania Gazette*, March 11, 1731; "The Speech of His Excellency James Glen, esq., Captain-General Governor, over the Province of South-Carolina, January 4, 1744," *Pennsylvania Gazette*, April 5, 1744; "Speech of Lft. Governour Robert Dinwiddie," *Maryland Gazette*, January 10, 1754; "Speech of His Excellency Charles Knowles, . . . to the Hon. Assembly [of Jamaica], November 8, 1754," *Maryland Gazette*, January 6, 1755; "Governour of New York's Speech to the General Assembly, April 15, 1741," *General Magazine*, April, 1741; "Speech of Thomas Broughton, Lft. Governour, to the Council and Assembly," *South Carolina Gazette*, May 31, 1735; "Speech of George Thomas, Lft. Governour of Pennsylvania to the House of Assembly, January 1, 1739," *South Carolina Gazette*, February 15, 1739.

86. "Governor Gabriel Johnson's Speech to the General Assembly of North Carolina, January 17, 1735," *C.R.N.C.*, 4:77-79.

87. "Report from the Upper House of South Carolina," *South Carolina Gazette*, April 28, 1733. For a study of the development of parliamentary privileges in American colonial legislatures, see Mary Patterson Clarke, *Parliamentary Privilege in the American Colonies* (New Haven: Yale University Press, 1943).

See also Breen, *Character of a Good Ruler*, 199; Bushman, *King and People*, 125; Jack P. Green, "Political Mimesis: A Consideration of the Historical and Cultural Roots of Legislative Behavior in the British Colonies in the Eighteenth Century," *Negotiated Authorities*, 192-202, *passim*.

88. *South Carolina Gazette*, May 8, 1736. For similar sentiments, see Philanthropos, "Postscript," *Maryland Gazette*, May 8, 1748; "Humble Address of the Maryland House of Delegates, June 25, 1755," *Maryland Gazette*, June 26, 1755

89. See Richard Bland, *The Colonel Dismounted*, Bailyn, *Pamphlets*, 322-323.

6

The Covenant Broken

Had our Creator been pleased to give us existence in a land of slavery, the sense of our condition might have been mitigated by ignorance and habit; but thanks to his adorable goodness, we were born the heirs of freedom, and ever enjoyed our rights under the auspices of your royal ancestors, whose family was seated on the British throne to rescue and secure a pious and gallant nation from the popery and despotism of a superstitious and inexorable tyrant. Your Majesty, we are confident, justly rejoices that your title to the crown is thus founded on the title of your people to liberty. — Petition of the Continental Congress to the King, January, 1775.[1]

No man was a warmer wisher for reconciliation than myself, before the fatal nineteenth of April 1775, but the moment the event of that day was made known, I rejected the hardened, sullen tempered Pharaoh of England for ever; and disdain the wretch, that with the pretended title of FATHER OF HIS PEOPLE can unfeelingly hear of their slaughter, and composedly sleep with their blood upon his soul. —Thomas Paine, *Common Sense.*[2]

On a late Spring morning in May 1766, some Bostonians awakened to the sounds of hammers, saws, and the voices of workmen busy at their tasks. When they looked out on the Common, they saw a great four story structure, a "magnificent Pyrimid," growing there.[3] At dusk the festivities began when twenty-four rockets were sent skyward. After that opening volley, revelers lit hundreds of lamps, brightly illuminating the figures in the windows of the pyramid, "making a beautiful appearance."[4] Prominently displayed in the windows of the four upper stories of the edifice were the symbolic guests of honor—the richly dressed effigies of King George III, the Queen, and members of the royal family.[5] From dusk until nearly midnight, candles, rockets, and pinwheels illuminated the city of Boston. To keep the festivities jolly, John Hancock treated the townsfolk to a pipe of Madeira wine, and "Mr. Otis, and some other Gentlemen who lived near the Common, kept open house the whole evening, which was very pleasant." Bostonians were on their best behavior and, apparently, in their best dress, as a "multitude of Gentlemen and Ladies who were continually passing from one place to another, added much to the brilliancy of the night." The Boston Sons of Liberty hosted the whole affair. The occasion of the celebration was the repeal of the Stamp Act.[6]

The repeal elicited joyous responses from all of the colonies. The evening after the Sons of Liberty held their popular celebration, the governor and council of Massachusetts met, dined, and drank toasts to the repeal. They likewise toasted William Pitt and King George III, whom they considered the principal supporters of the Stamp Act repeal in England.[7] At Annapolis on 5 June, to cap the daylong celebrations held there for the King's birthday, the governor of Maryland publicly read the Act that repealed the hated Stamp Act.[8] In Queen-Anne's County, Maryland, the Sons of Liberty held a solemn funeral for "DISCORD" and placed a plaque on the site of the mock burial that stated "in Memory of the Restoration of UNION, mutual Affection, and Tranquility to *Great-Britain* and her Colonies under the Auspices of GEORGE the Third."[9] On 30 June, the General Assembly of New York resolved to erect an equestrian statue of George III in New York City in order "to perpetuate to the latest Posterity, the deep Sense this Colony has of the eminent and singular Blessings received from His Majesty during his Auspicious Reign."[10] The Virginia House of Burgesses considered a similar bill to erect a statue to the King "as a grateful Acknowledgement for repealing the Stamp Act, and thereby restoring the Rights and Privileges of his *American* Subjects."[11]

Throughout the colonies Americans, for so they now often called themselves, celebrated the repeal with as much vigor and enthusiasm as they had resisted the Stamp Act. Often the Sons of Liberty organized and led the festivities. On 4 June, for instance, several hundred members of the Sons of Liberty of Woodbridge, New Jersey, gathered at the Liberty Oak to celebrate the King's birthday "and publicly to testify their Joy" at the repeal:

The Morning was ushered in with the Beat of Drum and the Sound of Trumpet, by which the Sons of Liberty were soon assembled. A large Ox was roasted whole, and Liquor of different Kinds in great Plenty provided for the Company. His Majesty's Colours were displayed in different Parts of the Square, and the Liberty Oak was handsomely decorated.

In the evening the assembled citizenry drank many toasts, the first of which were to King George III, the Queen, the Royal family, and to the glorious memory of the Duke of Cumberland. An observer announced that "his Majesty has no loyaler Subjects either in Europe or America, as the most firm loyalty seemed to glow in every Breast, and each endeavored to excell in honouring the Day."[12]

Colonial assemblies framed addresses to their governors and to London in which they pledged their loyalty to the King, and expressed their thanks for his intervention to restore the liberty of his American subjects. The Maryland House of Delegates expressed its deep sense of gratitude to the king for the "paternal Regard and Attention to the Interests" of his subjects that he displayed in assenting to the repeal of the odious Stamp Act.[13] The Assembly confessed an "invincible Attachment" to the King's "sacred Person and Government."[14] The Virginia Burgesses pledged their thanks for the "tender regard shown by his Majesty to the Rights and Liberties of his People" and acknowledged "that benign Virtue so distinguishable in him, that of protecting the Constitutional Privileges of his Subjects, even in the most distant part of his Realm, the American Dominions."[15]

Neither were American divines tardy in giving thanks to their God and their king for restoring to the colonies their just liberties. Jonathan Mayhew announced to his congregation at the Boston West Church that "I now partake no less in your common joy, on account of the repeal of that act; whereby these colonies are emancipated from a slavish, inglorious bondage; are re-instated in the enjoyment of their ancient rights and privileges."[16] Mayhew blamed Britain's enemies for the creation of the Stamp Act. The originators of the Act were "evil minded individuals," who, according to Mayhew, served the interests not of the king and good Britons wherever they might reside but were instead in league with "the houses of Bourbon, and the pretender," and sought to "bring about an open rupture between Great Britain and her colonies."[17] The Boston minister gave credit to God, King George, and William Pitt for the repeal. Mayhew observed:

> I am persuaded it would rejoice the generous heart of his majesty, if he knew that by a single turn of his scepter, when he assented to the repeal, he had given more pleasure to three million good subjects, than ever he and his royal grandfather gave them by all the triumphs of their arms, from Lake Superior to the Isles of Manilla.[18]

He warned his listeners that they should not be too hasty in placing blame on their king for giving his assent to the Stamp Act. After all, even "natural parents, thro' human frailty, and mistakes about facts, and circumstances, sometimes *provoke their children to wrath*, tho' they tenderly love them."[19] But, Mayhew noted, the king was quick to redress his subjects' grievances once he became aware of his error, and this fact ought to give his American subjects "a new spring, an additional vigor to their loyalty and obedience."[20] Completing the familial analogy, Mayhew reminded his congregation that "British kings are the political fathers of their people; the former are not tyrants, or even masters; the latter are not slaves, or even servants."[21]

The repeal of the Stamp Act represented something of another revolution, a return to first principles, for the American colonies. Americans perceived that they had been oppressed, their constitutional rights as Englishmen violated, and their liberties and property threatened. Yet, their resistence and their complaints had been noted by the king, who recognized their plight, redressed their grievances, and, in his paternal wisdom, repealed the "unconstitutional, oppressive, grievous, or ruinous" Stamp Act, thus restoring to Americans their ancient rights and privileges as Englishmen.[22] The Stamp Act crisis provided the first real rift between all of his Majesty's colonies in North America and the mother country in the Age of the Hanovers. It required Americans to reason out and reconfirm their understanding of their relationship with their king and their constitutional status in the British Empire for the first time since the Glorious Revolution. The central issue of the Stamp Act controversy, on its face, was simpler then those of the Revolution of 1689. There was no Catholic king, no invading Protestant Prince, no revolution in England, no abdication or desertion of the throne. The main issue of the Stamp Act crisis was the right of colonists to tax themselves through the agency of their own legislatures.[23] Yet, in the minds of American colonists, many of the same culprits, or at least their eighteenth-century equivalents, were involved. As Mayhew observed, the chief instigators of the heinous Act were evil Englishmen who supported the interests of the French and the exiled Stuarts.[24] Although the crisis had begun when the British Parliament enacted a statute that placed a direct tax upon Americans, most colonists were at some pains to absolve that body of guilt. Instead, they blamed evil ministers and their political machinations, and even colonial administrators like Governor Cadwallader Colden of New York and Governor Bernard of Massachusetts, whom colonists accused of betraying the colonies in order to further their own selfish ambitions.[25] King George III, unlike James II, was absolved of wrongdoing, and American colonists from divines to assemblies, even to the Sons of Liberty, hastened to show their loyalty to and support for their king. Indeed, colonists seemed to take every possible opportunity to stress that their quarrel was not with the king but with his ministry and the Parliament. Even the Sons of Liberty prefaced their manifestoes against the act with protestations of loyalty and allegiance to their ruler.[26] Americans, it seems, though prepared to resist the Stamp Act "to the last Extremity," had no intention of resisting their lawful and rightful king.[27]

The repeal of the Stamp Act confirmed American colonists' understanding of their constitution and the king's place in their system of government. A wrong had been done to Americans by evil ministers, Parliament, and even by colonial governors and fellow colonists who had misrepresented the facts to the government in London.[28] The repeal, after American resistence, indicated to colonists that the king could still give them relief. As Mayhew stated, "his Majesty and the Parliament were far too wise, just and good to persist in a measure, after they were convinced it was wrong, or to consider it any point of honor, to enforce an act so grievous to three million good subjects."[29] In short, in the minds of American colonists in 1766, the protection-allegiance covenant held; the system worked.

In one sense, a new epoch had begun in American political thought. During the Stamp Act crisis, colonists began to employ the "True Whig" opposition rhetoric and ideas in ways that they had rarely used them before the Stamp Act. Colonial writers began to apply opposition rhetoric to their controversies with the mother country. Bernard Bailyn, Caroline Robbins and others have shown convincingly that "True Whig" ideology and rhetoric had been well incorporated into American political discourse by the third decade of the eighteenth century.[30] These ideas were, however, used far more often in the give and take of internal political and religious controversies than in issues that concerned the relations between the colonies and the home government. Before the 1760s, colonial political writers were little concerned with the threat of corruption of the fabric of commonwealth government by the pervasive influence of a British "prime minister." Few Americans thought that the British Parliament had much to do with the internal life of the colonies, where colonial legislatures, authorized and protected by royal charter, were understood to hold sway in those legislative matters that had the greatest effect on the liberties of colonial Britons. While the British Parliament might justly pass laws that regulated trade throughout the Empire, or might otherwise benefit the whole, that body had not, as yet, passed any laws pertaining to the colonies that were generally construed as inimical to the liberties of British subjects in North America.[31]

Colonial governments and their agents had experienced good relationships with the Crown and ministry during the century, and, from the evidence of those relationships, it was apparent that neither the Crown nor its ministers had any malevolent design to deprive colonial subjects of their rights as Englishmen or to undermine their charters. That it was necessary to spread small bribes along the official paths of the London bureaucracy was understood by both colonial leaders and colonial agents. The latter noted in their accounts that these bribes were simply necessary expenses, and the colonial governments paid them with little comment.[32] The ancient system of tipping, bribery and the paying of posted fees (the traditional tips to civil servants were so widespread and uniform that they were codified and published in 1714), which were portrayed by the country opposition as exemplary of English corruption in government, were apparently dismissed by colonial agents and their employers as "the Expenses necessarily attending the negotiation of Business here."[33]

Opposition rhetoric was, however, employed in conflicts within the colonies. As Bailyn states, in these situations "the writings of the English radical and opposition leaders seemed particularly reasonable, particularly relevant . . . Everywhere groups seeking justification for concerted opposition to constituted governments turned to these writers."[34] When freedom of the press became an issue in the struggles between unseated minorities and the colonial assemblies in various colonies, the opposition writings of the English country party offered ready-made ammunition for both the minority and the majority. So, when Peter Zenger was brought forward by the New York Assembly on a charge of seditious libel, he "turned for authority to Trenchard and Gordon's *Cato's Letters.*"[35] When, in 1752, William Livingston and his circle of Presbyterians moved their perennial religious/political conflict with New York Anglicans into print with the publication of *The Independent Reflector*, Trenchard and Gordon's anti-episcopal, anti-clerical *Independent Whig* provided the perfect model.[36] When the Massachusetts Assembly passed an excise tax on alcoholic beverages in 1754, English country opposition writings against the Walpolian excises on cider and perry provided colonial opponents of the tax with a wealth of material.[37]

From the beginning of the Stamp Act crisis, Americans increasingly employed country opposition ideas and symbols as their language of grievance through the series of controversies with the mother country from 1765 to 1776. One possible explanation for the anti-ministerial tone of colonists' responses to the various bids for Parliamentary supremacy over provincial affairs may be the increased use of "True Whig" opposition rhetoric by William Pitt and various other members of the "Old Corps" of British ministerial politics who were ousted in the early years of George III's reign. Pitt, who consistently "cast himself in the role of patriot," based his political influence and prestige on political virtue, and criticized his political opponents with allegations of corruption, resigned from the ministry in 1761.[38] Pitt himself returned to politics in opposition in time to speak forcefully against the king's "Favorite," John Stuart, the Earl of Bute, and later, the Grenville ministry that had fostered the Stamp Act.[39] Americans' interpretations of the events that led to the Stamp Act and other incursions on their rights thereafter were colored by the opposition rhetoric of Pitt, his supporters, and others whose tenure as political players had come to an end in the first years of George III's reign.[40] Significant evidence is provided for this premise in the fact that Lord Bute became a symbol that colonists frequently employed in the Stamp Act opposition and even in later complaints by Americans against ministerial conspiracy and corruption, even though Bute's career as "Favorite" had ended before 1765.[41] Benjamin Church characterized Bute as "a primitive Aaron, leading the people into all manner of corruption."[42] The Sons of Liberty often employed symbols of Bute in their protests against local stamp officers, as in the case when Boston protesters hanged Andrew Oliver in effigy. Suspended next to the figure of the stamp collector was a large boot with a devil crawling out of it.[43] Bute died hard in American conspiracy theory. In 1769 Americans credited him with the "Townshend Acts," and again in 1775, he was accused of complicity in the promulgation of the Tea Act.[44] In a cartoon featured in the *Royal American Magazine* in 1774, Bute is depicted, kilted with a drawn sword, among the group of English politicians who are attempting to drown America in tea.[45] In 1775 Richard Henry Lee told John Adams that "we should inform his Majesty that we never can be happy, while the Lords Bute, Mansfield, and North, are his confidants and counsellors."[46] For American colonists, Bute represented a powerful and enduring symbol of conspiracy and corruption at the center of the British political world, a symbol manufactured by British politicians for their own political purposes.

When they tried to explain the chain of events over the last decade before the American Revolution, colonists searched for a "moral identity between cause and effect, between motive and deed."[47] As Gordon Wood argues, Americans of the Revolutionary Era generally preferred theories that involved conspiracy and corruption to either strictly mechanistic explanations for historical events, or to the notion that history was guided by a predetermined and unchangeable Providence. Thus, "colonists in effect turned their decade-long debate with the mother country into an elaborate exercise in the deciphering of British motives."[48] For Americans looking back on the acts of Parliament passed in reference to them since 1765 under several ministries, it must have seemed that the British constitution, as they understood it, had failed beyond all repair. They found their explanation for those constitutionally traumatic events in the Whig opposition rhetoric that had been a part of their political culture since the Robinocracy. They knew that the king could do no wrong. They also knew from the writings of Bolingbroke and other "True Whig" writers that "such as serve the Crown for *Reward* may in Time sacrifice the Interest of the Country to their *Wants*."[49] They knew that self-interested ministers employed their wiles, their money, and their patronage, to corrupt Parliament to their will. Americans saw no reason why the Parliament of Great Britain should threaten their constitutional rights of its own volition. It defied precedent. The Parliament would not pass such measures unless corrupted, and the king would surely not assent to them unless misadvised. The king could do no wrong, but the ministry certainly could, and two generations of English opposition writers had argued that the corrupt ministries of Great Britain wielded an undoe influence on Parliament. The king's ministers required greater wealth in order to extend their corrupting influence and rather than add to the tax burden of the mother country, they "extended their ravages to America."[50]

Although Americans often employed the language of "True Whig" opposition to frame their explanations of the causes of events that they came to view by 1776 as a systematic tyrannical usurpation of their English liberties by the British government, they never lost sight of the facts. Regardless of the origins of the legislation, by 1770 colonists had begun to see a pattern of arbitrary government that they could identify because they, or at least their grandparents, had seen it before. Given colonists' understanding of their relationship with the metropolitan government, their grievances were very real. By 1775, the specific wrongs had begun to look very much like those attributed to James II and his evil ministers. The British government maintained a standing army in the colonies even though the nation was at peace just as James had done in England before William of Orange rescued the English nation from Stuart oppression. The British government had established a military officer as the supreme commander of the colonies. If James II had his Andros, George III had his Gage. Since 1763 the number of lucrative offices and places in colonial service had been multiplied with tax agents, admiralty agents, and military officers. Arbitrary courts, such as the Admiralty Court, operated in the colonies just as they had in the days of James II, and agents of the courts were given powers that were inimical to the rights of Englishmen. Assemblies had been "frequently and injuriously dissolved" by royal governors, and the agents of the people "discountenanced."[51] Americans were taxed without their consent, and, in the case of New York and Massachusetts, their own popular assemblies had been either closed or rendered impotent to do the people's business. The government in England employed arbitrarily raised taxes to support royal governors and other officials in the colonies, giving provincial governors independence from the colonial legislatures, and thus having "a direct tendency to render assemblies useless."[52] This was the litany of the "destructive system of colony administration, adopted since the conclusion of the late war."[53] According to the Continental Congress, "to a sovereign who '*glories in the name of Britain,*' the bare recital of these acts, must, we presume, justify the loyal subjects, who fly to the feet of his throne, and implore his clemency for protection against them."[54]

For many colonists, the Quebec Act provided further proof of British tyranny. The statute was enacted in June 1774, less than a month after the passage of the Intolerable Acts. Parliament passed the latter in order "to reduce the colonies to a proper subordination" and to punish Massachusetts for what many friends and foes of the colonies in Britain considered the wanton destruction of property, the "Boston Tea Party."[55]

Because of its timing, colonists viewed the Quebec Act as another of the Intolerable Acts and therefore as further punishment directed by Parliament toward the errant Bay Colonists. The purpose of the Quebec Act was primarily to set the boundaries of the province of Quebec, to establish the authority of the governor and magistrates of the colony, and to protect the religious rights of citizens of the Canadian colony. "It is hereby declared," the Act stated, "That his Majesty's Subjects professing the Religion of the Church of *Rome*," in Quebec, "may have, hold, and enjoy, the free Exercise" of their religion, and that "the Clergy of the said Church may hold, receive, and enjoy their accustomed Dues and Rights, with respect to such Persons only as shall profess the said Religion."[56] Colonists saw the Act as an attempt by the government in London to place territory claimed by Virginia, Connecticut and Massachusetts under arbitrary prerogative government and officially sanctioned Papism.[57] That the King of England, the defender of English Protestantism, should preside over or even sanction a Roman Catholic colony many American colonists found suspect. In his apocalyptic sermon in January 1774, Samuel Sherwood described "the

Quebec Bill, for the establishment of popery," as one of the "instruments
that have been set to work" by a corrupt Parliament, to "strike at our
temporal interest and property, as well as our civil and religious
privileges."[58] Among the acts that the First Continental Congress protested
in their resolves of October 1774, was "the act . . . for establishing the
Roman Catholick Religion in the province of Quebec, abolishing the
equitable system of English laws, and erecting a tyranny there, to the great
danger, from so great a dissimilarity of Religion, law, and government of
the neighbouring British colonies."[59] The vision of history and precedent
ran strong in American minds. If the king and his ministry could establish
arbitrary government and Popery by statute in Canada, why not elsewhere?
If the evidence of tyranny was already apparent in the other American
colonies, might not Popery be far behind?

By the winter of 1775, colonists had begun to lose faith in their king. In
spite of their continued affirmations that they were still loyal subjects of the
British Crown, Americans were at war with Great Britain. Despite
entreaties, addresses, and petitions to the throne for redress and for peace,
the King turned a deaf ear to his faithful subjects in his American colonies.
He had, in fact, declared them in open insurrection. Still colonists were in
a quandary. Moses Mather summed up the problem when he observed that
Americans "have ever recognized" the authority of the king "as their
rightful sovereign, . . . and now call upon him as their liege lord for
protection, on pain of their allegiance, against the army, levied by the
British Parliament, against his loyal and dutiful subjects."[60] Mather
imagined George III's dilemma:

> Methinks I hear the king, retired with his hand upon his breast, in pensive
> solliloquy, saying to himself, who, and what am I? A king, that wears the
> crown, and sways the scepter of Great-Britain and America. . . . Do my
> subjects in America, refuse to resign their liberties and properties to the
> disposal of my subjects in Great-Britain? . . . Have not my subjects in Great-
> Britain rights that are sacred and inviolable, and which they would not
> resign but with their lives? They have. Have not my subjects in America
> rights equally sacred, and of which they are ought to be equally tenacious?
> They have. . . . What shall I do for the dignity of my crown, the peace of my
> dominions, and the safety of the nation?[61]

In his mind's eye, Mather envisioned the crux of the royal dilemma that
became inevitable once the Parliament of Great Britain hit upon the idea of
taxing American colonists directly in order to raise revenues. If the king
refused his assent to parliamentary bills aimed at the colonies and thus

fulfilled his role as protector of the rights of his American subjects, he broke with precedent, and by disallowing an act of Parliament, he wronged his ministry and his British subjects as represented in Parliament. If he allowed the bills to be enacted, he wronged his subjects in America and thus violated the protection-allegiance bond that colonists viewed as the most intimate constitutional link between each province and the mother country.

George III was no more likely to refuse his assent to parliamentary legislation than either of his two predecessors. By the beginning of his reign, political precedent and Whig ideological precept demanded that, while the king technically had the power of the royal veto, in practice he might not use it. The distinction between British constitutional theory and political reality was not as apparent to American colonists. Thomas Jefferson observed that Hanoverian kings were "conscious of the impropriety of opposing their single opinion to the united wisdom of two Houses of Parliament" and had therefore refrained from using the royal veto in the past. Jefferson argued that changes in the circumstances of the government in London and the Empire itself, had "produced an addition of new, and sometimes, opposite interests" between his Majesty's various dominions. This conflict of interests between Britain and other realms ruled by the British monarch obliged the king to resume the exercise of his veto prerogative over Parliament "to prevent the passage of laws by any one legislature of the empire, which might bear injuriously on the rights and interests of another."[62] Given both the prevailing philosophy of the executive in Britain and the political proclivities of the Hanovers, this was not a possibility.

The prevailing political idea of the Crown in the constitutional philosophy of Whig England in the Hanover period was that of the king in Parliament. This idea severely limited the powers of the Crown in terms of its ability to act as a balance in government. Saddled with a ministry theoretically chosen independently by the reigning monarch but actually usually comprised of members of the Court Whig political factions whose power base descended from the House of Commons, the king had lost much of the prerogative power attributed to him by constitutional theorists from Coke to Blackstone.[63] Among the most important royal functions that had fallen victim to the new political order was the king's ability to veto parliamentary legislation that threatened the rights and privileges of the people. By the middle of the eighteenth century, Parliament had become a paramount legislative body, its laws invulnerable to review.[64] Thus, although the king theoretically had the power to constrain Parliamentary legislation that was injurious to his subjects by using the royal veto in response to petitions for redress of grievances, in practice the king was powerless to do so.

The royal dilemma was further complicated by the disparity between English and American understandings of the constitutional status of the colonies. Most British political thinkers of the mid-eighteenth century reasoned that all Britons, no matter where they resided, were virtually represented in the House of Commons.[65] The idea of virtual representation was, and had to be, maintained by the British government not only as a means of subordinating the colonies to Parliament but also in order to govern and tax a growing population of unrepresented Englishmen. As Soame Jenyns, a member of Parliament and of the Board of Trade, observed:

> every Englishman is taxed, and not one in twenty represented: copyholders, leaseholders, and all men possessed of personal property only, chuse no representatives; Manchester, Birmingham, and many of our richest and most flourishing trading towns send no members to Parliament, [and] consequently cannot consent by their representatives, because they chuse none to represent them. . . . If the towns of Manchester and Birmingham, sending no representatives to Parliament, are notwithstanding there represented, why are not the cities of Albany and Boston equally represented in that Assembly? are they not alike British subjects? are they not Englishmen?[66]

American complaints that they could not constitutionally be taxed by a body that did not represent them fueled debate about representative government in Britain, and thus made it all the more important to institutional Whigs that the principle of virtual representation not be surrendered.[67]

Colonists had long asserted without serious contention from Britain that the American colonies were, essentially, "perfect States, no[t] otherwise dependent upon Great Britain than by having the same king, . . . having compleat legislatures within themselves."[68] According to the prevailing theory among most colonists, their forefathers, at great personal risk, had settled in the American wilderness and had set up their own governments modeled on the English constitution "within the king's allegiance."[69] The American colonies were thus separate realms that shared the same king, much as Ireland and Scotland (before the union) had been separate states with a shared king in the past. Unlike other past separate British realms, like Chester and Durham, Wales, and Scotland, and to some extent Ireland, the American colonies had never been annexed to the kingdom of Great Britain by statute or conquest.[70] Thus, Americans viewed each colony as a realm of the king of Great Britain, constitutionally distinct from each other, as well as distinct and independent from the government of Great Britain, and connected to the mother country only by their charters and a shared sovereign, the king.[71] Each colony had its own assembly that represented the king's provincial subjects and was the appropriate venue for the generation of taxes for that colony. Parliament had no right to tax any colony for the purpose of creating revenues because it did not represent the subjects there, nor even hold any authority over internal matters.[72] That the Parliament of Great Britain should presume to tax his Majesty's provinces in North America violated colonists' understanding of their fundamental relationship with the mother country. That their king should acquiesce to the arbitrary acts of a corrupt ministry and Parliament of Great Britain over the colonists' complaints, remonstrances, and active protest, Americans came increasingly to view as tyranny.

From the spring of 1776, matters went from bad to worse. New England had been in a state of war with British troops for a year, with blood spilled on both sides. Congress, the colonial assemblies, and even British colonies in the West Indies had sent petitions to London, all of which were ignored by the British government.[73] America had few friends in London and none in government. In August 1775, the King had declared Americans to be in "open and avowed rebellion," and in December Parliament had passed the American Prohibitory Act that halted trade with the colonies and gave American shipping the same status as enemy vessels. Henceforth American ships could be taken by the Royal Navy and "forfeited to his Majesty, as if the same were the ships and the effects of open enemies."[74]

By the beginning of the summer of 1776, while the Continental Congress still stalled on the question of independence, the conviction grew among many American colonists that their king had forsaken them. "Petition no more, save to the King of Kings," said one letter writer, who observed that an address to the king was, in effect, a petition to the very ministry that had caused the misery in America in the first place.[75] In May 1776, John Witherspoon admitted of the King, his ministry, and the Parliament and people of Great Britain that "many of their actions have probably been worse than their intentions." He added, however, that distance and differences made "a wise and prudent administration of our affairs" under the colonial system "as impossible as the claim of authority is unjust."[76] Moses Mather noted late in 1775 that "the king, by withdrawing his protection and levying war upon us, had discharged us of our allegiance, and of all obligations of obedience." Mather argued that, since the king had forsaken his obligation to protect his American subjects, he had violated the protection-allegiance covenant. Thus, Mather claimed, "we are necessarily become independent." For Mather the choice of independence was made, not in America, but in London, when the king abandoned his American realms to Parliament and his ministry. "Our affections are weaned from Great-Britain," he stated, "by similar means and almost as miraculously as the Israelites were from Egypt."[77]

Members of the Continental Congress made a similar argument in May 1776. The committee appointed to frame the preamble to another address to England returned a report in which they stated that the king, "in conjunction with the Lords and Commons of Great Britain," had withdrawn his protection from his subjects in North America. The report noted that the king had ignored the petitions and addresses sent from the American colonies and had resorted to force against the American people. The committee resolved that governments be established in the colonies "as shall, in the opinion of the representatives of the people, best conduce to the happiness and safety of their constituents, and America in general."[78]

By the spring of 1776 popular support for breaking ties with Great Britain had grown. An increasing number of Americans no longer viewed the king as their defender against the incursions of a renegade British ministry or a kept and corrupted Parliament. Instead colonists began to see the king as an active participant in their destruction. Much of the change of heart among American colonists was the result of the radical views of Thomas Paine, whose pamphlet *Common Sense* appeared in January, 1776. Paine's pamphlet was the first widely circulated work that presented the argument against Great Britain in purely republican terms. He abandoned the traditional "True Whig" approach to opposition writing and struck at the very heart of the connection between Britain and the colonies as Americans understood it.[79] The author of *Common Sense* employed evidence from Scripture and history to make the argument that monarchy, even the best and most benign of monarchies, was ultimately destructive to popular liberty. For Paine, monarchy was "the most prosperous invention the Devil ever set on foot."[80] He observed that "monarchy is ranked in Scripture as one of the sins among the Jews," that "monarchy in every instance is the Popery of government," and that hereditary kingship flies in the very face of nature, "otherwise she would not so frequently turn it into ridicule by giving mankind an *Ass for a Lion*."[81] Paine admitted that England had been ruled by a few good kings since the Norman Conquest, but he announced that it had "groaned beneath a much larger number of bad ones."[82] He even questioned the appropriateness of having a king as part of the English system of government. English kings, Paine argued, had "little more to do than make war and give away places; which in plain terms, is to impoverish the nation, and set it together by the ears." Paine noted that kings were the fount of patronage and, as such, were also the source of corruption and vice in the British Commonwealth. Britons, he noted, extolled their system of government because of "the republican and not the monarchical part of the constitution, . . . viz. The liberty of choosing an House of Commons from out of their own body." The monarchy that Americans clung to so tenaciously had done little more than sicken the English constitution—it had "poisoned the republic."[83]

Paine characterized the king, not as the protector of the colonies, but as a tyrant who had "shewn himself . . . as an inveterate enemy to liberty," who had "discovered . . . a thirst for arbitrary power." The king could, and often did, disallow colonial legislation at his whim. He would only be willing to allow colonial laws that suited his interests and purposes. Paine argued that, if Americans should become reconciled with Britain, the king, "the greatest enemy this continent hath, or can have, shall tell us 'there shall be no laws but such as I like.'"[84]

Thomas Paine's stand against monarchy in general, and the British monarchy in particular, went a long way toward dispelling Americans' notions of the king as their protector. It offered a timely interpretation of the troubling events that had plagued the colonies since 1765. It provided them with a new language, that of pure republicanism, with which to describe their situation. Whig opposition thought still characterized the monarchy in Whig terms. "True Whig" writers might complain of ministerial corruption and of the dire effects that the growth of ministerial power had on the British constitution, but they nevertheless viewed the Crown as a necessary and beneficial branch of government. In fact, Lord Bolingbroke saw the king as the potential savior of the constitution, the best hope for the restoration of virtue and good government in Britain.[85] Likewise, Americans had depended on the king as a defender and patriot, who would willingly protect their local autonomy from an arbitrary British ministry and Parliament. Paine's rhetoric placed the king, not on the side of the angels, but at the very center of the British conspiracy to deprive Americans of their liberties. He also appealed to Americans' interests. He offered them both an historical context that demanded separation and a rosy picture of the results of that separation from Britain.

In May 1776, a number of towns and counties began to send instructions to their representatives in which they communicated their sentiments on the future of colonial relations with Great Britain.[86] In one such from Buckingham County, Virginia, the freeholders reflected their own understanding of their changed view of the king. When differences between Virginia and the mother country began, they explained that "we felt our hearts warmly attached to the king of Great Britain and the Royal Family." The freeholders acknowledged that, at first, they had blamed the ministry and Parliament for their distress and had assumed that the king was "deceived and misguided" by his councillors. They had hoped that their king would "in the proper time, open his eyes, and become a mediator between his contending subjects."[87] Events of the recent past, especially the "King's speeches, addresses, resolutions and acts of Parliament," however, convinced the Buckingham County freeholders that they could no longer expect help from the king. They recommended that their representative vote against reconciliation with Great Britain. Significantly, the citizens of Buckingham County closed their address with the following historical observation:

> It was by Revolution, and the choice of the people, that the present Royal family was seated on the Throne of *Great Britain*, and we conceive the Supreme Being hath left it in our power to choose what Government we please for our civil and religious happiness, and when that becomes defective, or deviates from the end of its institution, and cannot be corrected, that the people may form themselves into another, avoiding the defects of the former. This we would now wish to have effected, as soon as the general consent approves, and the wisdom of our councils will admit; that we may, as far as possible, keep our primary object, and not lose ourselves in hankering after reconciliation with *Great Britain*.[88]

If Thomas Paine swept away the underpinnings of the alliance between king and people in America, Thomas Jefferson destroyed the covenant itself. In the *Declaration of Independence*, Jefferson laid the full blame for Americans' oppression, not on corrupt ministries or a renegade Parliament, but on King George III himself. Jefferson created, in effect, an American *Declaration of Right*, a summation of the "repeated injuries and usurpations" of a ruler who, like James II, had as his "direct object the establishment of an absolute tyranny over these states."[89]

Although the protection-allegiance covenant between the king and people was broken, the idea persisted in the new republican environment. For Thomas Paine, the covenant and the crown in a new American republic rested in the law, "for as in absolute governments the King is law, so in free countries the law *ought* to be King."[90] Though philosophically sound, perhaps this notion lacked the human touch. For John Witherspoon and other divines, the appropriate protector of the new American nation was the King of Kings.[91] Jacob Cushing, the minister of Waltham, Massachusetts, announced that, unlike an earthly king, God would not "cast off his people, nor will he forsake his inheritance."[92] Others placed the renewed covenant into the hands of their new secular leaders. For some, the new "fathers of their country," were the framers of new republican constitutions, and the "honorable Senate and House of Representatives," who it was hoped, would be "directed by supreme wisdom to such measures as will most effectively promote the best interests of their constituents."[93] As the covenant passed to public officials, so the accolade of loving father followed. One minister observed of the elected officials under the new national Constitution, that "the people call them father: we are willing to be their political children, as long as they are good parents. . . . Should they not be *ministers of God for good* to the people, in every possible way?"[94]

The lion's share of royal attributes fell on the shoulders of the United States' first martial hero, George Washington. Beginning as early as the summer of 1776, American Whigs launched a campaign that consciously compared the *personae* of the two Georges. George III, by his despotic and cruel behavior had forfeited the title of "father of his country." He had become, in the words of Whig propagandists, "an unnatural father."[95] George's claim to patriarchy was lost when, "by withdrawing his protection and levying war upon" his American subjects, he violated the compact that existed between the king and his civil progeny.[96] As George III's star waned, George Washington's grew.

As early as 1776, American Whigs began to bestow paternal appellations on Washington that hitherto had been reserved for the king. One writer called him "our political Father and head of a Great People." By 1778 the title "father of his country" was used with regularity in reference to the General. By 1779 Americans observed Washington's birthday with the same enthusiasm that they had once reserved for the king's birthday. American almanacs omitted the royal anniversary after 1778.[97]

Washington's virtues, as expressed by his devotees, took on monarchical trappings in the British Whig tradition, but also often resembled the moral characteristics of great republican leaders and heroes from ages past. American writers like Thomas Paine, Philip Freneau and Francis Hopkinson compared the General's character to that of Bolingbroke's Patriot King.[98] American writers praised him for his disinterest in political affairs, for his sacrifice for the sake of his people's liberty and property and for the "mild majesty of his morals and relgion."[99]

Others saw in Washington an American Cincinnatus.[100] According to Mercy Otis Warren, "though possessed of equal opportunities for making himself the despotic master of the liberties of his country," Washington "had the moderation repeatedly to divest himself of all authority, and retire to private life" to end his days on his plantation "in that tranquility which becomes the hero and the Christian."[101]

Unlike kings, presidents died, or, to put it more succinctly, eponymous republican magistrates passed from office. The virtues and strengths of the first President of the United States, the father of the new nation, were not to be expected in his successors. Americans accorded the paternal title to Washington only; it seems that future presidents could no longer claim to be nursing fathers to their people. Washington's title, thus, changed in meaning. The first president was the father of his country in the sense that he was its progenitor. Americans ascribed to future presidents, and indeed, Washington himself, republican rather than monarchical virtues. Thus, for a short time, the spirit of the covenant was sustained even after there was no king in America.

Historians generally recognize that American colonists' loyalty to their king remained strong until 1776. They are less clear, however, as to why colonists sustained their loyalty as long as they did. To answer this question it is necessary to understand how colonists viewed the king as an actor in their political life, to grasp the concept of British kingship in the minds of American colonists. Describing the colonial conception of true kingship, of the king as nursing father of his people—how and why it arose, how it changed over time in the colonies, how the circumstances of colonial life gave it a peculiarly American resonance in colonial minds by the mid-eighteenth century—has been the purpose of this study.

Although the notion that government existed for the preservation of the liberty, property and Protestant religion of the governed had been a basic tenet of English political thought since at least the early 1600s, only after the Glorious Revolution did Britons comprehend that their king was an active participant in preserving these essential rights of Englishmen. William of Orange's propaganda popularized the persona of the good English Protestant king, and Hanoverian publicists applied the image to the German rulers as part of their efforts to legitimize the dynasty and unite the nation under Whig Hanoverian rule.

The idea of good English kings traversed the Atlantic during the Glorious Revolution and subsequent reigns and became a prominent theme in American colonial political thought just as it was among Britons at home. The idea of Whig kingship resonated among Americans after their experience during the Stuart administrations in New England, New York, and elsewhere in the colonies. Americans, like many of their English brethren, viewed William III and his Hanoverian successors as champions of their civil and religious liberties against the forces of Romanism and oppression as represented by the Stuarts, their Jacobite supporters in Britain, and their allies on the Continent, the French and Spanish. Americans considered themselves active participants in the Glorious Revolution, as William of Orange's allies in the struggle to end Stuart oppression and restore the rights of Englishmen everywhere. As a result of the Glorious Revolution and the ensuing settlement, Americans embraced a new idea of governance, the protection-allegiance covenant, that assumed that the king and his subjects were united in the primary objectives of government—the preservation of the liberties, property and Protestant religion of Englishmen in the British colonies. This idea persisted until the American Revolution.

By the reign of George II the Whig image of kingship was an important part of colonists' political culture. While, as Gordon Wood observed, England possessed the most republican constitution of any European monarchy, the alterations in government, and particularly in the ruling dynasties of the seventeenth and eighteenth centuries, had the effect only of altering the nature of "kingly sanctity."[102] By the reign of George I, neither Americans nor most Britons subscribed to the notions of divine kingship and absolute monarchy associated with the Stuarts and Bourbons. American colonists, nevertheless, viewed their ruler as sacrosanct. Under the Whig image of kingship, monarchs ruled by the consent of their subjects, yet, paradoxically, so long as they continued to live up to their role as protectors and defenders of Englishmen's rights and religion, English kings were also the anointed of God. In the political sphere, Americans characterized their kings as "nursing fathers," benevolent and just toward their subjects and ever vigilant to protect their political children.

The democratization of colonial government grew substantially over the course of the eighteenth century as colonial assemblies achieved more and more power over royal governors and councils. The growth of popular institutions in the North American provinces did not, however, necessarily diminish the constitutional role of the monarch as colonists understood it. While American political institutions appeared, at first glance, increasingly republican, colonists' dependence on the king as a powerful ally in local affairs preserved the monarchical nature of their society. Although the medical careers of English rulers ended when George I abolished the royal touch, and the king's public persona was much reduced, especially in Britain, by the first two Hanovarian rulers' lack of enthusiasm for royal displays, Americans still considered their kings to be important figures in society and politics.[103]

Colonists viewed their rulers as arbiters of order and morality, and as political allies against any who would abridge their liberties. Since the king was seen to weigh in on the side of the people, he was often employed by the colonial assemblies as an ally against royal governors and other British officials, even when those officials were actively engaged in the promulgation of policies that originated with the Crown. Americans assumed that the king's prerogatives were their last defense against tyranny, that an appeal to the throne for protection against encroachments upon their English liberties would be heard, and that their king would defend them. Their evidence for this assumption included the fact that bad governors had been recalled and that, after long controversies on such issues as permanent salaries for governors and money emissions, the Crown had often allowed the colonists to have their way. When the British government repealed the hated Stamp Act in 1766, American colonists gave credit to their king. Through the crises of Empire that followed the repeal, American colonists continued to hope that their ruler would come to his senses and deliver his provinces from the grip of a corrupt ministry and British Parliament.

The events of the year preceding the Declaration of Independence gradually eroded Americans' faith in their king. New acts of Parliament, like the Coercive Acts and the Quebec Act, the escalation of the American crisis to open war and, finally, King George's announcement that the American provinces were in open rebellion, made it difficult for colonists to maintain their rationalization of the king as a nursing father in the face of so much evidence to the contrary. Yet the idea continued to persist for lack of another political paradigm. It remained for Thomas Paine, Thomas Jefferson, and other American political thinkers to provide a new paradigm that suggested that, in America, a functional republic was possible without a king. Although the protection-allegiance covenant between good English kings and the American people died with the Declaration of Independence, notions of political leaders as nursing fathers persisted into the Early Republic and beyond.

Notes

1. *Pennsylvania Magazine, or American Monthly Museum*, January, 1775, 49-50.

2. Thomas Paine, *Common Sense*, in *Common Sense, The Rights of Man, and Other Essential Writings of Thomas Paine*, Sidney Hook, ed. (New York: The New American Library, 1969), 44.

3. "Boston, May 22," *Maryland Gazette*, June 12, 1766.

4. "Boston, May 22. Account of the Rejoicings last Monday, on the Repeal of the STAMP ACT," *Virginia Gazette*, June 20, 1766.

5. "Boston, May 22," *Maryland Gazette*, June 12, 1766.

6. "Boston, May 22," *Virginia Gazette*, June 20, 1766.

7. "Boston, May 22," *Maryland Gazette*, June 12, 1766.

8. *Maryland Gazette*, June 5, 1766.

9. "Celebrations in Queen-Anne's County," *Maryland Gazette*, June 12, 1766.

10. "New York, June 30," *Maryland Gazette*, June 30, 1766.

11. "Annapolis, December 18," *Maryland Gazette*, December 18, 1766.

12. "Supplement to the *New York Gazette or Weekly Post Boy*, June 19, 1766," *N.J.C.D.*, 25: 143-145.

13. "Humble Address of the House of Delegates of Maryland, St. James, Feb. 7, 1767," *Maryland Gazette*, May 21, 1767. For similar sentiments see "A Message to the Governor from the Assembly [of Pennsylvania], June 3, 1766," *Minutes of the Provincial Council of Pennsylvania, From the Organization to the Termination of the Proprietary Government* (Harrisburg, Pennsylvania: Theo. Fenn & Co., 1852. Rep. New York: AMS Press, 1968), 9:312-313.

14. "Humble Address of the House of Delegates of Maryland, St. James, Feb. 7, 1767," *Maryland Gazette*, May 21, 1767.

15. "Address to his Honour the Governor, November 12, 7 Geo. III, 1766," *Journals of the House of Burgesses of Virginia, 1766-1769*, John Pendleton Kennedy, ed. (Richmond: Virginia State Library, 1906), 23.

16. Jonathan Mayhew, *The Snare Broken, A Thanksgiving Discourse, Preached at the Desire of the West Church, in Boston, N.E. Friday, May 23, 1766. Occasioned by the REPEAL of the Stamp Act . . .* (Boston: R. & S. Draper, 1766), in Ellis Sandoz, *Political Sermons of the Founding Era, 1730-1805* (Indianapolis: Liberty Press, 1990), 239.

17. Jonathan Mayhew, *The Snare Broken*, 242-243.

18. Jonathan Mayhew, *The Snare Broken*, 246.

19. Jonathan Mayhew, *The Snare Broken*, 252.

20. Jonathan Mayhew, *The Snare Broken*, 252.

21. Jonathan Mayhew, *The Snare Broken*, 252-253.

22. Jonathan Mayhew, *The Snare Broken*, 241.

23. For the constitutional questions and the Stamp Tax, see Reid, *The Authority to Tax*, 12-24, *passim*. For the politics and economics of taxes, both local and

Parliamentary, in the American colonies, see Robert A. Becker, *Revolution, Reform, and the Politics of Taxation, 1763-1783* (Baton Rouge: Louisiana State University Press, 1980), 8-112.

24. Jonathan Mayhew, *The Snare Broken*, 242.

25. See "New York, November 1," *London Chronicle*, December 14, 1765; "Instructions to the Representatives of Boston, September 18, 1765," *London Chronicle*, January 9, 1766; "Instructions from the Freeholders of BRAINTREE to their Representative relative to the STAMP-ACT, October 10," *London Chronicle*, January 11, 1766; "Governor Bernard's Reply to the House of Representatives, Boston, November 11," *London Chronicle*, July 1, 1766. See also Bernard Bailyn, *The Ordeal of Thomas Hutchinson* (Cambridge, Massachusetts: Belknap Press, 1974), 116-120, passim; Bailyn, *Ideological Origins*, 122-123.

26. See "To Mr. Green, Virginia, March 1, 1766," *Maryland Gazette*, March 27, 1766; "Annapolis, April 3," *Maryland Gazette*, April 3, 1766; "New York, January 9," *Pennsylvania Gazette*, January 16, 1766; "Connecticut," *Pennsylvania Gazette*, January 23, 1766; "New London, February 28," *Pennsylvania Gazette*, March 13, 1766; "Woodbridge, [New York,] February 21, 1766," *Pennsylvania Gazette*, March 13, 1766; "Wilmington, [North Carolina,] February 26," *Pennsylvania Gazette*, March 27, 1766; "Norfolk County Meeting, March 31," *Virginia Gazette*, April 14, 1766.

27. "New York, January 9," *Pennsylvania Gazette*, January 16, 1766. See also "South Carolina, March 10," *Maryland Gazette*, April 10, 1766.

28. See Mayhew, *The Snare Broken*, Sandoz, *Political Sermons*, 243; James Otis, *The Rights of the British Colonies Asserted and Proved* (Boston: Edes & Gill, 1764), Bailyn, *Pamphlets*, 449; [Benjamin Church,] *Liberty and Property Vindicated, and the St--pm-n Burnt . . .* (Boston, 1765) Bailyn, *Pamphlets*, 592, 596.

29. Mayhew, *The Snare Broken*, Bailyn, *Pamphlets*, 242.

30. Bailyn, *Ideological Origins*, 51-52, passim; Caroline Robbins, *Eighteenth-Century Commonwealthman*, 271, *passim.*

31. For discussions of the distinctions between "internal" and "external" taxes, and Parliamentary rights and trade regulation, see Reid, *The Authority to Tax*, 33-52; Morgan, *Stamp Act*, 53-58, 152-154; Carl Lotus Becker, *The Declaration of Independence: A Study in the History of Political Ideas* (1922, 1942. Rep. New York: Vintage Books, 1958), 89-91.

32. Michael G. Kammen. *A Rope of Sand: The Colonial Agents, British Politics, and the American Revolution* (Ithaca: Cornell University Press, 1968), 59-61.

33. William Bollan to Josiah Willard. April 19, 1754. Cited in Kammen, *Rope of Sand*, 59.

34. Bailyn, *Ideological Origins*, 53.

35. Bailyn, *Ideological Origins*, 52.

36. Bailyn, *Ideological Origins*, 53.

37. Leonard Levy, *Legacy of Suppression: Freedom of Speech and the Press in Early American History* (Cambridge, Massachusetts: Belknap Press, 1960), 39-41.

38. Brewer, *Party Ideology*, 96. For Pitt's resignation, see Brewer, *Party Ideology*, 103-104.

39. For a discussion of Pitt under George III, see Brewer, *Party Ideology*, 96-111. For Pitt and the politics of the Stamp Act repeal, see Morgan, *Stamp Act Crisis*, 329-336; Owen, *The Eighteenth Century*, 180-185. For the British side of the Stamp Act in general, see Peter David Garner Thomas, *British Politics and the Stamp Act Crisis: The First Phase of the American Revolution, 1763-1767* (Oxford: Clarendon Press, 1975).

40. For the use of the press by political factions in Britain, see Brewer, *Party Ideology*, 220-239. For coverage of the use of satire in the political contests of the period, and especially against Lord Bute, see, Vincent Carretta, *George III and the Satirists from Hogarth to Byron* (Athens, Georgia: University of Georgia Press, 1990), 57-87, *passim.*

41. Lord Bute's ministry ended in 1763. Richard Pares notes that George III had "recovered from his puerile admiration" of Bute by 1765, when he refused to meet with him anymore (Richard Pares, *King George III and the Politicians: The Ford Lectures, Delivered in the University of Oxford, 1951-2* (London: Oxford University Press, 1953), 107). For discussions of Bute as "Favorite," see Brewer, *Party Ideology,* 119-127, *passim.*; Pares, *King George III*, 46-47, 84-88, 116-117, *passim.* For Bute as a "secret influence" in British politics, see Bailyn, *Ideological Origins*, 145-148.

42. Church, *Liberty and Property Vindicated*, Bailyn, *Pamphlets*, 592.

43. See Robert Middlekauff, *The Glorious Cause* (New York: Oxford University Press, 1982), 90.

44. See Bailyn, *Ideological Origins*, 122-123.

45. "America Swallowing the Bitter Draught," *Royal American Magazine*, June, 1774, insert.

46. John Adams, *Diary*, in *Adams' Works*, 2:362.

47. Gordon Wood, "Conspiracy and the Paranoid Style: Causality and Deceit in the Eighteenth Century," *William and Mary Quarterly*, 3rd ser. 39 (January, 1982), 418. See also Bailyn, *Ideological Origins,* 144-159, *passim.*

48. Wood, "Conspiracy," 421.

49. "Extracts from the FREEHOLDER'S Political Catechism," *Lord Bolingbroke: Contributions to the Craftsman*, Simon Varey, ed. (Oxford: Clarendon Press, 1982), 162.

50. John Wilkes, cited in Bailyn, *Ideological Origins,* 131. See Bailyn's explanation of the ministerial conspiracy theory in *Ideological Origins*, 129-137.

51. "Petition of the Continental Congress to the King," *Pennsylvania Magazine*, 48.

52. "Philadelphia Resolutions Against the Tea Act," *Royal American Magazine,* January, 1774.

53. "Petition of the Continental Congress to the King," 48. Virtually all of the above complaints are enumerated in this petition.

54. "Petition of the Continental Congress to the King," 49.

55. Middlekauff, *The Glorious Cause,* 231.

56. The Quebec Act, June 22, 1774, cited in *Documents of American History,* 8th ed., Henry Steele Commager, ed. (New York: Appleton-Century-Crofts, Meredith Corp., 1968), 75.

57. See "The Mitred Minuet: A Vision," *Royal American Magazine,* October, 1774, 365; Moses Mather, *America's Appeal to the Impartial World,* Sandoz, *Political Sermons,* 480; Samuel Sherwood, *The Church's Flight into the Wilderness,* Sandoz, *Political Sermons,* 514; Samuel Langdon, *Government Corrupted by Vice, and Recovered by Righteousness* [election sermon] (Watertown, Massachusetts: Benjamin Edes, 1775), in A.W. Plumstead, *The Wall and the Garden: Selected Massachusetts Sermons, 1670-1775* (Minneapolis: University of Minnesota Press, 1968), 360. See also Bailyn, *Ideological Origins,* 119.

58. Samuel Sherwood, *The Church's Flight,* Sandoz, *Political Sermons,* 514, 513.

59. "Declaration and Resolves of the First Continental Congress, October 14, 1774," Commager, *Documents,* 84. See also "Address of the Continental Congress to the Inhabitants of Canada, May 29, 1775," Commager, *Documents,* 91-92. Interestingly, this document makes no mention of the religious aspects of the Quebec settlement, only informing Canadians that the Act created a despotic government.

60. Moses Mather, *America's Appeal to an Impartial World,* Sandoz, *Political Sermons,* 474.

61. Mather, *America's Appeal,* 484-485.

62. Thomas Jefferson, *A Summary View of the Rights of British America,* in Max Beloff, ed. *The Debate on the American Revolution, 1761-1783,* 3rd ed. (Dobbs Ferry, New York: Sheridan House, 1989), 168.

63. For a study of the political constraints placed on George III in the early years of his reign, see Brewer, *Party Ideology,* 112-126. See also Keir, *Constitutional History,* 296-298.

64. See Keir, *Constitutional History,* 295.

65. See Reid, *The Authority to Tax,* 115-121, 239-240; Morgan, *Stamp Act,* 105-112.

66. Soame Jenyns, *The Objections to the Taxation of Our American Colonies by the Legislature of Great Britain, Briefly Consider'd,* Beloff, *Debate on the American Revolution,* 79.

67. See H.T. Dickinson, *Liberty and Property,* 217-220; Brewer, *Party Ideology,* 208-216.

68. Sir Francis Bernard to Lord Barrington, 23 November, 1765, Beloff, *Debate on the American Revolution*, 86.

69. John Adams, "Novanglus No. VIII," *Adams' Works*, 4:122. See also Cook, *A Sermon*, Plumstead, *The Wall and the Garden*, 339; Mayhew, *the Snare Broken*, Sandoz, *Political Sermons*, 240-241; [John Jaochim Zubly,] *An Humble Inquiry into the Nature of Dependency of the American Colonies upon the Parliament of Great-Britain . . . by a Freeholder of South-Carolina* (1769), Sandoz, *Political Sermons*, 272-273; Thomas Pownall, *The Administration of the British Colonies. The Fifth Edition. Wherein Their Rights and Constitution are Discussed* (London: J, Walter, 1774), 1:50-51.

70. Adams, "Novanglus No. VIII," *Adams' Works*, 4:123. See also [Anon,] *The Liberty and Property of British Subjects Asserted In a Letter from an Assembly-man in Carolina To his Friend in London* (London: J. Roberts, 1727), 26-27.

71. John Adams, "Novanglus No. VIII," *Adams' Works*, 4:122

72. For a few examples of these sentiments, see Elliot, *Give Cesar His Due*, 14; Barnard (Harvard 1709), *The Presence of the Great God*, 22; Chauncy, *Civil Magistrates Must be Just*, 16; Samuel Cook, *A Sermon*, Plumstead, *The Wall and the Garden*, 328, 338-339; Mayhew, *The Snare Broken*, Sandoz, *Political Sermons*, 240; [Zubly,] *An Humble Inquiry*, Sandoz, *Political Sermons*, 270, passim; "To Mr. Green," *Maryland Gazette*, March 27, 1766; [John Dickinson,] "Letters from a Farmer in Pennsylvania, To the Inhabitants of Great Britain, No. 2," *Maryland Gazette*, December 31, 1767.

73. See "The Humble Petition and Memorial of the Assembly of Jamaica, December 28, 1774." *Pennsylvania Magazine*, January, 1775, 95-96.

74. Middlekauff, *The Glorious Cause*, 315.

75. "To the Editor," *Royal American Magazine*, December, 1774.

76. John Witherspoon, *The Dominion of Providence Over the Passions of Men*, Sandoz, *Political Sermons*, 550.

77. Moses Mather, *America's Appeal*, Sandoz, *Political Sermons*, 489. For a similar comparison with a more millenarian flavor, see Samuel Sherwood, *The Church's Flight*, Sandoz, *Political Sermons*, 500.

78. "Committee Report, May 15, 1776," *Adams' Works*, 3:46.

79. For a study of Paine and his works, see Eric Foner, *Tom Paine and Revolutionary America* (New York: Oxford University Press, 1976). For a short analysis of Paine's ideas equated with vicarious regicide, see Winthrop Jordan, "Familial Politics: Thomas Paine and the Killing of the King, 1776," *Journal of American History*, 60 (September, 1973), 294-308.

80. Paine, *Common Sense*, 30.

81. Paine, *Common Sense*, 30, 32-33.

82. Paine, *Common Sense*, 33.

83. Paine, *Common Sense*, 36.

84. Paine, *Common Sense*, 44-45.

85. See Kramnick, *Bolingbroke*, 163-168.

86. Six of them are published in Pauline Maier, *American Scripture: Making the Declaration of Independence* (New York: Alfred A. Knopf, 1997), 226-234.

87. "The Address and Instructions of the Freeholders of Buckingham County, Virginia, May 13, 1776[?]," in Maier, *American Scripture*, 226.

88. "Buckingham Freeholders' Address," Maier, *American Scripture*, 228-229. For similar sentiments, see "Cheraws District, South Carolina, May 20, 1776," in Maier, *American Scripture*, 229; "Charles County, Maryland Insrtructions, June, 1776," Maier, *American Scripture*, 231; "Town Meeting of Topsfield, Massachusetts, June 21, 1776," Maier, *American Scripture*, 233; Richard Henry Lee to Landon Carter, Philadelphia, 2d June 1776, James Curtis Ballagh, ed., *The Letters of Richard Henry Lee*, 2 vols. (New York: Macmillan Co., 1912), 1:200.

89. "The Declaration of Independence: The Jefferson Draft with Congress's Editorial Changes," in Maier, *American Scripture*, 237.

90. Paine, *Common Sense*, 49.

91. See Witherspoon, *The Dominion of Providence*, Sandoz, *Political Sermons*, 545, 547, passim; John Fletcher, *The Bible and the Sword: Or, the Appointment of the General Fast Vindicated . . .* (London, 1776), Sandoz, *Political Sermons*, 565; Abraham Keteltas, *God Arising*, Sandoz, *Political Sermons*, 589, *passim.*

92. Jacob Cushing, *Divine Judgements upon Tyrants: And Compassion to the Oppressed . . .* (Boston: Powars and Willis, 1778), Sandoz, *Political Sermons*, 619. See also Samuel Cooper, *A Sermon on the Day of the Commencement of the Constitution . . . of the Commonwealth of Massachusetts* (Boston: Fleet & Gill, 1780), Sandoz, *Political Sermons*, 646.

93. Samuel McClintock, *A Sermon on the Occasion of the Commencement of the New-Hampshire Constitution* (Portsmouth, New-Hampshire, 1784), Sandoz, *Political Sermons*, 802-803.

94. Israel Evans, *A Sermon Delivered at the Annual Election . . . of the State of New Hampshire* (Concord: George Hough, 1791), Sandoz, *Political Sermons*, 1070.

95. Cited in Paul K. Longmore, *The Invention of George Washington* (Berkeley: University of California Press, 1988), 204-205.

96. Moses Mather, *America's Appeal*, Sandoz, *Political Sermons*, 489.

97. Longmore, *Invention of George Washington*, 204-205.

98. See Longmore, *Invention of George Washington*, 207; Barry Schwartz, *George Washington: The Making of a Symbol* (Ithaca: Cornell University Press, 1978), 117.

99. Henry Holcombe, *A Sermon Ossasioned by the Death of Leiutenant-General George Washington, Late President of the United States of America. . .* (Savannah, Georgia: Seymour & Woolhopter, 1800), in Sandoz, *Political Sermons*, 1408.

100. See Schwartz, *George Washington*, 122-125.

101. Mercy Otis Warren, *History of the Rise, Progress and Termination of the American Revolution Interspersed with Biographical, Political and Moral Observations*. 2 Vols. (Boston: Manning and Loring, 1805; reprint, Indianapolis: Liberty Classics, 1988), 2:674-275.

102. Wood, *Radicalism*, 98.

103. Wood, *Radicalism*, 98.

Epilogue

Instead of the great tree that used to shelter the quiet little Dutch inn of yore, there now was reared a tall, naked pole, with something on the top that looked like a red nightcap, and from it was fluttering a flag, on which was a singular assemblage of stars and stripes–all this was strange and incomprehensible. He recognized on the sign, however, the ruby face of King George, under which he had smoked so many a peaceful pipe; but even this was singularly metamorphosed. The red coat was changed for one of blue and buff, a sword was held in the hand instead of a scepter, the head was decorated with a cocked hat, and underneath was painted in large characters, GENERAL WASHINGTON.

Washington Irving, "Rip VanWinkle"

Bibliography

Primary Sources

Newspapers and Periodicals
British Mercury (London)
Common Sense (London)
The Craftsman (London)
Daily Gazeteer (London)
The Evening Post (London)
Extract from the Political State of Great Britain (Boston)
The Flying-Post; or Post-Master (London)
Fog's Weekly Journal (London)
The General Magazine and Historical Chronicle (Philadelphia)
The Independent Reflector (New York)
John Englishman, In Defence of the English Constitution (New York)
London Chronicle
London Gazette
London Journal
Maryland Gazette
New England Courant (Boston)
New York Weekly Journal
North Carolina Gazette
The Patriot (London)
Pennsylvania Gazette
Pennsylvania Journal
Pennsylvania Magazine, Or American Monthly Museum
The Plebian (London)
The Royal American Magazine (Boston)
South Carolina Gazette
The St. James Journal (London)
Virginia Gazette
The Weekly Rehearsal (Boston)

Other Primary Sources

A Woman of Quality. *The Amours of Messalina, Late Queen of Albion, in Which are Briefly Couch'd Secrets of the Imposture of the Cambrion Prince, The Gothic League, and Other Court Intrigues of the Four Last Years Reign, Not Yet Made Publick.* London: John Lyford, 1689.

A Woman of Quality. *The Second Part of the Amours of Messalina, Late Queen of Albion, Wherein the Secret Court Affairs of the Last Four Years Reign Are Pursued; Particularly the Imposture of the Child.* London: John Lyford, 1689.

A Woman of Quality. *The Amours of the French King with the Late Queen of Albion, Being the Fourth Part of the History of Messalina.* London: John Lyford, 1689.

Abbadie, James. *A Panegyric on Our Late Sovereign Lady Mary Queen of England, Scotland, France, and Ireland, Of Glorious and Immortal Memory who Died at Kensington, on the 18th of December, 1694.* London: Hugh Newman, 1695.

Adams, Charles Francis, ed. *Works of John Adams.* 10 vols. Boston: Little & Brown, 1850-1856.

Addison, Joseph. *The Freeholder.* James Leheny, ed. Oxford: Clarendon Press, 1979.

------. *The Works of Joseph Addison: Including The Whole Contents of B.P. Hurd's Edition, With Letters and Other Pieces Not Found in Any Previous Collection...,* 6 vols., George Washington Greene, ed. (Philadelphia: J.B. Lippincott & Co., 1880).

Anderson, John. *The Book of the Chronicles of His Royal Highness, William Duke of Cumberland: Being an Account of the Rise and Progress of the Current Rebellion.* (New York, 1746).

Andrews, Charles M. *Narratives of the Insurrections, 1675-1690.* New York: Charles Scribner's Sons, 1915.

Andros, Edmund. *The Andros Papers: Files of the Provincial Secretary of New York During the Administration of Governor Sir Edmund Andros, 1674-1680.* 2 vols. Peter R. Christoph and Florence A. Christoph, eds. With Translation from the Dutch by Charles T. Gehring. *The New York Historical Manuscript Series,* vols. XXIV-XXV. Syracuse, New York: Syracuse University Press, 1989.

[Annet, Peter?]. *A Discourse on Government and Religion, Calculated for the Meridian of the Thirteenth of January, By an Independent . . .* Boston, 1750.

[Anon.] *The Abdicated Prince: or, The Adventures of Four Years. A Tragi-Comedy, as it was Lately Acted at the Court of Alba Regalis, by Several Persons of Great Quality* . . . London, 1690.

[Anon.] *An Appeal to the Men of New England.* Boston, 1689.

[Anon.] *A Brief Account of the Moral and Political Acts of the Kings and Queens of England.* London, 1793.

[Anon.] *The Character of His Royal Highness William Henry Prince of Wales.* London, 1689.

[Anon.] *The Confession of Mrs. Judith Wilks the Queen's Midwife, With a full Account of Her Running Away by Night; and Going into France.* London[?], 1689.

[Anon.] *The Humble Address of the Publicans of New-England, To Which King You Please, With Some Remarks Upon it. (A Publican is a Creature that Lives Upon the Common-Wealth).* London, 1691.

[Anon.] *A Letter to a Gentleman at Brussels Containing an Account of the Causes of the Peoples Revolt from the CROWN.* London, 1689.

[Anon.] *A Letter from a Gentleman at St. Germians to his Friend in London.* London, 1697.

[Anon.] *A Letter from a Lawyer in the Country to a Member of Parliament: or, Indemnity the Effect of Vacancy.* London, 1689.

[Anon.] *A Letter to a Lord in ANSWER to a Late Pamphlet Intituled, The Causes of the Present Fears and Dangers of the Government, in a DISCOURSE between a Lord-Lieutenant and One of his Deputies.* London, [?].

[Anon.] *A Letter Writ by a Clergy-Man to his Neighbour. Concerning the Present Circumstances of the Kingdom, and the Allegiance that is Due to the King and Queen.* London, 1689.

[Anon.] *The Liberty and Property of British Subjects Asserted In A Letter from an Assembly-Man in Carolina To his Friend in London.* London: J. Roberts, 1727.

[Anon.] *The Lords and Commons Reasons for the Deprivation and Disposal of James II. From the Imperial Throne of England. Being in Full Satisfaction to all the Princes of Europe, and an Answer to all Objections, Domestic and Foraign.* London, 1689.

[Anon.] *Loyalty Vindicated. Being an Answer to the Late* False, Seditious & Scandalous *Pamphlet Entituled, A Letter to a Gentleman of the City of New York* . . . *Published for the Sake of Truth and Justice. By a Hearty Lover of King William and the Protestant Religion.* Boston: B. Green & J. Allen, 1698.

[Anon.] *The Pagan Prince: Or a Comical History of the Heroick Achievements of the Palatine of Eboracum. By the Author of the Secret History of King* Charles *II and K.* James *II.* Amsterdam, 1690.

[Anon.] *The Plain Case Stated.* Boston, 1689.

[Anon.] *The Present Dangerous Crisis.* London, 1763

[Anon.] *A Rara Show, A Rara Shight! A Strange Monster (the Like Not in Europe) To be Seen Near* Tower-Hill, *a Few Doors Beyond the Lion's Den.* London: R. Janeway, 1689.

[Anon.] *A Short Account Touching the Succession of the Crown* (London[?], 1689[?]).

[Anon.] *A Short Historical Account Touching the Succession of the Crown.* (London, 1689).

[Anon.] *A Short Review of the Remarkable Providences Attending Our Gracious Sovereign William the IIId Continued from the Year 1693, Down to this Day.* London: Tho. Ax, 1799?.

[Anon.] *A Suppliment to the Muses, Farewell to Popery and Slavery, or a Collection of Miscellany Poems, Satyrs, Songs, &c, Made by the Most Eminent of Wits in the Nation, as the Shams, Intreaques, and Plots of Priests and Jesuits gave Occasion.* London, 1690.

[Anon.] *Two Letters Discovering the Designs of the Late King James in* Ireland *Written from a Person of Quality to a Noble Peer Sitting in the* HOUSE *of* LORDS. London, 1689.

[Anon.] *Tyrconnel's Letter to the French King from Ireland.* (London, 1690).

Appleton, Nathaniel. *The Cry of Oppression Where Judgement is Looked for . . .* Boston: J. Draper, 1748.

------. *The Great Blessing of Good Rulers, Depends Upon God's Giving his Judgements & His Righteousness to Them. A Sermon Preached Before His Excellency William Shirley, Esq;... May 26, 1742. Being the Day for the Election of His Majesty's Council . . .* Boston: J. Draper, 1742.

Bailyn, Bernard, ed. *Pamphlets of the American Revolution, 1750-1776.* Vol. I. Cambridge, Mass.: Harvard University Press, 1965

Balch, William. *A Public Spirit, as Express'd in Praying for the Peace and Seeking the Good of Jerusalem, Recommended to Rulers and People . . .* [Massachusetts election sermon] Boston, 1749.

Ballagh, James Curtis, ed. *The Letters of Richard Henry Lee*, 2 vols. New York: Macmillan Co., 1912.

Bancroft, George, et al., eds. "Documents Relating to the Administration of Leisler." *Collections of the New York Historical Society For the Year 1868*. New York, 1868, 241-423.

Banks, John. *The History of the Life and Reign of William III, King of England, Prince of Orange, and Hereditary Stadtholder of the United Provinces* . . . London, 1744.

Barnard, John (Harvard, 1709). *The Presence of the Great God in the Assembly of Political Rulers* . . . [Massachusetts election sermon, May 28th, 1746]. Boston: J. Draper.

Barnard, John. *The Throne Established by Righteousness* . . . Boston, 1734.

Bellof, Max, ed. *The Debate on the American Revolution, 1761-1783*. 3rd ed. Dobbs Ferry, New York: Sheridan House, 1989.

Burnet, Gilbert. *An Abridgement of Bishop Burnet's History of His Own Times*. London, 1724.

------. *A Compleat History of the Glorious Life and Reign of the Most Renowned Monarch, William the Third* . . . London, 1702.

Calendar of State Papers. Colonial Series, America and the West Indies, Preserved in Her Majesty's Public Record Office. W. Noel Sainsbury, J.W. Fortescue, and Cecil Headlam, eds. 42 vols. (London, 1860-1953).

Carswell, Francis. *England's Restoration Parallel'd in Judah's: or The Primative Judge and Counsellor. In a Sermon Before the Honourable Judge at Abbington Assizes, for the County of Berks. Aug. 6, 1689*. London, 1689.

Chauncy, Charles. *Civil Magistrates Must be Just, Ruling in the Fear of God* . . . [Massachusetts election sermon, 1747]. Boston, 1747.

------. *The Council of Two Confederate Kings to Set the Son of Tabeal on the Throne Represented as Evil... A Sermon Occasion'd by the Present Rebellion in Favour of the Pretender...February 6th, 1745[/6]* . . . Boston: D. Gookin, 1746.

Checkley, Samuel. *The Duty of a People to Lay to Heart and Lament the Death of a Great KING* . . . [Sermon preached August 20, 1727]. Boston, 1727.

Claridge, Richard. *A Looking Glass for Religious Princes: or, The Character and Work of Josiah Delivered in a Sermon . . ., April 5, 1692, at Peeshore in Worcester-shire*. . . London, 1691.

"The Clarendon Papers," *Collections of the New York Historical Society for the Year 1869*. New York: New York Historical Society, 1870. 1-159.

Clay, Charles. *Sermon on Psalm 22.28.* Unpublished sermon notebook, ca. 1760. Clay Family Papers. Mss 1 C5795 no. 18-23, Virginia Historical Society.

Colden, Cadwallader. "Letters on Smith's History of New York," *Collections of the New York Historical Society For the Year 1868.* (New York, 1868), 175-235.

Colman, Benjamin. *Fidelity to Christ . . .* Boston: T. Fleet, 1727.

------. *God is a Great King . . .* Boston: S. Kneeland, 1733.

------. *Government the Pillar of the Earth. . .* Boston, 1730.

------. *A Sermon for the Reformation of Manners . . .* (Boston: Fleet & Crump, 1716.

------. *A Sermon Preach'd at Boston in New England, on Thursday the 23rd of August, 1716. Being the Day of Public Thanksgiving, for the Suppression of the Late Vile and Traitorous Rebellion in Great Britain.* Boston: Fleet & Crump, 1716.

Colonial Records of North Carolina. William L. Saunders, ed. Vols. 3-4. Raliegh: P.M. Hale, 1886.

[Comber, Thomas.] *The Protestant Mask Taken Off from the Jesuited Englishmen; Being an Answer to a Book, Entituled* GREAT BRITAIN'*s* Just Complaint. London, 169²/₃.

Commager, Henry Steele, ed. *Documents of American History.* 8th ed. New York: Appleton-Century-Crofts, 1968.

Cook, Samuel. *An Election Sermon.* Boston, 1770.

Cooper, Samuel. *A Sermon on the Day of the Commencement of the Constitution . . .* Boston[?], 1780.

Cradock, Thomas. *The Poetic Writings of Thomas Cradock, 1718-1770.* David Curtis Skaggs, ed. Newark: University of Delaware Press, 1983.

------. *Two Sermons...Preached on the Occasion of the Suppression of the Scotch Rebellion . . .* Annapolis, Jonas Green, 1747.

Cummings, Archibald. *The Character of a Righteous Ruler. A Sermon Upon the Death of the Honourable Patrick Gordon. Christ's Church, Philadelphia, August 8, 1736 . . .* Philadelphia: Andrew Bradford, 1736.

Davies, Samuel. *Religion and Patriotism the Constituents of a Good Soldier . . . Hanover County, Virginia, August 17, 1755 . . .* Philadelphia: James Chattin, 1755.

Dickens, Lilian, and Mary Stanton, eds. *An Eighteenth Century Correspondence.* London: John Murray, 1910.

Dilworth, W.H. *The Protestant Hero: Or the History of William the Third, the Great Restorer of British Liberty . . .* London[?]: G. Wright, 1758.

Documentary History of the State of New York. Edmund B. O'Callaghan, ed. 4 vols. Albany: Weed, Parsons, & Co., 1850.

"Documents Relating to the Colonial History of the State of New Jersey: Journal of the Governor and Council, Vol. 4, 1748-1755," *Archives of the State of New Jersey*. 1ˢᵗ Series. Vol. XVI. Frederick W. Ricord, ed. Trenton: John L. Murphey Publishing Co., 1891.

Documents Relative to the Colonial History of the State of New York; Procured in Holland, England and France. John R. Brodhead, Edmund B. O'Callghan, Berthold Fernow, eds. 15 vols. Weed, Parsons, & Co., 1853-1885.

Dongan, Thomas. *The Dongan Papers, 1683-1688*. 2 vols. Peter R. Christoph, ed. *The New York Historical Manuscripts Series*, vols. 34-35. Syracuse, New York: Syracuse University Press, 1993, 1996.

Eells, Nathaniel. *The Wise Ruler, a Loyal Subject . . .* [Connecticut election sermon] Hartford, 1748.

Eliot, Jared. *Give Cesar [sic] His Due: or, an Obligation that Subjects are Under to their Civil Rulers . . . A Sermon Preached before the General Assembly of Connecticut, May 11th, 1736*. New London: T. Green, 1738.

[Eyre, William]. *A Vindication of the Letter out of the North, Concerning Bishop Lake's Declaration of his Dying in the Belief of the Doctrine of Passive Obedience, &c . . .* London, $16^{89}/_{90}$.

Fagel, Gaspar. *A Letter writ by Mijn Heer Fagel, Pensioner of Holland, to Mr. James Stewart, Advocate, Giving an Account of the Prince and Princess of Orange's Thoughts Concerning the Repeal of the Test, and the Penal Laws*. Amsterdam[?],1688.

Filmer, Sir Robert. *Patriarchia: or the Natural Power of Kings*, in *Two Treatises of Government, by John Locke. With a Supplement Patriarchia by Robert Filmer*. Thomas I. Cook, ed. New York: Hafner Press, 1947, 249-310.

Fraser, J. *A Friendly Letter to the Father Petre, Concerning his Part in the Late King's Government: Publish'd for his Defence and Justification*. London: Richard Baldwin, 1690.

Gay, Ebenezer. *The Character and Work of a Good Ruler, and Duty of an Obliged People . . .* [Massachusetts election sermon] Boston: D. Gookin, 1745.

------. *The Duty of a People to Pray for and Praise their Rulers . . .* Boston: Thomas Fleet, 1730.

Gordon, John. *A Sermon on the Suppression of the Late Unnatural Rebellion*. Annapolis: Jonas Green, 1746.

Hall, Michael, G., Lawrence H. Leder, and Michael G. Kammen, eds. *The Glorious Revolution in America: Documents on the Colonial Crisis of 1689.* Chapel Hill: University of North Carolina Press, 1964.

Hancock, John. *Rulers Should be Benefactors . . .* Boston, 1722.

Hobbes, Thomas. *Leviathan.* C.B. MacPherson, ed. London: Penguin Books, 1981.

Holyoke, Edward. *Integrity and Religion Pricipally Regarded, by such as Design Others to Stations of Public Trust . . .* [Massachusetts election sermon, May 26, 1736]. Boston, J. Draper, 1736.

Hughes, Thomas. *The Court of Neptune. A Poem Address'd to the Right Honourable Charles Montague, Esq.* London: Jacob Jonson, 1700.

Hume, David. *Essays Moral, Political, and Literary.* ed. T.H. Green and T.H. Grose. 2 Vols. New York: Longmans, Green & Co., 1907.

Hunn, Nathaniel, *The Welfare of the Government Considered . . .* [Connecticut election sermon] New London: T. Green, 1747.

Jensen, Merrill. *English Historical Documents: American Historical Documents to 1776.* Vol. IX. London: Eyre & Spottiswoode, 1955.

Johnson, Samuel. *Samuel Johnson's Dictionary of the English Language.* Alexander Chalmers, ed. London: Studio Editions, 1994.

Journals of the House of Burgesses of Virginia, 1727-1734, 1736-1740. H.R. McIlwane, ed. Richmond, Virginia, 1910.

Journals of the House of Burgesses of Virginia, 1742-1747, 1748-1749. H.R. McIlwane, ed. Richmond, Virginia, 1909.

Journals of the House of Burgesses of Virginia, 1766-1769. John Pendleton Kennedy, ed. Richmond, Virginia, 1906.

Keteltas, Abraham. *God Arising and Pleading the People's Cause . . .* Newburyport, Massachusetts, 1777.

Larabee, Leonard Woods, ed. *Royal Instructions to British Colonial Governors, 1670-1776.* 2 Vols. Prepared under direction of the American Historical Association. New York: D. Appleton, 1935.

Lewes, Daniel. *Good Rulers, the Fathers of their People, and the Marks of Honour Due Them. . .* [Massachusetts election sermon, 1748]. Boston: John Draper, 1748.

Locke, John. *Second Treatise of Civil Government By John Locke. With a Supplement Patriarcha by Robert Filmer.* Thomas I. Cook, ed. New York: Hafner Press, 1947.

[Mather, Cotton?] *A Letter of Advice to the Churches of the Non-Conformists in the English Nation. . .* London, 1700.

Mather, Cotton. *The Glorious Throne: A Short View of Our Great Redeemer on his Throne . . . What has Occurred in the Death of Our Late Memorable Sovereign and the Legal Succession of the British Crown to the Illustrious House of Hanover . . .* Boston: B. Green, 1714.

------. *Magnalia Christi Americana: Books I and II.* Kenneth B. Murdock, ed. Cambridge, Massachusetts: Belknap Press of Harvard University, 1977.

------. *The Present State of New-England.* Boston: Samuel Green, 1690.

------. *Souldiers Counselled and Comforted: A Discourse Delivered unto Some Part of the Forces Engaged in the Just War of New-England Against the Northern & Eastern Indians, Sept. 1, 1689.* Boston: Samuel Green, 1689.

------. *The Way to Prosperity . . .* [Massachusetts election sermon, 1689]. Boston: Richard Pierce, 1690

Mather, Increase. *A Vindication of New-England, From the Vile Aspersions Cast Upon that Country By a Late ADDRESS of a Faction there, Who Denominate themselves of the Church of England in Boston.* London, 1690[?].

Mather, Moses. *America's Appeal to an Impartial World.* Hartford, 1775.

Mather, Samuel. *The Fall of the Mighty Lamented. A Funeral Discourse Upon the Death of Her most Excellent Majesty Wilhelmina Dorothea Carolina.* Boston, 1738.

------. *A Funeral Discourse Preached on the Occasion of the Death of the High, Puissant, and Most Illustrious Prince Frederick Lewis, Prince of Great Britain . . .* Boston: J. Draper, 1751.

------. *The Life of the Very Reverend and Learned Cotton Mather . . .* Boston, 1729.

Mayhew, Jonathan. *An Election Sermon, May 29, 1754* [Massachusetts election sermon]. Boston, 1754.

------. *A Discourse Concerning Unlimited Submission. . .* Boston, 1750.

------. *A Discourse Occasioned by the Death of King George II. And the Happy Accession of His Majesty King George III.* Boston, 1761.

------. *A Sermon Preached at Boston in New England, May 26, 1751, Occasioned by the Much Lamented Death of His Royal Highness, Frederick, Prince of Wales . . .* Boston: Richard Draper, 1751.

------. *The Snare Broken, A Thanksgiving Discourse, Preached at the Desire of the West Church in Boston, N.E., Friday, May 23, 1766. Occasioned by the Repeal of the Stamp Act . . .* Boston: R. & S. Draper, 1766.

Merchant, John. *A Genuine and Impartial History of the Late Rebellion in Great-Britain.* New York: James Parker, 1747.

Miner, Earl. "Poems on the Reign of William III (1690, 1696, 1699, 1702)," *The Augustan Reprint Society No. 166.* Los Angeles: William Andrews Clark Memorial Library, University of California, 1974.

Minkema, Kenneth P., ed. *The Works of Jonathan Edwards.* New Haven: Yale University Press, 1997.

Minutes of the Provincial Council of Pennsylvania, From the Organization to the Termination of the Proprietary Government. Vol. 9. Harrisburg, Pennsylvania: Theo. Fenn & Co., 1852. Rep. New York: AMS Press, 1968.

"Minutes of the Supreme Court of Judicature, April 4, 1693 to April 1, 1701," *Collections of the New York Historical Society for the Year 1912.* New York, 1912. 41-214.

Paine, Thomas. *Common Sense, The Rights of Man, and Other Essential Writings of Thomas Paine.* Sidney Hook, ed. New York: New American Library, 1969.

Palfrey, John Gorham. *History of New England,* Vol. 3-4. Boston: Little, Brown & Co., 1882.

Paltsits, Victor Hugo. *Minutes of the Executive Council of the Province of New York, Administration of Francis Lovelace, 1668-1673.* 2 Vols. Albany: J.B. Lyon & Co. For the state of New York, 1910.

Parker, Henry. *The True Portraiture of the Kings and Queens of England.* London, 1688.

Pemberton, Ebenezer. *A Sermon Preached at the Presbyterian Church in New-York, July 31, 1746. Being a Day of Solemn Thanksgiving... for the Late Victory Obtained by His Majesty's Arms, Under the Conduct of His Royal Highness the Duke of Cumberland, Over the Rebels in North Britain . . .* New York: James Parker, 1746.

Plumstead, A.W., ed. *The Wall and the Garden: Selected Massachusetts Election Sermons, 1670-1775.* Minneapolis: University of Minnesota Press, 1968.

Pownall, Thomas. *The Administration of the British Colonies, The Fifth Edition. Wherein Their Rights and Constitution are Discussed.* Vol. 1. London: J. Walter, 1774.

Prince, Thomas. *The People of New-England Put in Mind of the Righteous Acts of the Lord to Them and Their Fathers. . .* [Massachusetts election sermon]. Boston: B. Green, 1730.

------. *A Sermon on the Sorrowful Occasion of the Death of His Late Majesty King George of Blessed Memory . . .* Boston, 1727.

"Proceedings of the Council of Maryland, 1687/8-1693," *Archives of Maryland*. Vol. 8. William Hand Brown, ed. Baltimore, Isaac Friedenwald for the Maryland Historical Society, 1890.

"Proceedings of the General Court of Assizes, Held in the City of New York, October 6, 1680, to October 6, 1682," *Collections of the New York Historical Society for the Year 1912*. New York, 1913, 3-38.

Quincy, Samuel. *Twenty Sermons...Preached in the Parish of St. Philip, Charles-Town, South-Carolina*. Boston: John Draper, 1750.

Rae, Peter. *The History of the Late Rebellion: Rais'd Against His Majesty King George, By the Friends of the Popish Pretender*. Dumfries, 1718.

Randolph, Edward. *Edward Randolph, Including his Letters and Official Papers from the New England, Middle, and Southern Colonies in America, with Other Documents Relating Chiefly to the Vacating of the Royal Charter of the Colony of Massachusetts Bay, 1676-1703. With Historical Illustrations and a Memoir by Robert Noxon Toppan....* Robert N. Toppan, ed. vols. 27, 28. The Prince Society, Boston, Vol. XXVII, 1899. Reprint. New York: Burt Franklin, 1967.

[Rawson, Edward and Samuel Sewall]. *The Revolution in New England Justified, and the People there Vindicated from the Aspersions Cast upon them by Mr. Joseph Palmer, in his Pretended Answer to the Declaration, Published by the Inhabitants of Boston, and the Country Adjacent . . ., By E.R. & S.S.* Boston, 1691.

Sandoz, Ellis, ed. *Political Sermons of the American Founding Era, 1730-1805*. Indianapolis: Liberty Press, 1991.

Sewall, Samuel. *Diary of Samuel Sewall, 1674-1729.* 3 Vols. *Collections of the Massachusetts Historical Society*, Vol. V, Fifth Series. Cambridge, Massachusetts: University Press, 1878.

------. *Letter Book of Samuel Sewall. Collections of the Massachusetts Historical Society*, Vol. I, Sixth Series. Cambridge, Massachusetts: University Press, 1886.

Sherlock, William. *A Sermon Preached at the Temple-Church, May 29, 1692. . .* London, 1692.

------. *A Sermon Preached at White-hall, Before the Queen, on the 17th of June, 1691, Being a Fast Day.* London, 1691.

Shower, Sir Bartholomew. *The Justice of the Parliament, In Inflicting Punishments Subsequent to Offenses, Vindicated. And the Lawfulness of the Present Government Asserted . . .* London, 1689.

Shute, John Viscount Barrington. *A Dissuasive from Jacobitism: Shewing in General what the* NATION *is to Expect from a Popish King, and in Particular, from the Pretender . . .* 2nd ed. London, 1713.

Sidney, Algernon. *Discourses Concerning Government.* Thomas G. West, ed. Indianapolis: Liberty Press Classics, [no date].

Stoughten, William. *A Narrative of the Proceedings of Sir Edmund Androsse and Accomplices, Who Acted by an Illegal and Arbitrary Commission from the Late K. James . . .* Boston, 1691.

Swift, John. *Election Sermon.* Boston: B. Green, 1732.

Swift, Jonathan. *The Portable Swift.* Carl Van Doren, ed. New York: Viking Press, 1948.

------. *The Prose Works of Jonathan Swift.* H. Davis, ed. Vol. III. Oxford: Clarendon Press, 1939-62.

Tennant, Gilbert. *A Sermon Preach'd at Philadelphia, January 7, 174$^7/_8$* Philadelphia: W. Bradford, 1748.

Tillotson, John. *Sermons Preached upon Several Occasions. By John, Late Lord Archbishop of Canterbury. Vol. 4.* London, 1695.

Tyrell, Sir James. *A Brief Enquiry into the Ancient Constitution and Government of England, As Well in Respect to the Administration, and Succession Thereof. Set forth in a Dialogue, and Fitted for Men of Ordinary Learning and Capacities. By a True Lover of His Country.* London, 1695.

Van Laer, A.J.F., ed. and trans. *Correspondence of Jeremias Van Renselaer, 1651-1674.* Albany: University of the State of New York, 1932.

------ , ed. and trans. *Correspondence of Maria Van Renselaer, 1651-1674.* Albany: University of the State of New York, 1935.

Van Rensselaer, Mrs. Schuyler. *History of the City of New York in the Seventeenth Century.* Vol. 2. New York: The Macmillan Co., 1909.

Varey, Simon, ed. *Lord Bolingbroke: Contributions to the Craftsman.* Oxford: Clarendon Press, 1982.

W.G.A. *A Letter from a Country Gentleman: Setting Forth the CAUSE of the Ruin of Trade. To Which is Annexed a LIST of NAMES of Some Gentlemen who were Members of the Last Parliament, and are now (or lately were) in Public Employment.* London, 1698.

Waller, Edward. *Poems &c. Written upon Several Occasions, and to Several Persons.* 6th ed. London: H. Herrington & Thomas Bennes, 1693.

Wake, William. *A Sermon Preached before the Lord-Mayor and Court of Aldermen, in the Church of St. Mary le Bow; on Thursday the 26th of November, being a Day of Public Thanksgiving.* London, 1691.

Wellwood, James. *An Answer to the Late King JAMES Last Declaration, Dated at St. Germains, April 17, S.N. 1693.* London, 1693.

------. *Memoirs of the Most Material Transactions in England, for the Last Hundred Years, Preceding the Revolution of 1688*. London, 1700.

------. *A Vindication of the Present Great Revolution in England; in Five Letters Pass'd betwixt* James Wellwood, *M.D. and* Mr. John March, *Vicar of* Newcastle *upon* Tyne. *Occasion'd by a Sermon Preach'd by him on January 30 168⁸/₉ Before the Mayor and Aldermen, for* Passive Obedience *and* Non-Resistence. London, 1689.

Whitefield, George. *Britain's Mercies, Britain's Duties... Represented in a Sermon Preach'd at the New Building in Philadelphia... Occassion'd by the Suppression of the Late Unnatural Rebellion*, Boston: S. Kneeland, 1746.

Whitman, Elnathan. *The Character and Qualifications of Good Rulers, and the Happiness of Their Administrations . . .* New London: T. Green, 1745.

[Whittel, John]. *A Short Review of the Remarkable Providences: Attending Our Gracious Sovereign William the IIId. Continued From the Year 1693, Down to this Day.* London, 1699.

Wigglesworth, Samuel. *The Blessedness of Such as Trust in* CHRIST *the King Whom* GOD *Hath Exalted.* Boston: S. Kneeland, 1755.

------. *God's Promise to an Obedient People, of Victory Over Their Enemies.* Boston: S. Kneeland, 1755.

Williams, Elisha. *The Essential Rights and Liberties of Protestants. . .* Boston: S. Kneeland, 1744.

Secondary Sources

Appleby, Joyce. *Economic Thought and Ideology in Seventeenth Century England.* Princeton, New Jersey: Princeton University Press, 1978.

------. *Liberalism and Republicanism in the Historical Imagination.* Cambridge, Massachusetts: Harvard University Press, 1992.

Archdeacon, Thomas J. *New York City, 1664-1710: Conquest and Change.* Ithaca, New York: Cornell University Press, 1976.

Ashley, Maurice. *The Glorious Revolution of 1688.* New York: Charles Scribner's Sons, 1966.

Atherton, Herbert M. *Political Prints in the Age of Hogarth: A Study of the Ideographic Representation of Politics.* Oxford: Clarendon Press, 1974.

Bailyn, Bernard. *Faces of the Revolution: Personalities and Themes in the Struggle for American Independence.* New York: Vintage Books, 1992.

------. *Ideological Origins of the American Revolution*, Cambridge, Mass.: Belknap Press of Harvard University, 1967.

------. *The Ordeal of Thomas Hutchinson*. Cambridge, Massachusetts: Belknap Press, 1974.

------ , and John B. Hench, ed. *The Press and the American Revolution*. Boston: Northeastern University Press, 1980.

Barnes, Viola Florence. *The Dominion of New England: A Study in British Colonial Policy*. New Haven: Yale University Press, 1923.

Batinski, Michael C. *Jonathan Belcher: Colonial Governor*. Lexington: Kentucky: University Press of Kentucky, 1996.

Baxter, Stephen B. *William III and the Defense of European Liberty, 1650-1702*. New York: Harcourt, Brace & World, 1966.

Beard, Charles A. *An Economic Interpretation of the Constitution*. New York: Macmillan & Co., 1913.

Becker, Carl Lotus. *The Declaration of Independence: A Study in the History of Political Ideas*. Rep. New York: Vintage Books, 1958.

------. *The History of Political Parties in the Province of New York*. Madison, Wisconsin: University of Wisconsin Press, 1909.

Becker, Robert A. *Revolution, Reform, and the Politics of American Taxation, 1763-1783*. Baton Rouge: Louisiana State University Press, 1980.

Bennett, William Harper. *Catholic Footsteps in Old New York: A Chronicle of Catholicity in the City of New York from 1524 to 1808*. New York, 1909, Rep. Yonkers, New York: United States Catholic Historical Society, 1973.

Black, Jeremy. *The English Press in the Eighteenth Century*. London: Croom Helm, Ltd., 1987.

Bonomi, Patricia. *A Factious People: Politics and Society in Colonial New York*. New York: Columbia University Press, 1971.

------. *Under the Cope of Heaven: Religion, Society and Politics in Colonial America*. New York: Oxford Press, 1986.

Boorstin, Daniel. *The Americans: The Colonial Experience*. New York: Random House, 1958.

------. *The Genius of American Politics*. Chicago: University of Chicago Press, 1953.

Bradley, James E. *Popular Politics and the American Revolution in England: Petitions, the Crown, and Public Opinion*. Macon, Georgia: Mercer University Press, 1986.

Breen, T.H. *The Character of a Good Ruler: A Study of Puritan Political Ideas in New England, 1630-1730*. New Haven: Yale University Press, 1970.

Brewer, John and John Styles, ed. *An Ungovernable People: The English and Their Law in the Seventeenth and Eighteenth Centuries*. New Brunswick, New Jersey: Rutgers University Press, 1980.

------. *Party Ideology and Popular Politics at the Accession of George III*. Cambridge: Cambridge University Press, 1976.

------. *The Sinews of Power: War, Money and the English State, 1688-1783*. Cambridge, Massachusetts: Harvard University Press, 1990.

Brown, Robert E. *Middle-Class Democracy and the Revolution in Massachusetts, 1691-1780*. Ithaca, New York: Cornell University Press, for the American Historical Association, 1955.

------, and Katherine T. *Virginia, 1705-1780: Democracy or Aristocracy?* East Lansing: Michigan State University Press, 1964.

Bucholz, R.O. *The Augustan Court: Queen Anne and the Decline of Court Culture*. Stanford, California: Stanford University Press, 1993.

Bushman, Richard L. *King and People in Provincial Massachusetts*. Williamsburg: University of North Carolina Press, 1985.

Calvert, Karen. "Children in American Portraiture, 1670-1810," *William and Mary Quarterly*, 3rd Series, 39 (1982), 87-113.

Cannon, John, ed. *The Whig Ascendancy: Colloquies in Hanoverian England*. New York: St. Martin's Press, 1981.

Carretta, Vincent. *George III and the Satirists from Hogarth to Byron*. Athens, Georgia: University of Georgia Press, 1990.

Clark, Charles E. *The Public Prints: The Newspapers in Anglo-American Culture, 1665-1740*. New York: Oxford University Press, 1994.

Clark, J.C.D. *Revolution and Rebellion: State and Society in England in the Seventeenth and Eighteenth Centuries*. Cambridge: Cambridge University Press, 1986.

Clarke, Mary Patterson. *Parliamentary Privilege in the American Colonies*. New Haven: Yale University Press, 1943.

Cruickshanks, Eveline, Hayton, D. and Jones, C. "Division in the House of Lords on the Transfer of the Crown and Other Issues, 1689-1694: Ten New Lists," *Bulletin of the Institute of Historical Research*, 53 (1980), 56-87.

------ , ed. *Ideology and Conspiracy: Aspects of Jacobitism, 1689-1759*. Edinburgh: John Donald Publishers Ltd., 1982.

------. *Political Untouchables: The Tories and the '45*. New York: Holmes and Meier Publishers, Inc., 1979.

Curti, Merle. *The Growth of American Thought*. New York: Harper and Row, 1943.

------. *Human Nature in American Historical Thought*. Columbia Missouri: University of Missouri Press, 1968.

Davidson, Philip. *Propaganda and the American Revolution, 1763-1783*. Chapel Hill: University of North Carolina Press, 1941.

De Michele, Michael D. "The Glorious Revolution in Maryland: A Study in the Provincial Revolution of 1689." PhD. Dissertation. Pennsylvania State University, 1967.

Dickinson, H.T. *Liberty and Property: Political Ideology in Eighteenth Century Britain*. New York: Holmes and Meier, 1977.

------, ed. *Politics and Literature in the Eighteenth Century*. London: J.M. Dent & Sons, Ltd., 1974.

Draper, Theodore. *A Struggle for Power: The American Revolution*. New York: Times Books, A Division of Random House, 1996.

Dunn, John. "Consent in the Political Theory of John Locke," *The Historical Journal*, Vol. 10, No. 2, 1967, 153-182.

Dunn, Richard S. *Puritans and Yankees: The Winthrop Dynasty of New England, 1630-1717*. New York: W.W. Norton & Co., 1962.

Egnal, Marc and Joseph Ernst, "An Economic Interpretation of the American Revolution," *William and Mary Quarterly*, 3rd series, 29 (January, 1972), 3-33.

Fischer, David Hackett. *Albion's Seed: Four British Folkways in America*. New York: Oxford University Press, 1989.

Foner, Eric. *Tom Paine and Revolutionary America*. New York: Oxford University Press, 1976.

Foote, Henry Wilder. *Annals of King's Chapel from the Puritan Age of New England to the Present Day*. Vol. I. Boston: Little, Brown and Company, 1882.

George, Dorothy M. *English Political Caricature to 1792: A Study of Opinion and Propaganda*. Vol. 1. Oxford: Clarendon Press, 1959.

Goldgar, Bertrand A. *Walpole and the Wits: The Relation of Politics to Literature, 1722-1742*. Lincoln, Nebraska: University of Nebraska Press, 1976.

Greene, Evarts Boutell. *The Provincial Governor in the English Colonies of North America, Harvard Historical Studies*, Vol. VII. New York: Longman, Green and Co., 1907.

Greene, Jack P. *Negotiated Authorities: Essays in Colonial Political and Constitutional History*. Charlottesville: University Press of Virginia, 1994.

------. *The Quest For Power: Lower Houses of Assembly in the Southern Colonies, 1689-1776.* New York: W.W. Norton Company & Co., 1972.

Gregg, Edward. *Queen Anne.* London: Routledge & Kegan Paul, 1980.

Grob, Gerald N. and George Athan Billias, eds. *Interpretations of American History: Patterns and Perspectives.* 6th ed., 2 vols. New York: The Free Press, Macmillan, Inc., 1992.

Hatton, Ragnold. *George I Elector and King.* Cambridge, Massachusetts: Harvard University Press, 1978.

Henretta, James A. *"Salutory Neglect": Colonial Administration Under the Duke of Newcastle.* Princeton: Princeton University Press, 1972.

Hibbard, Caroline. *Charles I and the Popish Plot.* Chapel Hill: University of North Carolina Press, 1983.

Hill, B.W. *The Growth of Parliamentary Parties, 1689-1742.* Hamden, Connecticut: The Shoestring Press, 1976.

Hill, Christopher. *The Century of Revolution, 1603-1714.* New York: W.W. Norton & Co., 1982.

Hill, Hamilton Andrews. *History of the Old South Church (Third Church), Boston, 1669-1884.* Vol. I. Boston: Houghton, Mifflin and Co., 1890.

Hofstadter, Richard. *America at 1750: A Social Portrait.* New York: Vintage Books, 1973.

Holmes, Geoffrey. *British Politics in the Age of Anne* New York: St. Martin's Press, 1967.

Horwitz, Henry. "Parliament and the Glorious Revolution," *Bulletin of the Institute of Historical Research*, 47 (1974), 36-52.

Hutchinson, Thomas. *History of the Colony and Province of Massachusetts Bay.* ed. Lawrence Shaw Mayo. 2 Vols. Cambridge, Massachusetts: Harvard University Press, 1936.

Isaac, Rhys. *Transformation of Virginia, 1740-1790.* New York: W.W. Norton & Co., 1988.

Jameson, J. Franklin. *The American Revolution Considered as a Social Movement.* Princeton: Princeton University Press, 1926.

Jones, Alice Hanson. *Wealth of a Nation to Be.* New York: Columbia University Press, 1980.

Jones, J.R., ed. *Liberty Secured? Britain Before and After 1688.* Stanford: Stanford University Press, 1992.

------. *The Revolution of 1688 in England.* New York: W.W. Norton & Co., 1972.

Jordan, Winthrop. "Familial Politics: Thomas Paine and the Killing of the King, 1776," *Journal of American History*, 60 (September, 1973), 294-308.

Judd, Jacob, and Irwin H. Polishook, eds. *Aspects of Early New York Society and Politics*. Tarrytown, New York: Sleepy Hollow Restorations, 1974.

Kammen, Michael G. *A Rope of Sand: The Colonial Agents, British Politics, and the American Revolution*. Ithaca: Cornell University Press, 1968.

------. *Colonial New York: A History*. New York: Charles Scribner's Sons, 1975.

------. "The Causes of the Maryland Revolution of 1689," *Maryland Historical Magazine*, Vol. 55, No. 4 (December, 1960), 293-333.

Keir, David Lindsay. *The Constitutional History of Modern Britain Since 1485*. 9th ed. New York: W.W. Norton & Co., 1966.

Kellogg, Louise Phelps. *The American Colonial Charter*. Washington, D.C., 1904.

Kendrick, T.F. "Sir Robert Walpole, the Old Whigs and the Bishops, 1733-1736: A Study in Eighteenth-Century Parliamentary Politics," *The Historical Journal*, Vol. 11, No. 3 (1968), 421-445.

Kenyon, J.P. *The Popish Plot*. London: Heinemann, 1972.

------. *Revolution Principles: The Politics of Party, 1689-1720*. Cambridge: Cambridge University Press, 1977.

------. *Stuart England*. London: Penguin Books, 1985.

Kishlansky, Mark, *A Monarchy Transformed: Britain, 1603-1714*. London: The Penguin Press, 1996.

Kramnick, Isaac. *Bolingbroke and His Circle: The Politics of Nostalgia in the Age of Walpole*. Cambridge, Massachusetts: Harvard University Press, 1968.

Kulikoff, Allan. "The Progress of Inequality in Revolutionary Boston," *William and Mary Quarterly*, 3rd series, 28 (July, 1971), 375-412.

Kupp, Jan. "Aspects of New York-Dutch Trade, 1670-1674," *New York Historical Quarterly*, Vol. 58, April, 1974.

Larabee, Leonard Wood. *Royal Government in America: A Study of the British Colonial System Before 1783*. New Haven: Yale University Press, 1930.

Leder, Lawrence. *Robert Livingston, 1654-1728, and the Politics of Colonial New York* (Published for the Institute of Early American History and Culture at Williamsburg, Virginia). Chapel Hill: University of North Carolina Press, 1961.

------. "The Unorthodox Domine: Nicholas Van Rensalaer," *New York History Quarterly,* Vol. 35, No. 2, (April, 1954), 166-176.

Lemisch, Jesse. *Jack Tar vs. John Bull: The Role of New York's Seamen in Precipitating the Revolution.* New York: Garland Publishing, 1997.

Lenman, Bruce. *Jacobite Risings in Britain, 1689-1746.* London: Methuen, 1980.

Levy, Leonard. *Legacy of Suppression: Freedom of Speech and the Press in Early American History.* Cambridge, Mass.: Belknap Press of Harvard University, 1960.

Lewis, Theodore Burnum, Jr. "Massachusetts and the Glorious Revolution, 1660-1692." Ph.D. diss. University of Wisconsin, 1967.

Linebaugh, Peter. *The London Hanged: Crime and Civil Society in the Eighteenth Century.* Cambridge: University Press, 1992.

Lockridge, Kenneth. *A New England Town: The First Hundred Years.* New York: W.W. Norton, 1985.

Longmore, Paul K. *The Invention of George Washington.* Berkeley: University of California Press, 1988.

Lovejoy, David S. *The Glorious Revolution in America.* New York: Harper and Row, Publishers, 1972.

Macaulay, Thomas Babbington. *The History of England.* Edited and Abridged by Hugh Trevor-Roper. New York: Penguin Books, 1968.

------. *Macaulay's History of England.* 4 Vols. Introduction by Douglas Jerrold. Reprint. London: Everyman's Library, 1962.

Maier, Pauline. *American Scripture: Making the Declaration of Independence.* New York: Alfred Knopf, 1997.

------. *From Resistance to Revolution: Colonial Radicals and the Development of American Opposition to Britain, 1765-1776.* New York: W.W. Norton & Co., 1991.

Maitland, F.W. *The Constitutional History of England.* Cambridge: Cambridge University Press, 1963.

Marston, Jerrilyn Greene. *King and Congress: The Transfer of Political Legitimacy, 1774-1776.* Princeton: University Press, 1987.

Matthews, Richard K. *Virtue, Corruption and Self-Interest: Political Values in the Eighteenth Century.* Cranbury, New Jersey: Associated University Press, 1994.

McAnear, Beverly, ed. "Mariland's Grevances Wiy The Have Taken Op Arms," *The Journal of Southern History.* 8 (August, 1942), 392-409.

McMahon, Marie P. *The Radical Whigs, John Trenchard and Thomas Gordon: Libertarian Loyalists to the New House of Hanover.* Lanham, Maryland: University Press of America, 1990.

Merwick, Donna, "Becoming English: Anglo-Dutch Conflict in the 1670s in Albany, New York," *New York History* (October 1981), 389-414.

Middlekauff, Robert. *The Glorious Cause: The American Revolution, 1763-1789.* New York: Oxford University Press, 1982.

Miller, James. *James II: A Study in Kingship.* London: Methuen, 1989.

Miller, John. *Popery and Politics in England, 1660-1688.* Cambridge: Cambridge University Press, 1973.

------. "The Glorious Revolution: 'Contract' and 'Abdication' Reconsidered," *Historical Journal*, 25 (1982), 541-555.

Miller, Perry. *The New England Mind: From Colony to Province.* Reprint. Boston: Beacon Press, 1961.

------. *The New England Mind: The Seventeenth Century.* 2nd ed. Reprint. Boston: Beacon Press, 1961.

------. *Orthodoxy in Massachusetts.* Rep. Boston: Beacon Press, 1968.

Morgan, Edmond S. *Inventing the People: The Rise of Popular Sovereignty in England and America.* New York: W.W. Norton & Co., 1988.

------. *The Puritan Dilemma: The Story of John Winthrop.* Boston: Little Brown & Co., 1958.

------ , and Helen M. *The Stamp Act Crisis: Prologue to Revolution.* New York: Macmillan, 1962.

Morton, Richard L. *Colonial Virginia.* 2 Vols. Published for the Virginia Historical Society. Chapel Hill: University of North Carolina Press, 1960.

Motley, Daniel Esten. "The Life of Commissary Blair," *Johns Hopkins University Studies in History and Political Science.* Ser. 19, No. 10 (October, 1901).

Namier, Louis B. *England in the Age of the American Revolution.* 2nd ed. London: Macmillan & Co., 1961.

------. *The Structure of Politics at the Accession of George III.* 2 Vols. London: Macmillan & Co., Ltd., 1929.

Nash, Gary B. *The Urban Crucible: The Northern Seaports and the Origins of the American Revolution.* Cambridge, Massachusetts: Harvard University Press, 1979.

Nenner, Howard. *The Right to be King: The Succession to the Crown of England, 1603-1714.* Chapel Hill: University of North Carolina Press, 1995.

Olson, Alison Gilbert. *Anglo-American Politics 1660-1775: The Relationship Between Parties in England and Colonial America.* New York: Oxford University Press, 1973.

Owen, John B. *The Eighteenth Century, 1714-1815.* New York: W.W. Norton & Co., 1974.

Pares, Richard. *King George III and the Politicians: The Ford Lectures Delivered at the University of Oxford, 1951-2.* London: Oxford University Press, 1953.

Pencak, William. *War, Politics & Revolution in Provincial Massachusetts.* Boston: Northeastern University Press, 1981.

Perkins, Edwin J. *The Economy of Colonial America*, 2nd ed. New York: Columbia University Press, 1988.

Pinkham, Lucile. *William III and the Respectable Revolution: The Part Played by William of Orange in the Revolution of 1688.* Cambridge, Massachusetts: Harvard University Press, 1954.

Plumb, J.H. *England in the Eighteenth Century.* London: Penguin Books, 1990.

------. *The Growth of Stability in England.* London: Macmillan & Co., 1967.

Pocock, J.G.A. *The Machiavellian Moment: Florentine Political Thought and the Atlantic Republican Tradition.* Princeton, New Jersey: Princeton University Press, 1975.

Pole, J.R. *Political Representation In England and the Origins of the American Republic.* New York: St. Martin's Press, 1966.

Pomfret, John E. *Colonial New Jersey: A History.* New York: Charles Scribner's Sons, 1973.

Potter, David. *The Impending Crisis, 1848-1861.* Completed and edited by Don E. Fehrenbacher. New York: Harper & Row, 1976.

Pratt, John Webster. *Religion Politics, and Diversity: The Church-State Theme in New York History.* Ithaca, New York: Cornell University Press, 1967.

Rahe, Paul A. *Republics Ancient and Modern: Classical Republicanism and the American Revolution.* Chapel Hill: University of North Carolina Press, 1992.

Raper, Charles. *North Carolina: A Royal Province, 1729-1775.* Chapel Hill: The University Press, 1901.

Reed, James Morgan. "Atrocity Propaganda and the Irish Rebellion," *Public Opinion Quarterly*, 2 (April, 1938), 229-244.

Reich, Jerome R. *Leisler's Rebellion: A Study of Democracy in New York, 1664-1720.* Chicago: University of Chicago Press, 1953.

Reid, John Phillip. *The Concept of Liberty in the Age of the American Revolution.* Chicago: University of Chicago Press, 1988.

------. *Constitutional History of the American Revolution: The Authority to Tax.* Madison: University of Wisconsin Press, 1987.

Richards, James O. *Party Propaganda under Queen Anne: The General Elections of 1702-1713.* Athens, Georgia: University of Georgia Press, 1972.

Ritchie, Robert. "The Duke of York's Commission of Revenue," *New York Historical Society Quarterly*, 58 (July, 1974), 177-187.

------. *The Duke's Province: A Study of New York Colonial Politics and Society, 1664-1691.* Chapel Hill: University of North Carolina Press, 1977.

Robbins, Caroline. *The Eighteenth Century Commonwealthsman: Studies in the Transmission, Development and Circumstance of English Liberal Thought from the Restoration of Charles II until the War with the Thirteen Colonies.* Harvard University Press, 1959. Rep. New York: Atheneum, 1968.

Rogers, Nicholas. *Whigs and Cities: Popular Politics in the Age of Walpole and Pitt.* Oxford: Clarendon Press, 1989.

Rose, Craig. "'Seminarys of Faction and Rebellion': Jacobites, Whigs and the London Charity Schools, 1716-1724," *The Historical Journal,* 34 (December, 1991), 831-855.

Sack, James J. *From Jacobite to Conservative: Reaction and Orthodoxy in Britain, 1760-1832.* Cambridge: Cambridge University Press, 1993.

Schlesinger, Arthur M. *The Colonial Merchants and the American Revolution, 1762-1776.* 1918. Rep. New York: The Facsimile Library, 1938.

------. *Prelude to Independence: The Newspaper War on Britain, 1764-1776.* New York: Knopf, 1958.

Schwartz, Barry. *George Washington: The Making of a Symbol.* Ithaca: Cornell University Press, 1978.

Schwoerer, Lois G. "Propaganda in the Revolution of 1688-89," *American Historical Review*, Vol. 82, No. 4, (October 1977), 843-874.

------. *The Declaration of Rights, 1689.* Baltimore: Johns Hopkins University Press, 1981.

------, ed. *The Revolution of 1688-1689: Changing Perspectives.* Cambridge: Cambridge University Press, 1992, 843-874.

Seaward, Paul. *The Cavalier Parliament and the Restoration of the Old Regime, 1661-1667.* Cambridge: Cambridge University Press, 1989.

Shagan, Ethan Howard. "Constructing Discord: Ideology, Propaganda, and the English Responses to the Irish Rebellion of 1641," *Journal of British Studies*, 36 (January, 1997), 4-34.

Sharpe, Kevin and Peter Lake, eds. *Culture and Politics in Early Stuart England*. Stanford, California: Stanford University Press, 1993.

Shipton, Clifford K. *Sibley's Harvard Graduates: Biographical Sketches of Those Who Attended Harvard College*. Vols. 6-9. Boston: Massachusetts Historical Society, 1951.

Sibley, John Langdon. *Biographical Sketches of Graduates of Harvard University, in Cambridge, Massachusetts*. 4 Vols. Cambridge, Massachusetts: C.W. Sever., 1873-1919.

Smith, Daniel Blake. "Study of the Family in Early America," *William and Mary Quarterly*, 3rd Series, 39 (1982) 3-28.

Smith, William Jr. *The History on the Province of New York*. Vol. 1. Michael Kammen, ed. Cambridge, Massachusetts: Belknap Press of Harvard University, 1972.

Sparks, Francis Edgar. "Causes of the Maryland Revolution of 1689," *Johns Hopkins University Studies in Historical and Political Science*, Herbert Adams, ed. 14th Series, 11-12 (November-December, 1896), 7-108.

Speck, W.A. "The Orangist Conspiracy Against James II," *Historical Journal*, 30 (1987), 453-462.

------. *Reluctant Revolutionaries: Englishmen and the Revolution of 1688*. Oxford: Oxford University Press, 1988.

Stephenson, Carl and Frederick George Marcham. *Sources of English Constitutional History: A Selection of the Documents from the Interregnum to the Present*. Vol. II. New York: Harper and Row Publishers, Inc., 1972.

Stern, Steve. "Knickerbockers who Insisted and Asserted: The Dutch Interest in New York Politics, 1664-1691," *New York Historical Society Quarterly*, 58 (April, 1974), 113-138.

Stevenson, John. *Popular Disturbances in England, 1700-1832*. 2nd edition. New York: Longman Publishing, 1992.

Stone, Lawrence. *The Family, Sex and Marriage in England, 1500-1800*. London: Weidenfeld & Nicholson, 1977.

------. "Literacy and Education in England," *Past and Present*, 42 (February, 1969), 69-139.

Szechi, D. *Jacobitism and Tory Politics, 1710-1714*. Edinburgh: John Donald Publishers, Ltd., 1984.

Taylor, Robert J., et al. ed. *Papers of John Adams*, Vol. I. Cambridge, Massachusetts: Belknap Press of Harvard University, 1977

Thomas, Peter David Garner. *British Politics and the Stamp Act Crisis: The First Phase of the American Revolution, 1763-1767.* Oxford: Clarendon Press, 1975.

Thompson, E.P. *Whigs and Hunters: The Origin of the Black Act.* New York: Random House, 1975.

Trevelyan, George Macaulay. *England Under Queen Anne.* 3 vols. London: Longman and Green & Co., 1930-1934.

------. *The English Revolution, 1688-1689.* Rep. London: Oxford University Press, 1965.

Trevor-Roper, Hugh. *From Counter-Reformation to Glorious Revolution.* Chicago: University of Chicago Press, 1992.

Underdown, David. *Revel, Riot and Rebellion: Popular Politics and Culture in England, 1603-1660.* Oxford: Clarendon Press, 1985.

Voorhees, David William. "'In Behalf of the True Protestants Religion': The Glorious Revolution in New York." PhD. Dissertation, New York University, 1988.

------. "The Fervent Zeale of Jacob Leisler," *William and Mary Quarterly,* 3rd ser. 51 (July, 1994), 447-472.

Walcott, Robert. *English Politics in the Early Eighteenth Century.* Oxford: Oxford University Press, 1956.

Walsham, Alexandra. "'The Fatall Vesper': Providentialism and Anti-Popery in Late Jacobean London," *Past and Present,* 144 (August, 1994), 36-84.

Warren, Mercy Otis *History of the Rise, Progress and Termination of the American Revolution Interspersed with Biographical, Political and Moral Observations.* 2 Vols. (Boston: Manning and Loring, 1805; reprint, Indianapolis: Liberty Classics, 1988).

Webking, Robert H. *The American Revolution and the Politics of Liberty.* Baton Rouge: Louisiana State University Press, 1988.

Wertenbaker, Thomas J. *Virginia Under the Stuarts, 1607-1688.* Princeton: Princeton University Press, 1914.

Western, J.R. *Monarchy and Revolution: The English State in the 1680s.* Totowa, New Jersey: Rowman & Littlefield, 1972.

Wheeler, Joseph Towne. "Reading Interests of the Professional Classes in Colonial Maryland, 1700-1776," *The Maryland Historical Magazine.* 36, (June, 1941), 184-201.

Wiles, R.M. *Freshest Advices: Early Provincial Newspapers in England.* Columbus, Ohio: Ohio State University Press, 1965.

Wood, Gordon, *The Creation of the American Republic, 1776-1787.* New York: W.W. Norton & Co., 1969.

------. "Conspiracy and the Paranoid Style: Causality and Deceit in the Eighteenth Century," *The William and Mary Quarterly*, 3rd Series, 39 (July, 1982), 401-441.

------. "Rhetoric and Reality and the American Revolution," in *In Search of Early America: The William and Mary Quarterly, 1943-1993*. Richmond, Virginia: William Byrd Press, 1993.

------. *The Radicalism of the American Revolution*. New York, Alfred A. Knopf, Inc., 1992.

------. "Virtues and Interests," *The New Republic*, February 11, 1991, 32-35.

Wright, Langdon G. "In Search of Peace and Harmony: New York Communities in the Seventeenth Century," *New York History*, 64, January, 1980, 5-21.

Wrightson, Keith. *English Society, 1580-1680*. New Brunswick, New Jersey: Rutgers University Press, 1982.

Wroth, Lawrence. "The First Sixty Years of the Church of England in Maryland, 1632-1692," *Maryland Historical Magazine*, 11 (March, 1916), 1-41.

Young, Alfred F., ed. *Beyond the American Revolution: Explorations in the History of American Radicalism*. DeKalb, Illinois: Northern Illinois University Press, 1993.

Index

About the Author

Benjamin Lewis Price was born in Baton Rouge, Louisiana, on March 1, 1951. He graduated from Leysin American High School, Leysin, Vaud, Switzerland in 1969. He received a B.A. in Anthropology from Louisiana State University, Baton Rouge in 1973. While employed as the fencing instructor at Baton Rouge Magnet High School (1976-1985), Price completed his M.A. in Classical History from Louisiana State University in 1985. He was employed as a teacher of social studies at the Scotlandville Magnet High School in Baton Rouge, Louisiana, from the fall 1986 through the spring 1989. While working on his PhD., which he obtained in 1997, Mr. Price was a member of the Faculty of the Louisiana State University Evening School, teaching the first semester survey in American History. He is currently the historical adviser for the Louisiana History Project at Louisiana Public Broadcasting in Baton Rouge, Louisiana.

DATE DUE